IMAGES
of America

OUTER BANKS SCENIC BYWAY

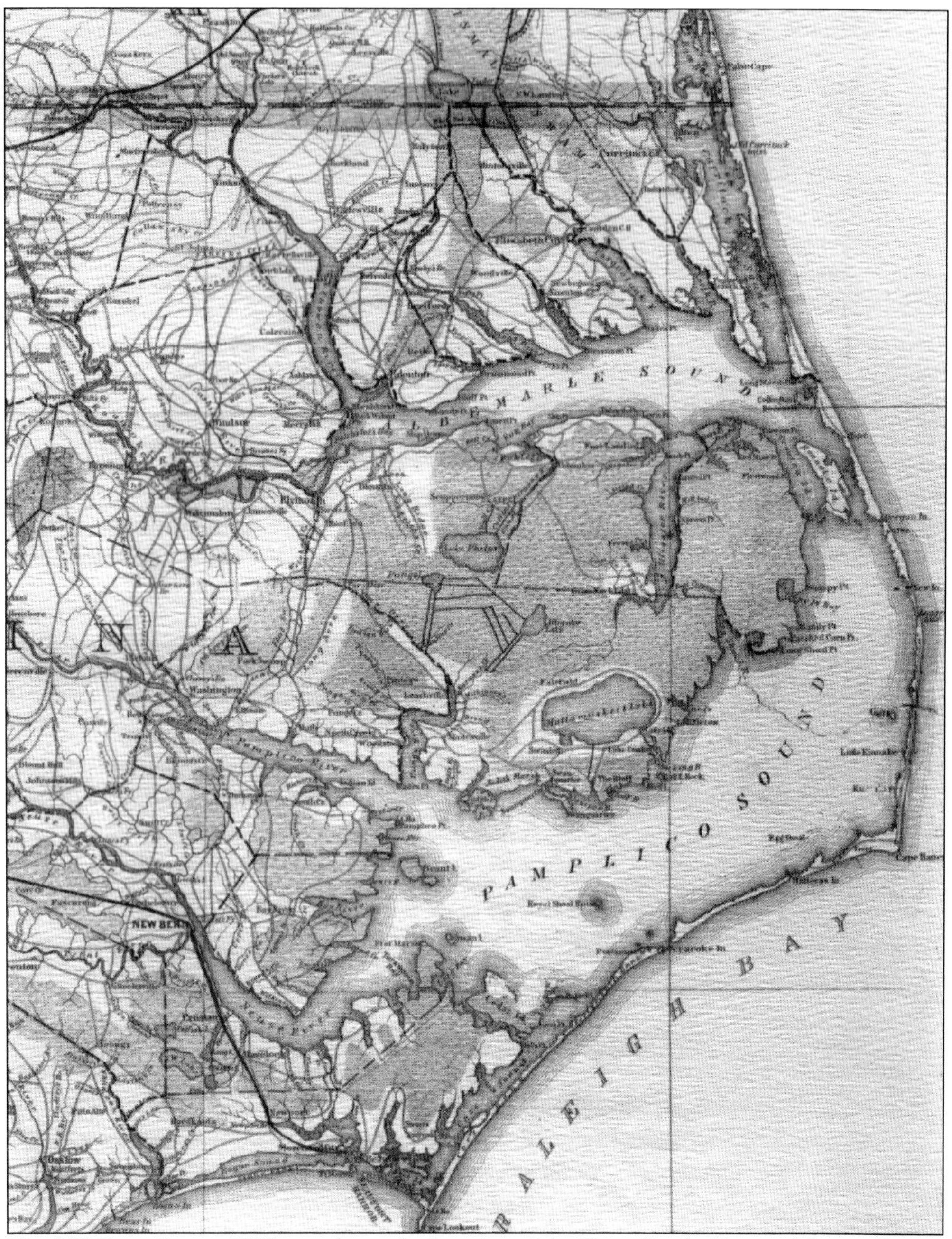

This US Coast Survey 1865 map shows the location of the Outer Banks National Scenic Byway, North Carolina. (Courtesy of the North Carolina Department of Archives and History.)

On The Cover: Pictured here in 1952 are the Bodie Island Old Coast Guard Station and a car driving on the newly paved NC 12 Highway, what is today the Outer Banks National Scenic Byway. (Courtesy of the Cape Hatteras National Seashore.)

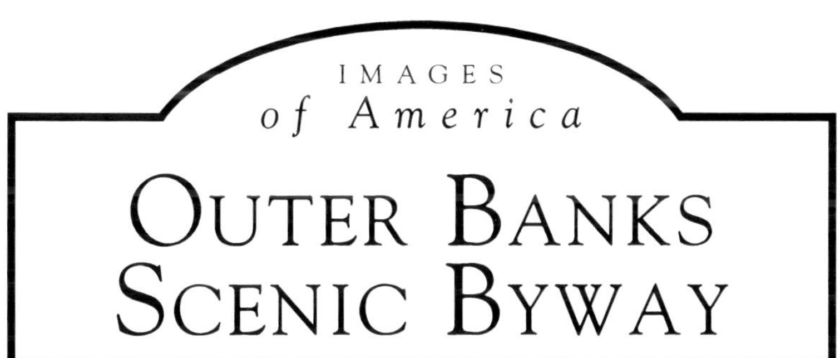

Douglas Stover

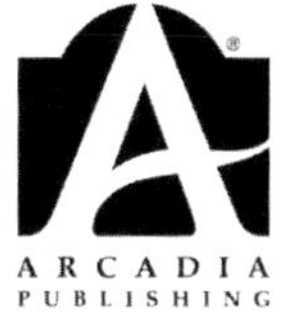

ISBN 978-1-4671-1553-7

Published by Arcadia Publishing
Charleston, South Carolina

Printed in the United States of America

Library of Congress Control Number: 2015953253

For all general information, please contact Arcadia Publishing:
Telephone 843-853-2070
Fax 843-853-0044
E-mail sales@arcadiapublishing.com
For customer service and orders:
Toll-Free 1-888-313-2665

Visit us on the Internet at www.arcadiapublishing.com

Contents

ACKNOWLEDGMENTS

I am pleased to make available this collection of historic images of the Outer Banks National Scenic Byway. Help was provided by many sources and research material from the Cape Hatteras National Seashore, Outer Banks History Center, Cape Lookout National Seashore, Core Sound Waterfowl Museum & Heritage Center, and Lynn Doggett Anderson, collections manager at the North Carolina Maritime Museum in Beaufort. Special thanks go to Jami Lanier, cultural resource manager, Outer Banks Group, National Park Service for allowing me access to the National Park Service archives and the Cape Hatteras and Cape Lookout National Seashores collection of over 500 photographs. Special thanks go to KaeLi Schurr (curator), Tama Creef (archivist), and Stuart Parks (archivist) at the Outer Banks History Center in Manteo, North Carolina.

I want to thank the Outer Banks National Scenic Byway Advisory Committee, Mary Helen Goodloe-Murphy, Chair & Dare Co., Karen Willis Amspacher, Core Sound Waterfowl Museum and Heritage Center, Carteret Co., Melinda Sutton, Hyde County, and specially Cyndy Holda, the advisory committee's secretary and public information officer, Outer Banks Group, National Park Service for reviewing and editing the photographs and text.

Thanks go to my wife, Joan, for allowing me during my semiretirement years to author another book within two years and assisting me with reviewing photographs.

I want to thank Matt Todd, title manager at Arcadia Publishing, as well as the production staff for allowing me to research and write this book and working with me through the various stages of publication.

INTRODUCTION

The Outer Banks National Scenic Byway was designated by the US Department of Transportation in 2009 to recognize, preserve, and enhance the many cultural traditions of a distinctive region. The byway stretches for nearly 200 miles along the famed North Carolina barrier islands. The unique maritime culture shared by the 21 coastal villages along this route led to the national byway designation.

Leave the nation's mainland behind, slow down, and come to the land of beginnings to tour historic villages centered on a rich maritime culture. Explore beautiful beaches and scenic marshlands with thriving wildlife, well-known lighthouses, and stunning sunrises and sunsets. Visit Bodie, Hatteras, and Ocracoke Islands, and "Down East" communities for an up-close look at the region's life and its bountiful plenty.

The byway's 21 villages possess centuries of maritime history and monumental firsts in our nation's history. The Outer Banks National Scenic Byway connects the communities of Hatteras (Dare County), Ocracoke (Hyde County), and Down East (Carteret County) to provide visitors with a beautiful travel experience along the dynamic eastern edge of the continent, an area rich and diverse in many natural and cultural resources.

Scattered the length of the byway, these 21 villages share a maritime heritage, one shaped by wind and water on shifting sands of the barrier islands, the domineering Atlantic Ocean, and the shallow but expansive Pamlico, Core, and Back Sounds.

Weather rules life here, and the families that have lived along the byway for generations have great stories to share. Village residents of the Outer Banks were traditionally boatbuilders, fishermen or waterfowl hunters, ferry operators, or guardians of the coast. All have amazing stories to tell about life on the edge of the continent. Their lives are constantly influenced, both beneficially and in sometimes disastrous ways, by the marine environment.

Enter the Outer Banks National Scenic Byway from the north along NC 12 at Whalebone Junction, Nags Head, North Carolina, or from the south at the North River and US 70, six miles outside of Beaufort, North Carolina.

Today's ground transportation features paved roads, a far cry from sand trails of yesteryear. On the water, modern state-owned ferries transport byway travelers and vehicles across two inlets. The magnificent Herbert C. Bonner Bridge connects Bodie and Hatteras Islands across Oregon Inlet, formed in 1846. More bridges on Ocracoke and Down East reinforce that watery paths slice through land.

Ferry rides provide amazing sights and sounds of this vibrant edge of life teeming with birds and fish and sometimes sightings of dolphin and sea turtles. At inlets, frothy, salty seawater meets calmer sound waters. Few who travel these ferry routes can resist the temptation to leave vehicles once underway and stand on the ferry deck to take in this exhilarating encounter with nature.

Crossing Hatteras Inlet to Ocracoke Island is about a 60-minute route, and the Swanquarter-to-Ocracoke trip is 2 hours and 40 minutes. The ride between Ocracoke and Cedar Island is about 2 hours and 15 minutes.

These byway transportation corridors traverse one of the nation's great coastal landscapes. These scenic views are preserved by the Cape Hatteras National Seashore, the Cape Lookout National Seashore, the Pea Island National Wildlife Refuge, and the Cedar Island National Wildlife Refuge. That great coastal landscape captures the historical imagination, as miles of sand and marsh border the byway in the national seashore at the north ends of Hatteras and Ocracoke Islands, Cedar Island Wildlife Refuge, and between the Down East villages. Visitor information for these federal areas is found at visitors' centers at Bodie Island Lighthouse, Cape Hatteras Lighthouse, Hatteras Village Weather Bureau, Ocracoke, and Cape Lookout on Harkers Island.

Rising above the coastal landscape are four iconic lighthouses, sentinels of the sea and the nation's history.

Bodie Island Lighthouse, built in 1872, is 156 feet tall with 22-foot black-and-white-striped bands. Also on the lighthouse grounds are the 1878 Bodie Island Life-Saving Station, the 1916 boathouse, and the two-story 1925 Coast Guard station, currently being used as modern-day National Park Service offices. This lighthouse, like two others on the byway, is open for climbing seasonally. The lightkeepers' quarters building serves as the visitors' center and bookstore.

Cape Hatteras Lighthouse, in Buxton, marks the cape and the dangerous Diamond Shoals. Built in 1870, the structure is the tallest masonry lighthouse in the United States. The black-and-white candy-striped tower, famous the world over, is open for climbing seasonally. The lighthouse is operated by the National Park Service. The visitors' center is open year-round. Just down the road from the lighthouse is a two-grave British cemetery holding the remains of two World War II soldiers who lost their lives defending the Hatteras Island coastline.

Ocracoke Lighthouse is one of the oldest operating lighthouses on the Atlantic coast. It is located on Silver Lake, the harbor for the village of Ocracoke. The 75-foot-tall lighthouse, built in 1823, is topped with its original fourth-order Fresnel lens, which still guides mariners to Silver Lake. The lighthouse is not open for climbing, but on special occasions, volunteers open the entrance of the lighthouse for a peek inside.

Cape Lookout Lighthouse can be seen from the tower at the Core Sound Waterfowl Museum and Heritage Center on Harkers Island, from Marshallberg Harbor and Davis. The lighthouse is operated by the Cape Lookout National Seashore. Painted with its distinctive black diamonds, the 169-foot-tall lighthouse is open for climbing seasonally. This lighthouse is accessible by private ferry leaving from Beaufort and the Byway's Harkers Island.

Lighthouses warned of dangers, but storms sent ships ashore or to the bottom of the ocean. Outer Banks men responded to calls for help, creating a lifesaving tradition along the byway. Historic and modern-day lifesaving stations dot the Outer Banks.

The Chicamacomico Life-Saving Station is among the most completely restored historic US Life-Saving Service stations in the nation. The original 1874 building and its successor erected in 1911 grace the grounds in Rodanthe. Owned by the Chicamacomico Historical Association, the station is open for tours April through November.

Other publicly owned historic Life-Saving stations are Little Kinnakeet, located between Salvo and Avon on Hatteras Island, the North Carolina Center for the Advancement of Teaching in Ocracoke, Portsmouth Island, and Cape Lookout. Modern-day Coast Guard facilities are found at Oregon Inlet and Hatteras village. Two surf-rescue teams also operate on Hatteras Island.

An entire museum is devoted to the shipwreck history of the Outer Banks. The state-owned Graveyard of the Atlantic Museum is located in Hatteras Village.

A traditional maritime trade along this byway is fishing. In villages along the scenic route, watermen ply an age-old trade of harvesting bounty from the sea and sound and bringing it to shore. Harbors are found in most villages. Watermen operations are found in Rodanthe, Hatteras, Ocracoke, Cedar Island, Atlantic, Marshallberg Davis, and Harkers Island. Today, that maritime trade is augmented with sports fishing. Beautifully crafted boats, some made along the byway, are moored in marinas, awaiting a visit to the Gulf Stream to chase billfish. Oregon Inlet Fishing Center, the marinas along the dock at Hatteras Village, and Ocracoke's Silver Lake are homes to these sleek oceangoing boats.

The villages along the Outer Banks National Scenic Byway cherish stories and traditions. For those traveling the byway from the north, Rodanthe, Waves, and Salvo are the first villages embedded in Cape Hatteras National Seashore. The Chicamacomico Life-Saving Station, the Rodanthe harbor, the Rasmus Midgett home, and the old Salvo Post Office are all places with stories to tell.

In the Pea Island National Wildlife refuge and between Salvo and Avon are long stretches of ocean and sound beaches undisturbed by development. The beaches are perfect for surf fishing, windsurfing, kiteboarding, shell hunting, and sunbathing. South of Salvo and elsewhere in the Cape Hatteras National Seashore are access points for beach drivers and walkers.

The Little Kinnakeet Life-Saving Station is just north of Avon. The station, built in 1871, sits all alone in the national seashore. Further south, the community of Avon was originally named Kinnakeet.

The villages of Avon, Buxton, Rodanthe, Waves and Salvo have paved pathways established by the Outer Banks National Scenic Byway for walking, jogging, biking, and skating.

Buxton, at the elbow of Hatteras Island, features the Cape Hatteras Lighthouse historic district. The lighthouse was moved back from the encroaching ocean in 1999, a worldwide engineering sensation. The district hosts a walking trail, campground, bookstore, visitors' center, ranger presentations, and a lifeguarded beach. Cape Hatteras Lighthouse is also known as a wave magnet, drawing surfers to its beach. At Cape Point, two ocean currents collide, creating an astounding place for fishing and watching sunrises and sunsets.

Buxton merges gently into Frisco. The village was settled in 1795. It hosts the Frisco Native American Museum, the Billy Mitchell Air Field (the only one on Hatteras Island), a National Park Service campground, and other amenities for travelers.

Stop to visit the unique shops in Hatteras Village. Walk the docks. Show up for a Saturday night fish fry, which Hatteras folks have been hosting for over half a century. Then journey to the Hatteras Ferry Docks for a ride across Hatteras Inlet.

Ocracoke is an island destination experience second to none on the Eastern Seaboard. Ocracoke Island, except for the privately owned lands of the village, is part of the Cape Hatteras National Seashore and has miles of beautiful sandy beaches and marshy sound shorelines to explore on foot, by vehicle, or by boat.

Ocracoke's historic streets are filled with points of interest, like the 2,290-square-foot parcel that is a British cemetery, the final resting place for four British sailors defending the East Coast of the United States during World War II. Explore the Ocracoke Preservation Society's museum and Springers Point, where the November 22, 1718, death of the notorious pirate Blackbeard is reenacted annually.

The byway's longest ferry ride crosses Ocracoke Inlet heading for Down East. The Ocracoke Island–to–Cedar Island Ferry travels over Pamlico Sound waters for 2 hours and 15 minutes. The trip signals a quieter way of life. From this ferry ride, the byway steps back in time with a view of Portsmouth Island, to the east of the ferry route and on the northern tip of Cape Lookout National Seashore. Settled in the 1700s and incorporated in 1753, Portsmouth was one of North Carolina's busiest ports of entry before the Civil War.

Known at one time as the shipping capital of the Outer Banks, it was named after Portsmouth, England. Today, the restored buildings on the island include a home, the church, a general store, the post office, the lifesaving station, and a school for townsfolk, the last of whom left the island in 1971. A private ferry service offers visitors a way to the island from Ocracoke. Portsmouth Island is a National Register Historic District and managed by the National Park Service, Cape Lookout National Seashore.

Cedar Island, the northern end of Down East, is an emersion into spectacular, expansive salt marshes, home to migrating waterfowl and Cedar Island National Wildlife Refuge. Wildlife viewing and photography buffs can find plenty of exciting scenes and gorgeous sunsets and sunrises to capture from this little-known treasure. This entry sets up a regular Down East rhythm of coastal village, marsh, coastal village, marsh.

The byway follows NC 12 from Whalebone Junction until about 10 miles south of the Cedar Island ferry terminal. NC 12 ends and becomes US 70 West. Sound names change from Pamlico to Core and Back Sounds with Nelson and Jarrett Bay. In Down East, the byway follows two loops through coastal villages. The villages are marked with old windblown oaks and harbors, a rich fishing heritage, and small coastal community way of life.

One loop features Atlantic and Sea Level around Nelson Bay. Atlantic was once called Hunting Quarters because of the abundance of game. Stacy, Davis, Williston, and Smyrna are arrayed along US 70. The enormous Davis Marsh surrounds Jarrett Bay. Williston and Smyrna are beside creeks feeding Jarrett Bay. Stacy is home of some of the area's best-known waterfowl decoy carvers, a tradition that continues today.

The second byway loop highlights Marshallberg, Gloucester, whose annual Wild Caught festival celebrates root music, local seafood, and produce, and Straits. The maritime village of Marshallberg, a working harbor, was known for its wooden boatbuilding traditions and skills. Today, Glouchester and Straits are both small coastal villages.

Straits Road leads across a causeway to Harkers Island, and the village features island homes and small cottage business dedicated to decoy carving, model boats, fresh seafood, and boatbuilding. The pronounced flare to the bow of a Harkers Island fishing vessel is a centuries-old boatbuilding tradition unique to the surrounding regional waters. Today, boatbuilding is primarily done on Harkers Island, with larger operations on the mainland and Jarrett Bay.

At the end of the road, the Core Sound Waterfowl Museum & Heritage Center celebrates these traditions. The center built by Down East communities reinforces an experience of place with stories, objects, and exhibits. Harkers Island Elementary School hosts the decoy festival, and the museum hosts Waterfowl Weekend simultaneously the first weekend of December.

Hiking trails connect the museum to the Cape Lookout National Seashore Visitor Center with informative exhibits and ferry rides to the Cape Lookout Lighthouse.

In the first or last stretch of the byway, the landscape features farmland. Otway and Bettie are two farming towns separated by Ward's Creek. Otway is named for Otway Burns, a privateer who fought the British in the War of 1812. Bettie once had a mill powered by the tides of the North River, which marks the start or end of the Outer Banks National Scenic Byway.

One

Transportation and the Highway

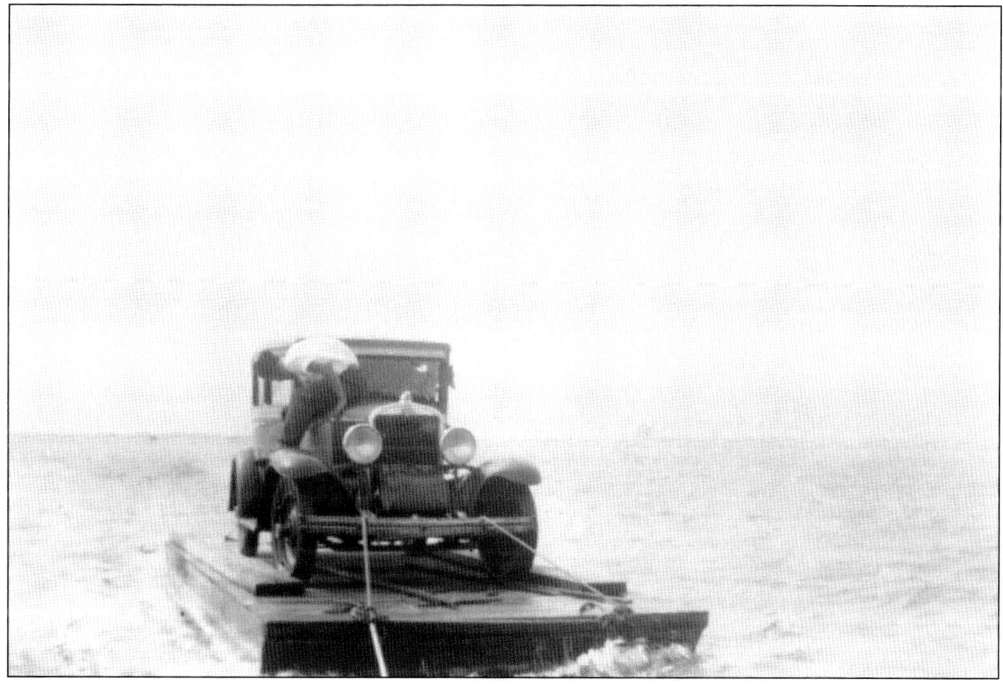

Prior to the 1930s, visitors coming to the Outer Banks of North Carolina had to endure treacherous travel conditions. Ferries and other modes of transportation were primitive, and few people were hardy enough to endure the long and arduous trip to the barrier islands. In 1931, Walker Styron of Portsmouth Island ferried his 1929 Chevrolet from Core Banks to the village of Atlantic. The trip, an all-day endeavor at best, was accomplished only if the weather permitted. (Courtesy of the Cape Lookout National Seashore.)

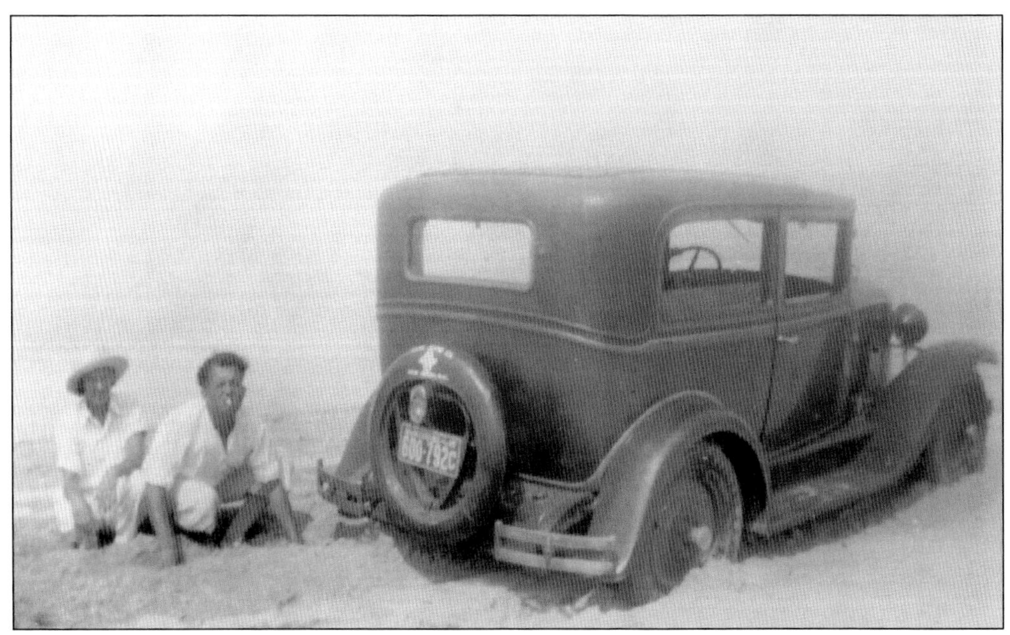

Originally, island residents and visitors used the beaches or sound-side sand trails to traverse the barrier islands of Hatteras, Ocracoke, and Core Banks. Travel was difficult, and it was a common occurrence for vehicles to become mired in the sand. (Courtesy of the Cape Lookout National Seashore.)

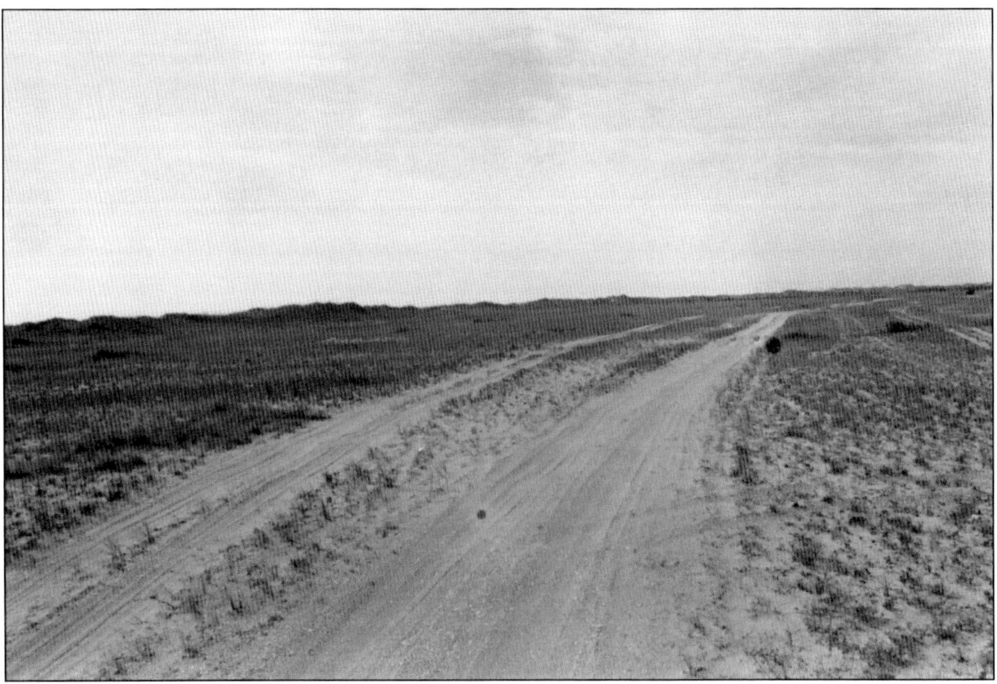

The first vehicles arrived on the Outer Banks around 1915, the same year the US Life-Saving Service became part of the US Coast Guard. The only open roads on Hatteras Island were sand routes that were later used as today's highway, known as the Outer Banks National Scenic Byway Highway. (Courtesy of the Cape Hatteras National Seashore.)

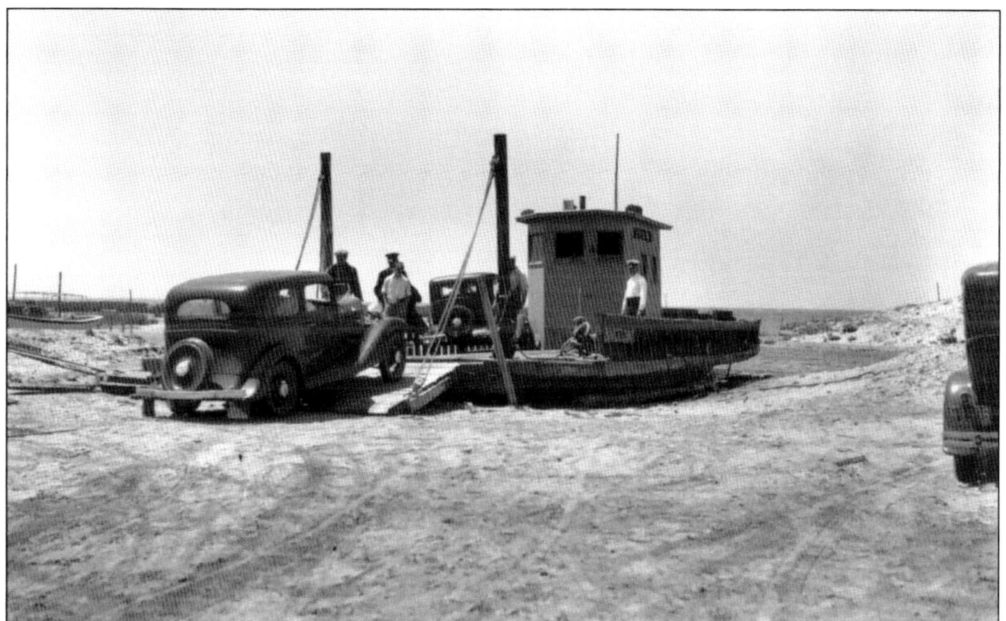

In the 1920s and 1930s, Hatteras, Ocracoke, and Core Banks residents occasionally needed to leave the islands. Vehicles were loaded on makeshift ferries run by local entrepreneurs who possessed the navigational skills to cross the treacherous inlets. In the 1920s, the State of North Carolina recognized that a system of ferries was needed to provide reliable service to the islands. Visitors soon fell in love with the wildness of the islands and abundant fishing opportunities and flocked to the area. (Courtesy of the Cape Hatteras National Seashore.)

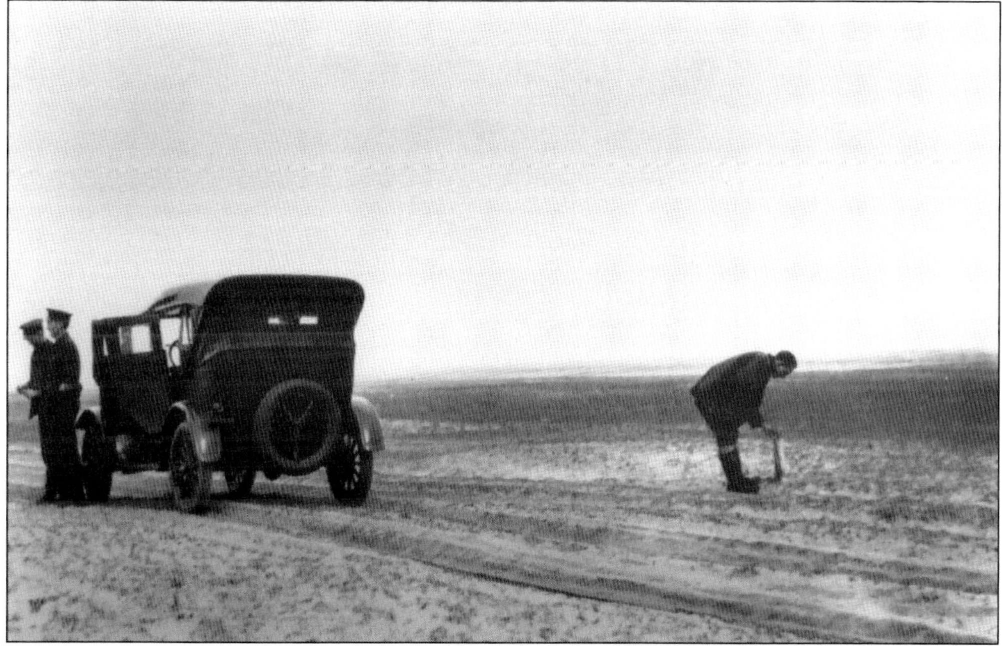

By 1935, surveyors were mapping the roads and land along the Outer Banks. The vehicles followed existing tire tracks in order to attempt to stay on solid ground along barrier islands. (Courtesy of the Cape Hatteras National Seashore.)

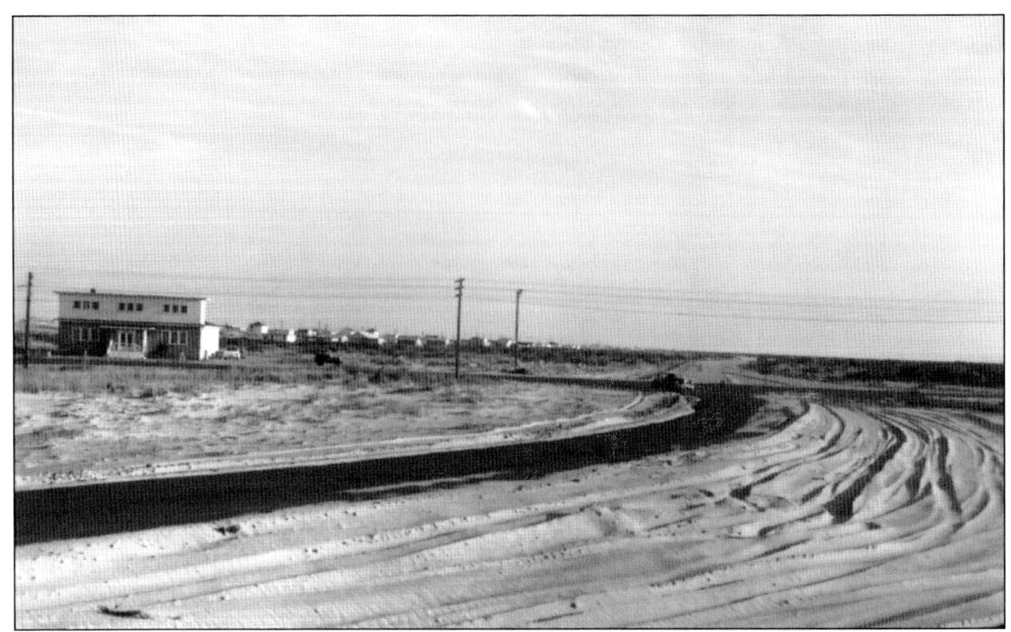

Pictured here in 1958 is construction of the new road at Whalebone Junction in Nags Head, North Carolina, at the north entrance to Cape Hatteras National Seashore begun in the 1950s. Today, travelers enter the scenic byway from the north at Whalebone Junction in Nags Head or from the south at the North River Bridge on US 70 East, just past Beaufort, North Carolina. (Courtesy of the Cape Hatteras National Seashore.)

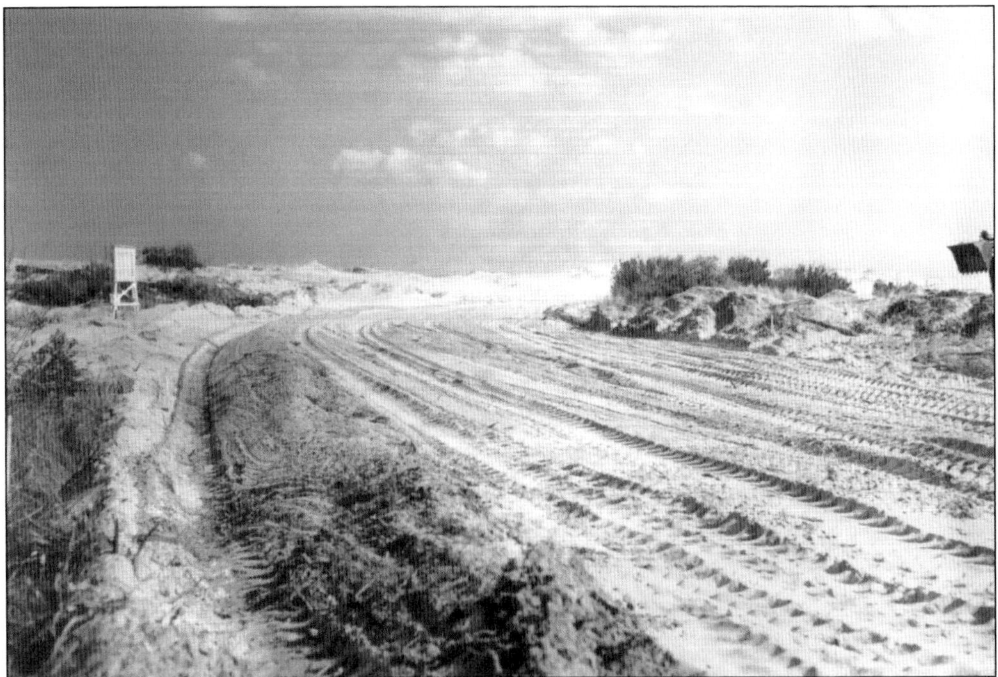

Coquina Beach, located on Bodie Island at the north entrance of the Outer Banks National Scenic Byway, is one of the most popular beaches. A new entrance road to the parking lot was built in 1955. (Courtesy of the Cape Hatteras National Seashore.)

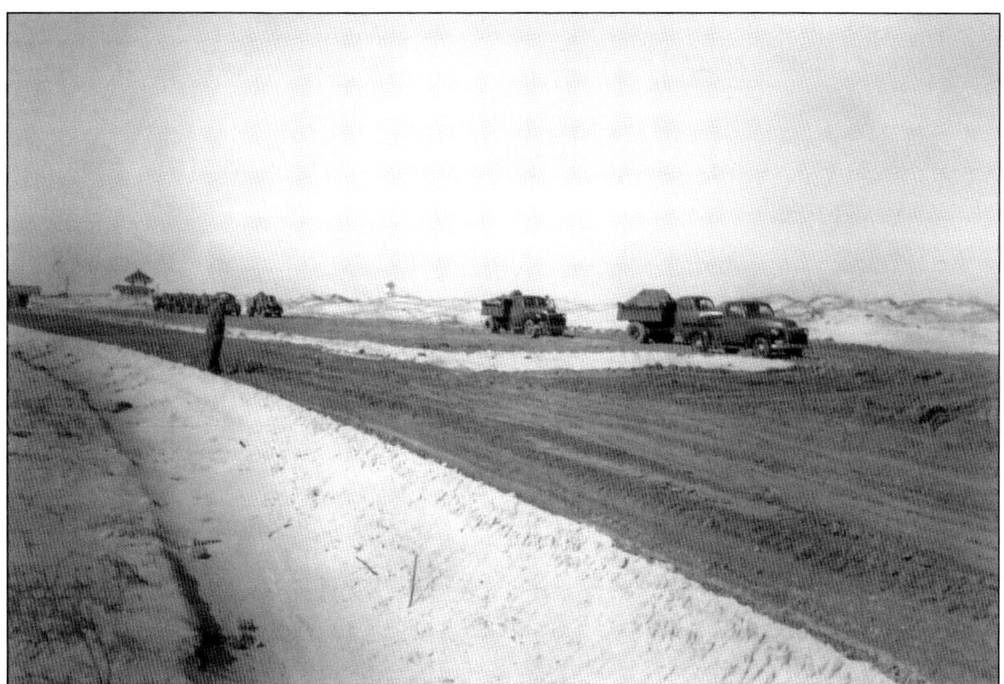

By the early 1950s, the construction of a new road provided a hardened, more dependable surface for travel and access to Hatteras Island and points further south flourished. (Courtesy of the Cape Hatteras National Seashore.)

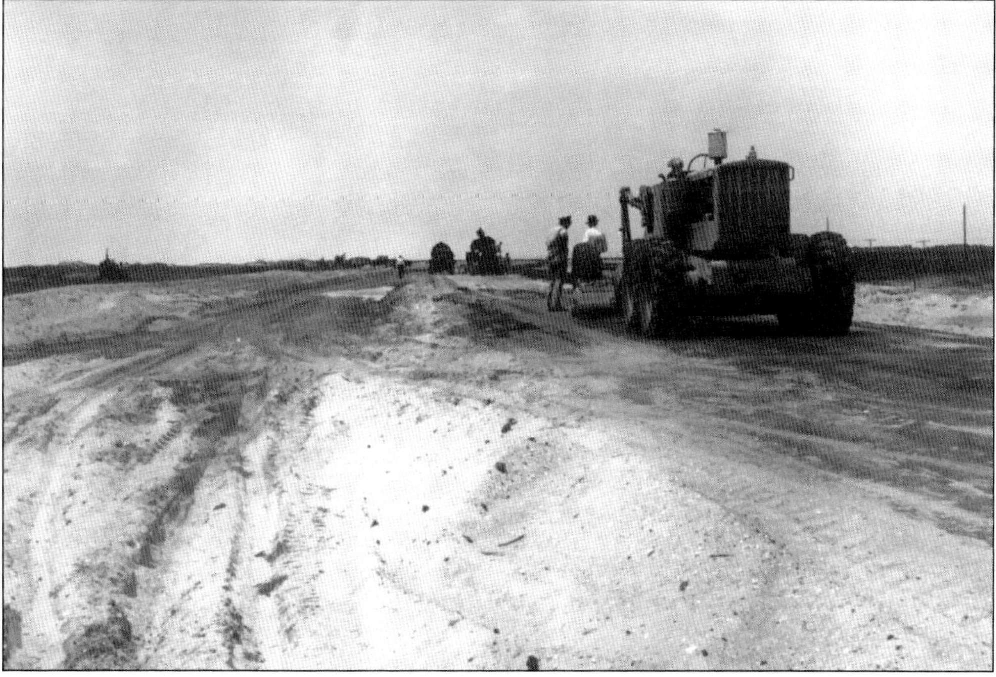

Work vehicles line up in 1955 to deliver gravel to one of the newly constructed parking lots, which provided access to beaches of what is now known as Cape Hatteras National Seashore, America's first national seashore. (Courtesy of the Cape Hatteras National Seashore.)

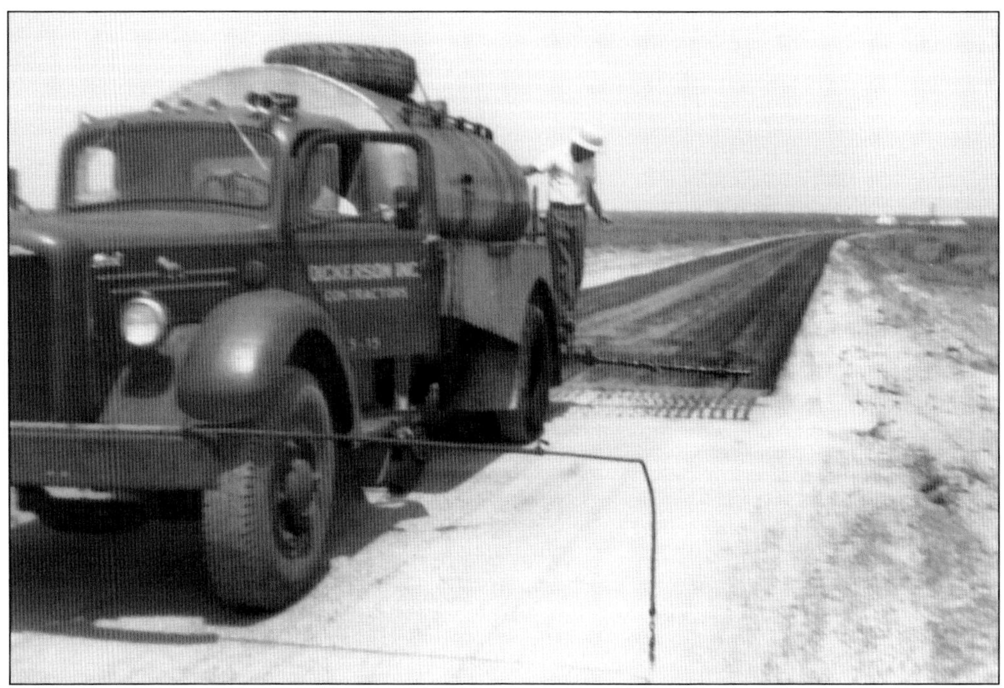

NC Route 12 was not completed until 1952. The paved road forever changed the island, making it easier for its residents to travel between the villages as well as enabling the island to host thousands of visitors each year. (Courtesy of the Cape Hatteras National Seashore.)

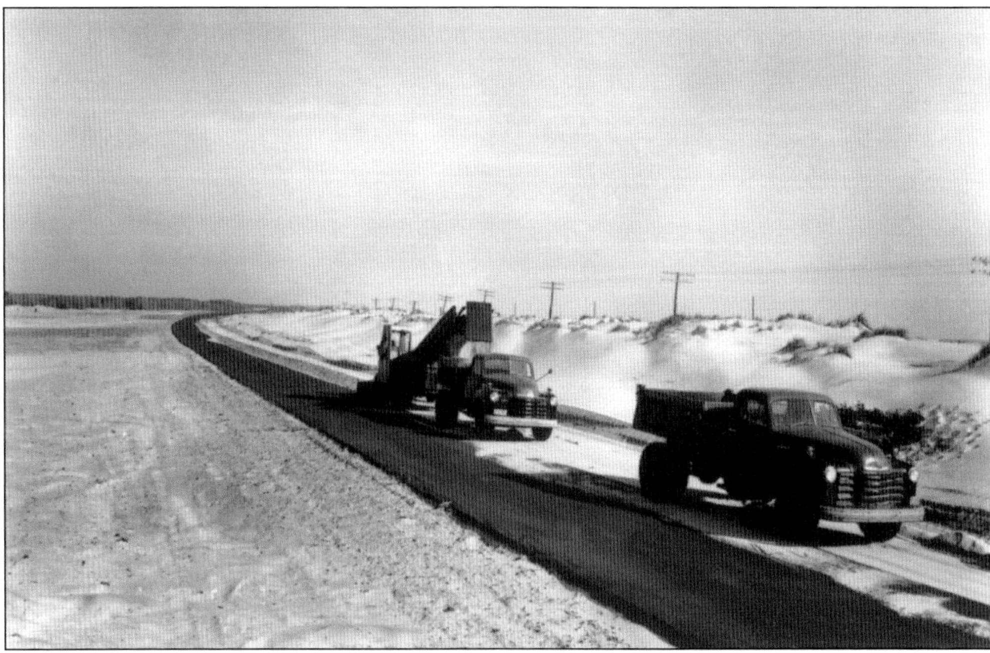

Pictured here in 1958 is the view north along the newly paved road leading through Pea Island National Wildlife Refuge. In the background, note the large sand dunes on the ocean side, built by the Civilian Conservation Corps (CCC) in the 1930s. (Courtesy of the Cape Hatteras National Seashore.)

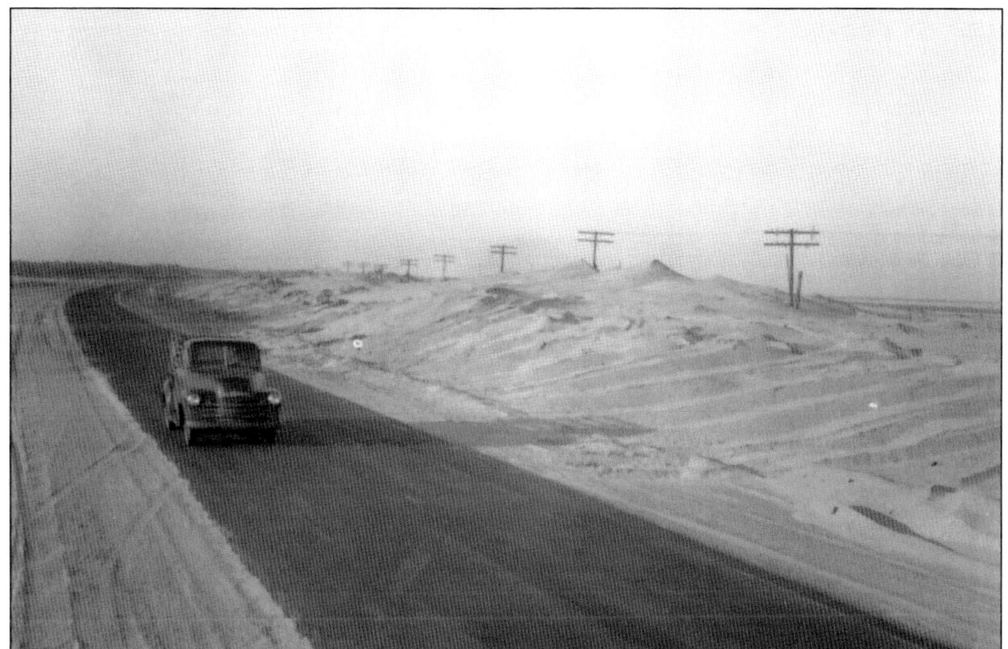

By 1959, the road through Pea Island National Wildlife Refuge had been paved and made automobile travel much easier. Travelers and their vehicles appreciated the new hard-surface road, as it was much more navigable than the former difficult maneuvering through sand, mud, and water along the banks. (Courtesy of the Cape Hatteras National Seashore.)

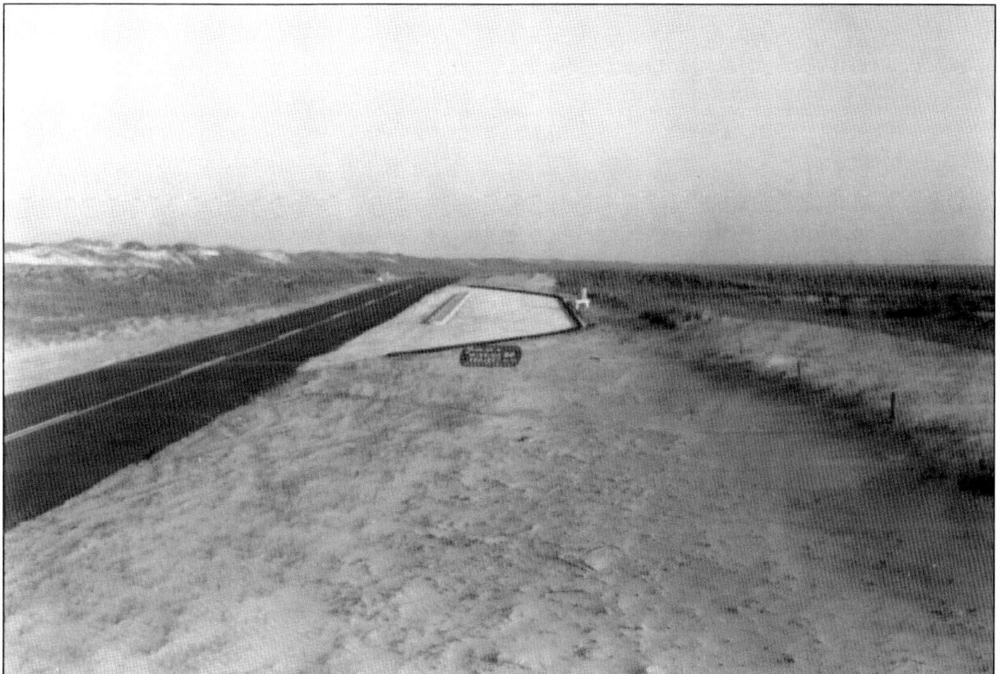

The newly paved NC Route 12 highway included an addition of a parking overlook, which allowed visitors to view the birds that inhabited the refuge. The overlook shown here in 1959 is at the south dike of the North Pond. (Courtesy of the Cape Hatteras National Seashore.)

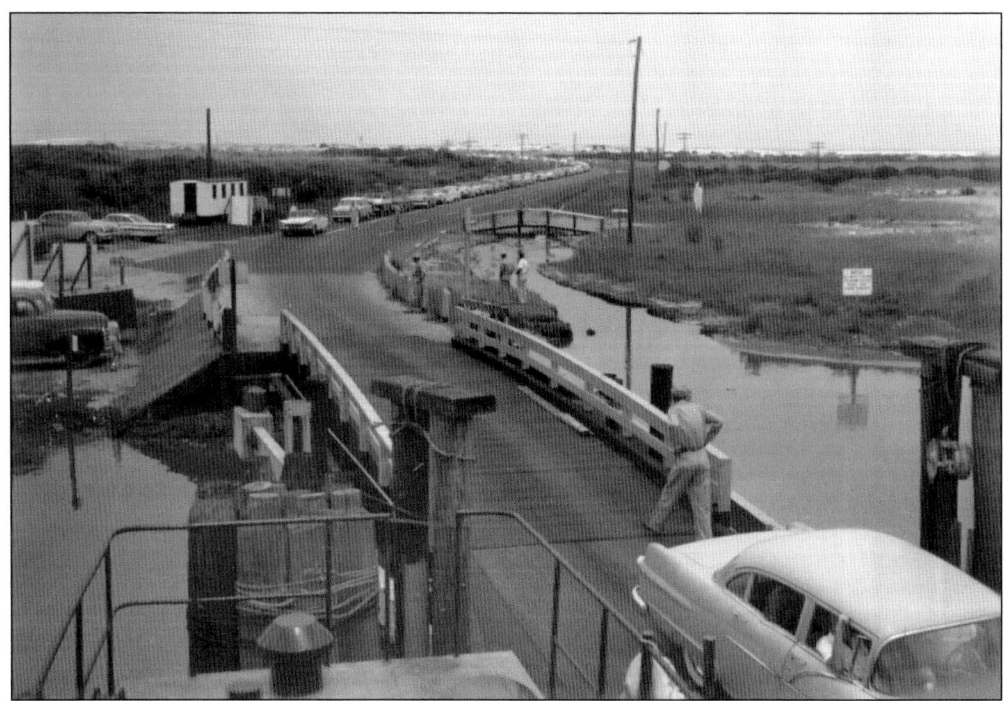

Here is a 1960 view of the Oregon Inlet Ferry, which served the long line of vehicles awaiting the ferry transport across Oregon Inlet to Hatteras Island. With the completion of NC Route 12 as far south as Oregon Inlet, the increasing numbers of vehicles prompted the State of North Carolina to offer larger vessels for a more efficient ferry service to the islands. (Courtesy of the Cape Hatteras National Seashore.)

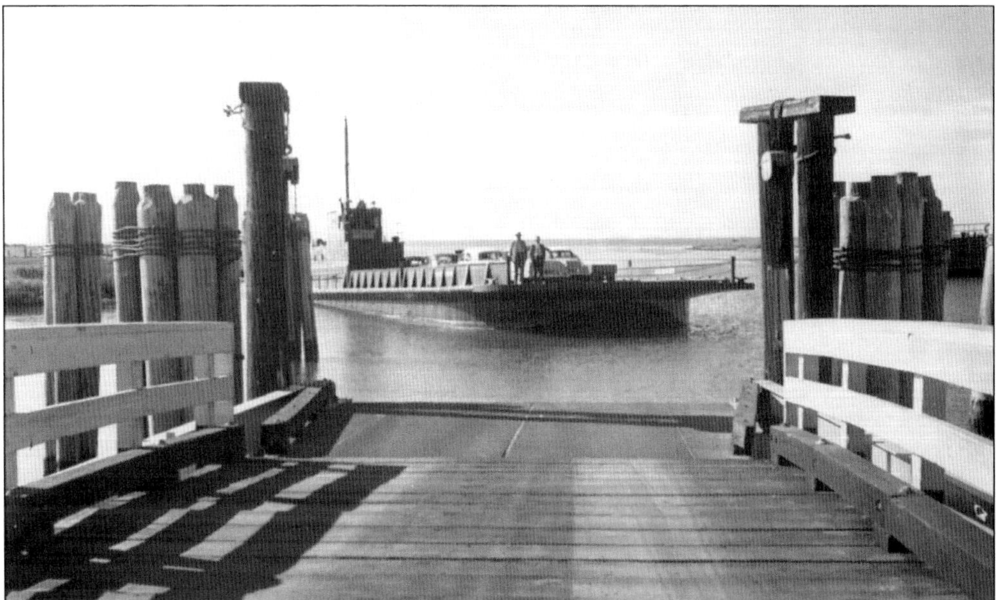

A ferry is pictured here approaching North Slip at Oregon Inlet in 1960. The regular scheduled ferry on the Oregon Inlet route was discontinued in 1963 after the opening of the Herbert C. Bonner Bridge. (Courtesy of the Cape Hatteras National Seashore.)

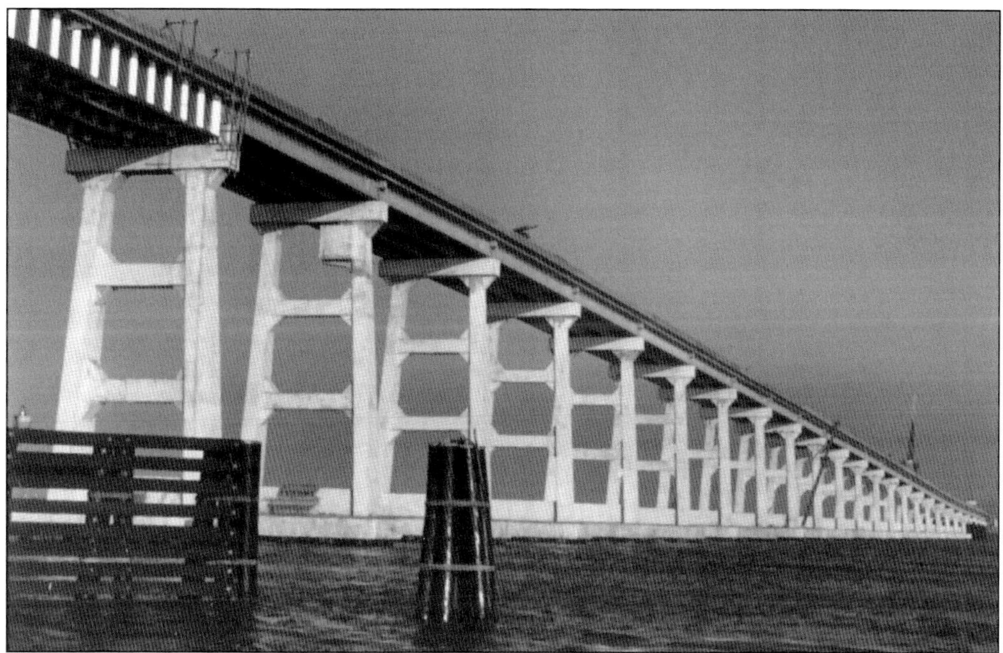

Prior to the construction of the Herbert C. Bonner Bridge, Hatteras Island was only accessible by small aircraft or ferry. Ferries could carry a maximum of 2,000 people per day. When the Herbert C. Bonner Bridge was completed in 1963, Hatteras Island was changed forever. Vacationers have been streaming onto the island ever since. (Courtesy of the Cape Hatteras National Seashore.)

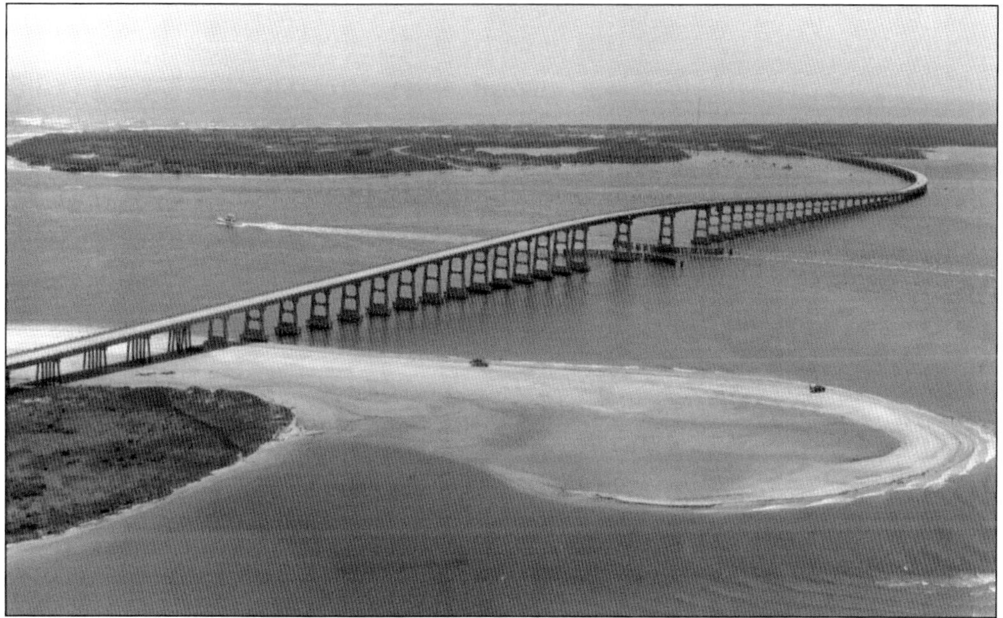

This aerial view of the Herbert C. Bonner Bridge, a 2.5-mile bridge spanning Oregon Inlet, was captured in 1963. The waters of the Pamlico Sound join the Atlantic Ocean and separate Bodie Island from Hatteras Island. Oregon Inlet has a nearby harbor, home of the preeminent offshore Gulf Stream charter fishing fleets on the East Coast—the Oregon Inlet Fishing Center. (Courtesy of the Cape Hatteras National Seashore.)

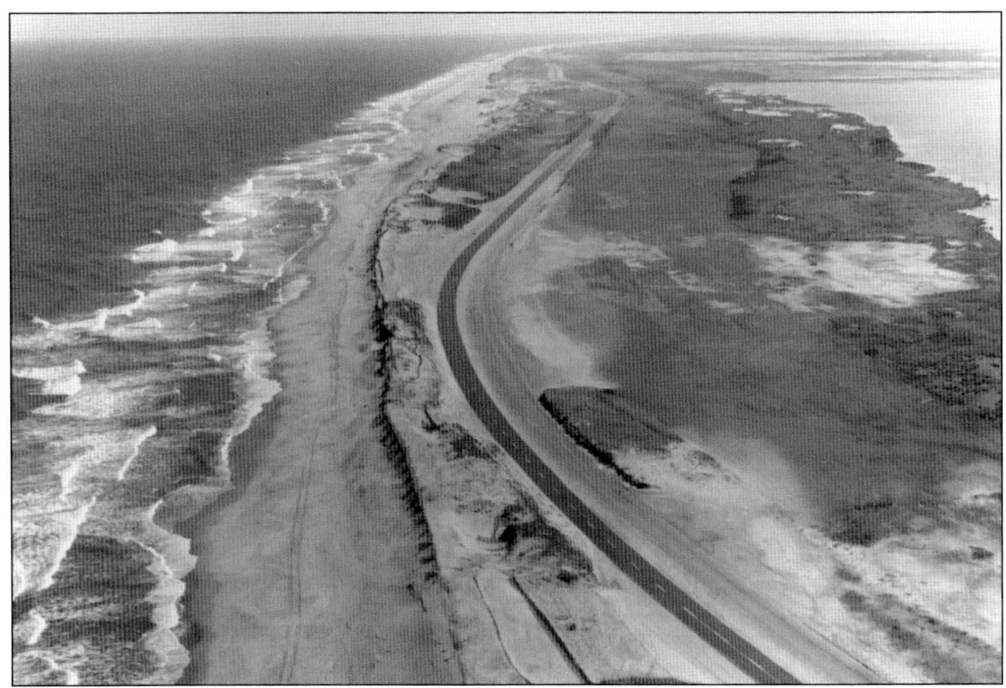

This is an aerial view of NC Route 12 looking south through Pea Island NWR from 1965. The Atlantic Ocean is on the left and dike ponds are on the right. (Courtesy of the Cape Hatteras National Seashore.)

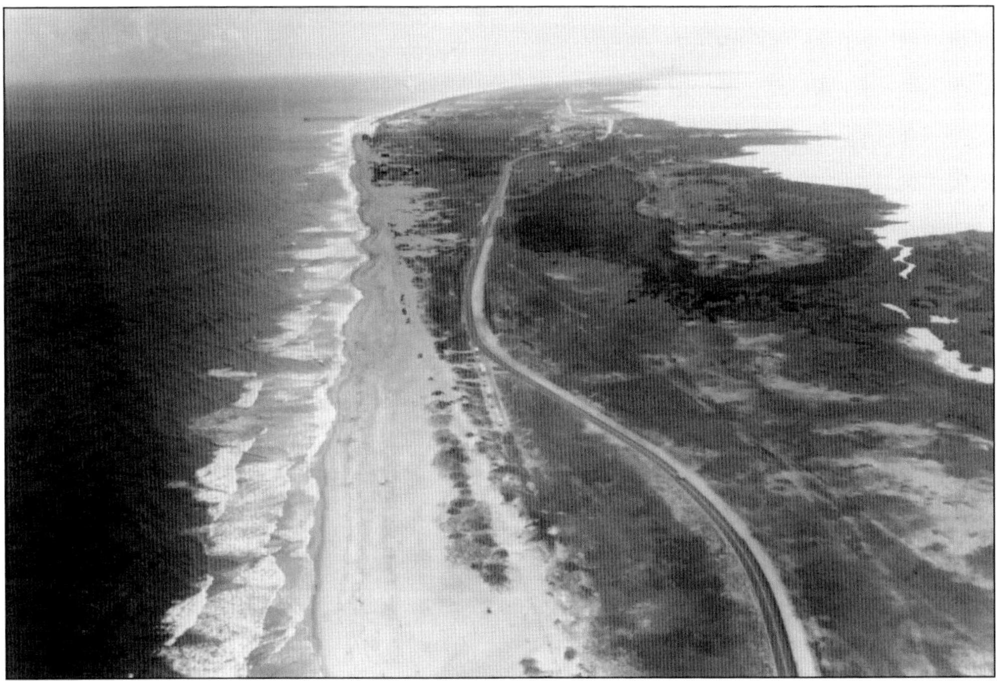

NC Route 12 is pictured here from above as it heads south through the community of Rodanthe, Waves, and Salvo. The Rodanthe Fishing Pier (extending into the ocean) can be seen in the far distance. (Courtesy of the Cape Hatteras National Seashore.)

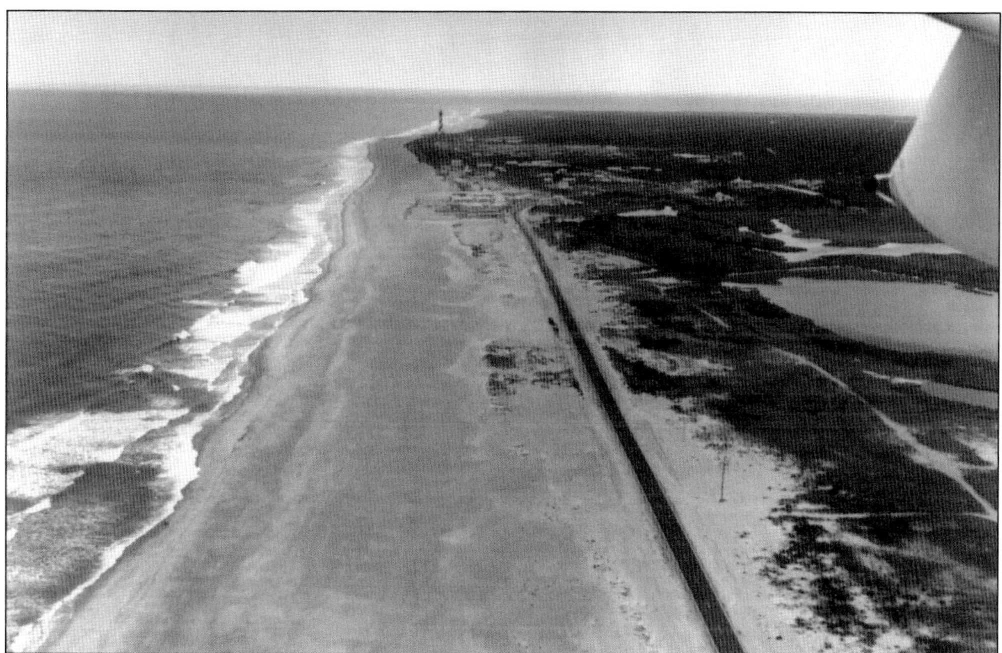

This is a 1974 aerial view of NC Route 12 and points south toward Buxton, North Carolina. The Cape Hatteras Lighthouse is visible in the background at its former location. By 1999, the severely eroded shoreline necessitated the move of the lighthouse a distance of 2,900 feet from the immediate surf zone. (Courtesy of the Cape Hatteras National Seashore.)

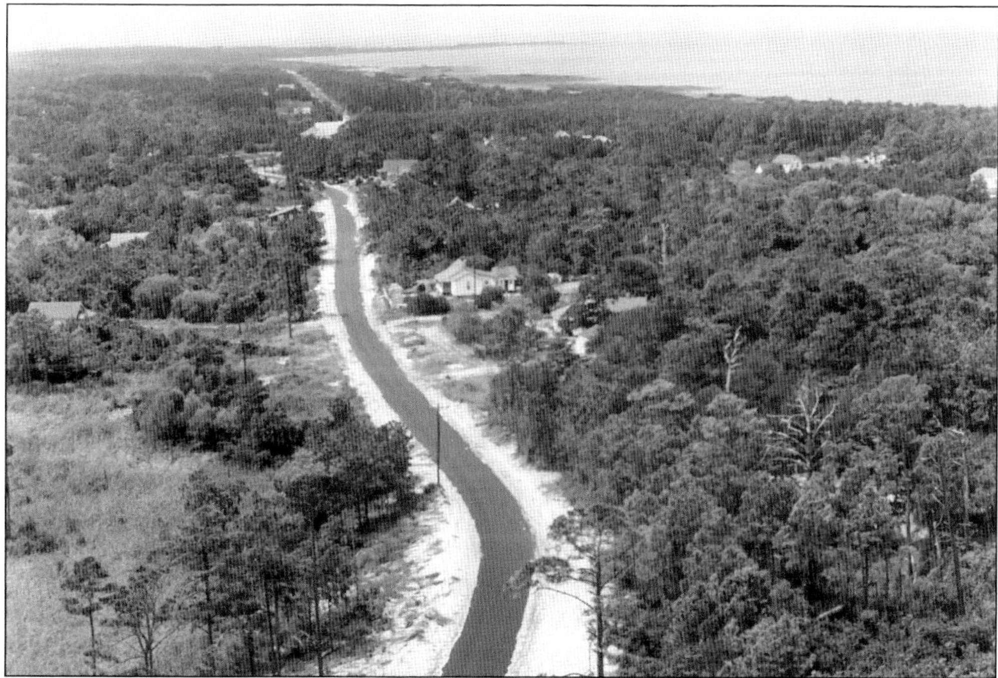

The photograph is a 1974 aerial view of NC Route 12 through Buxton Woods (today a designated coastal reserve) leading toward the community of Frisco, North Carolina. (Courtesy of the Cape Hatteras National Seashore.)

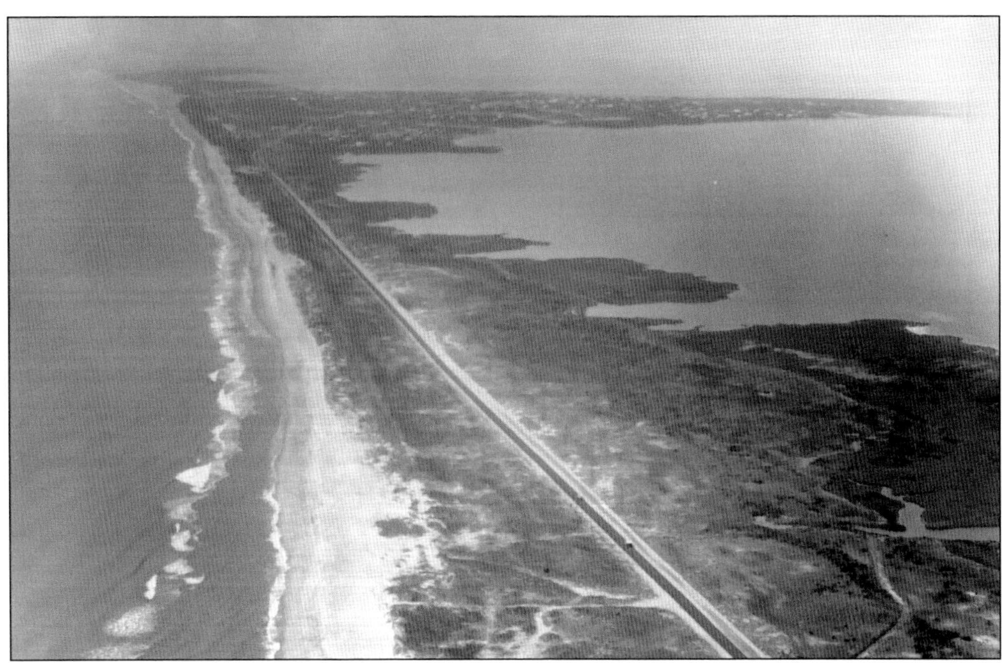

NC Route 12 winds through the narrow island section known as Sandy Bay, which leads to the village of Hatteras. The two structures on the left of the highway, in the foreground, are part of Creeds Hill Life-Saving Station (active 1878–1918), now a private home. (Courtesy of the Cape Hatteras National Seashore.)

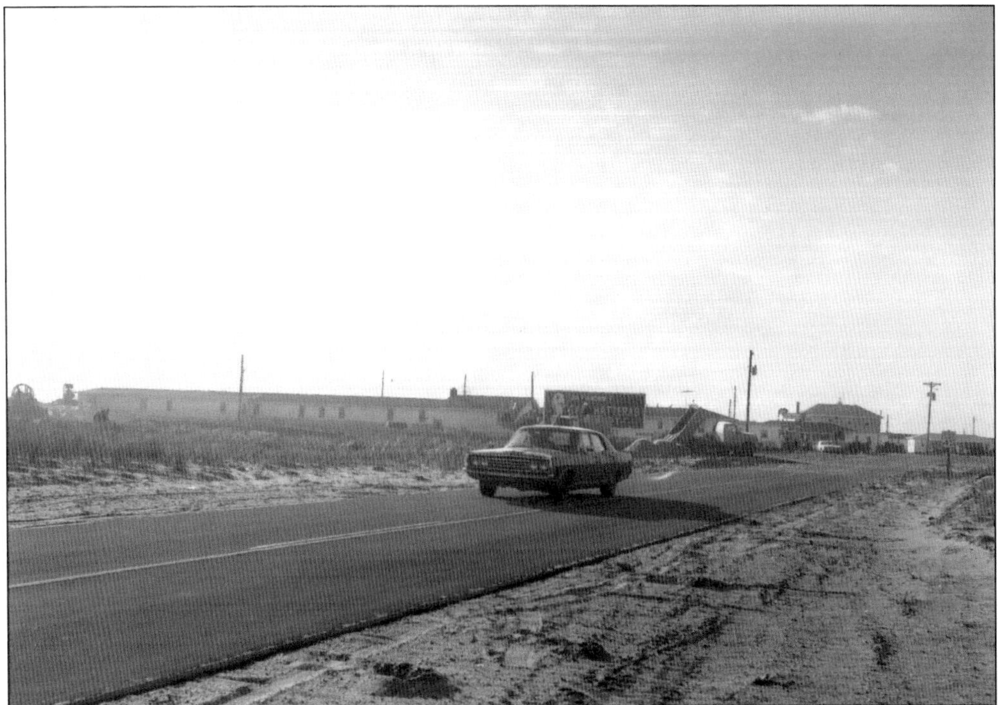

The 1970 photograph shows a newly paved section of the highway after a passing storm damaged the road near Hatteras Village. (Courtesy of the Cape Hatteras National Seashore.)

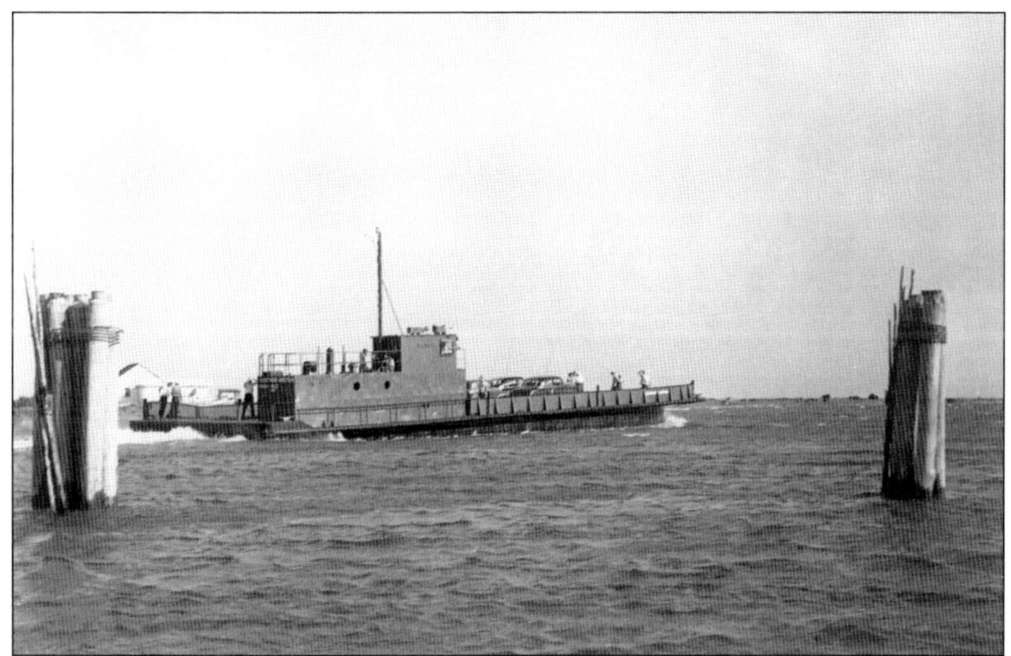

By 1953, the ferries leaving Hatteras Island en route to Ocracoke Island were operating daily runs. Between the 1920s and 1950s, other privately operated ferry routes were subsidized or bought outright by the North Carolina Department of Transportation to keep the fares low or nonexistent. (Courtesy of the Cape Hatteras National Seashore.)

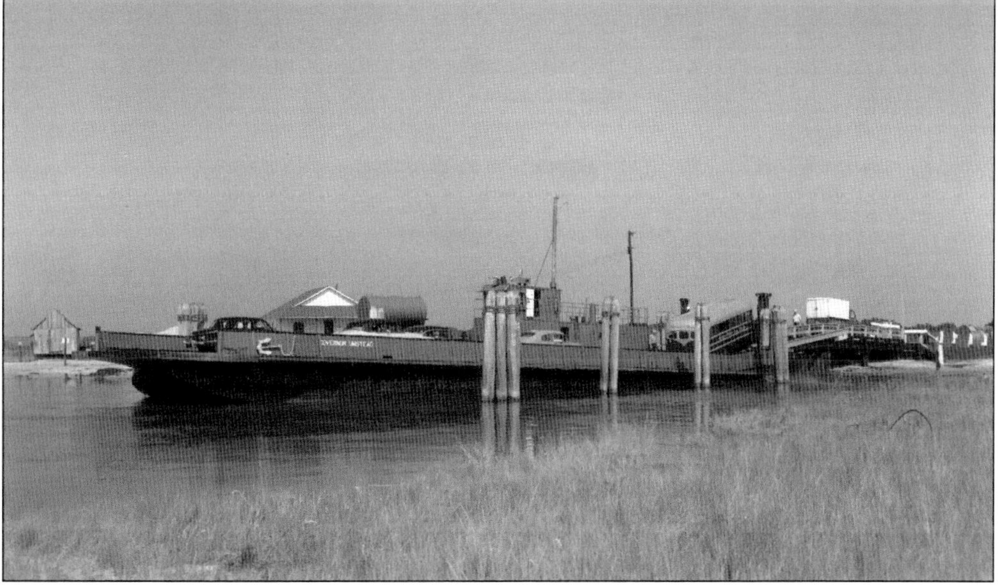

On August 8, 1953, a newly built ferry, the *William B. Umstead*, named after a former senator and governor of North Carolina, began departing Hatteras en route to Ocracoke Island. The state-owned and -operated ferry system soon replaced all the local entrepreneurs and provided more dependable access to destinations farther south. Once established, the transportation link to Ocracoke Island and Cedar Island enhanced access, allowing both areas to become popular vacation destinations. (Courtesy of the Cape Hatteras National Seashore.)

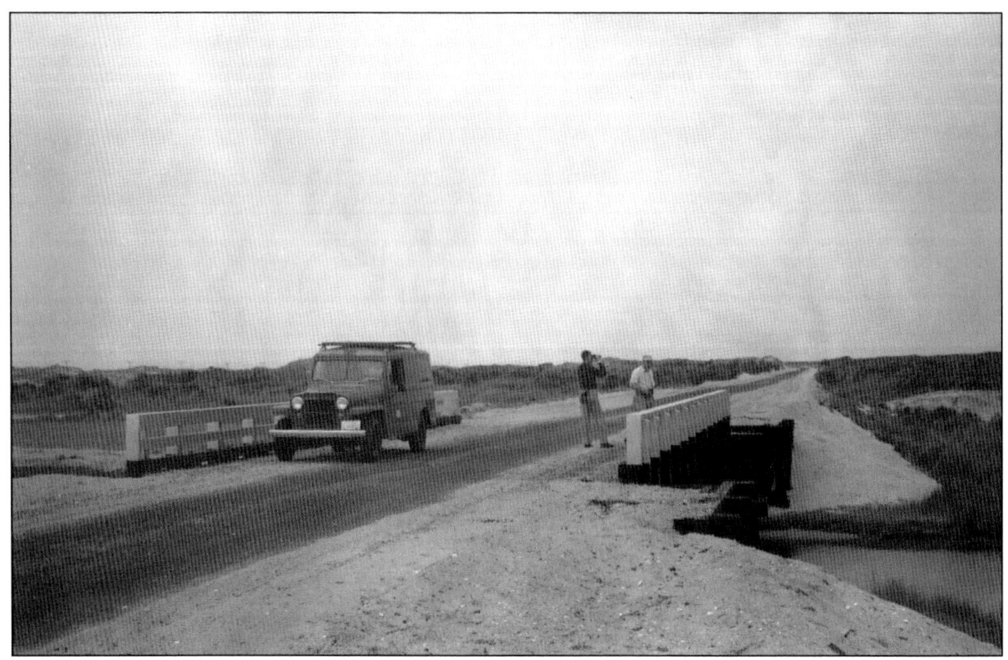

Ocracoke Island's NC Route 12 lanes were paved in the 1950s throughout the village. By 1956, a paved highway ran the length of the 13-mile-long island from the northern Ocracoke Ferry Terminal to Ocracoke Village, including seven small bridges built in the 1950s and replaced in 2008. (Courtesy of the Cape Hatteras National Seashore.)

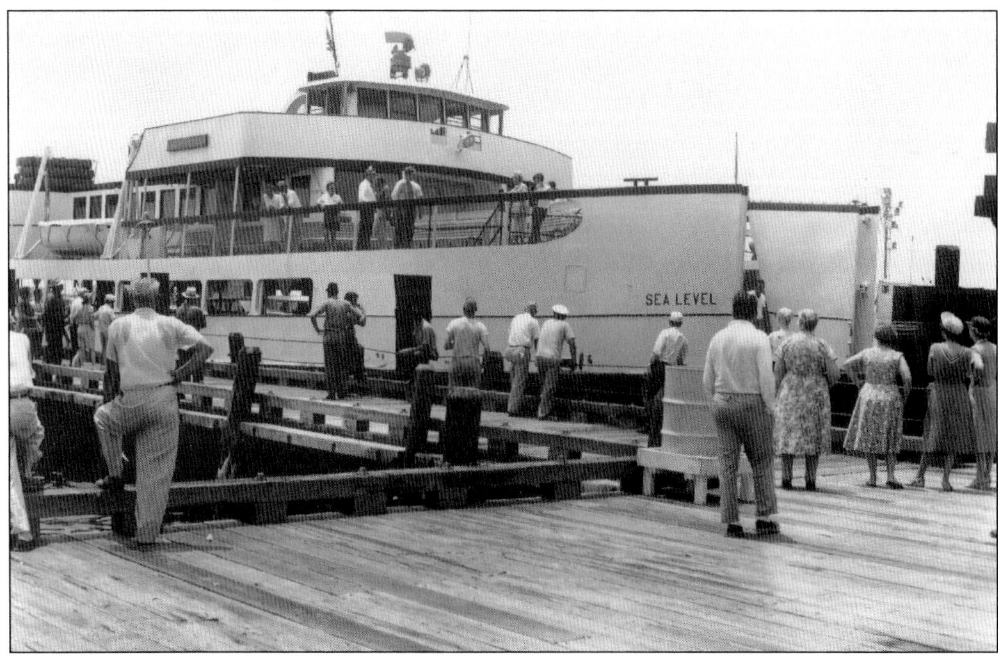

In 1961, service began between Ocracoke and Cedar Island. The *Sea Level* ferry carried passengers and vehicles on this 2.5-hour journey from Ocracoke to Cedar Island. The route provided a southern connection to the mainland and allowed improved access for the motoring public to the Outer Banks across the expansive Pamlico Sound. (Courtesy of the Cape Lookout National Seashore)

Two

Nation's History Passing By

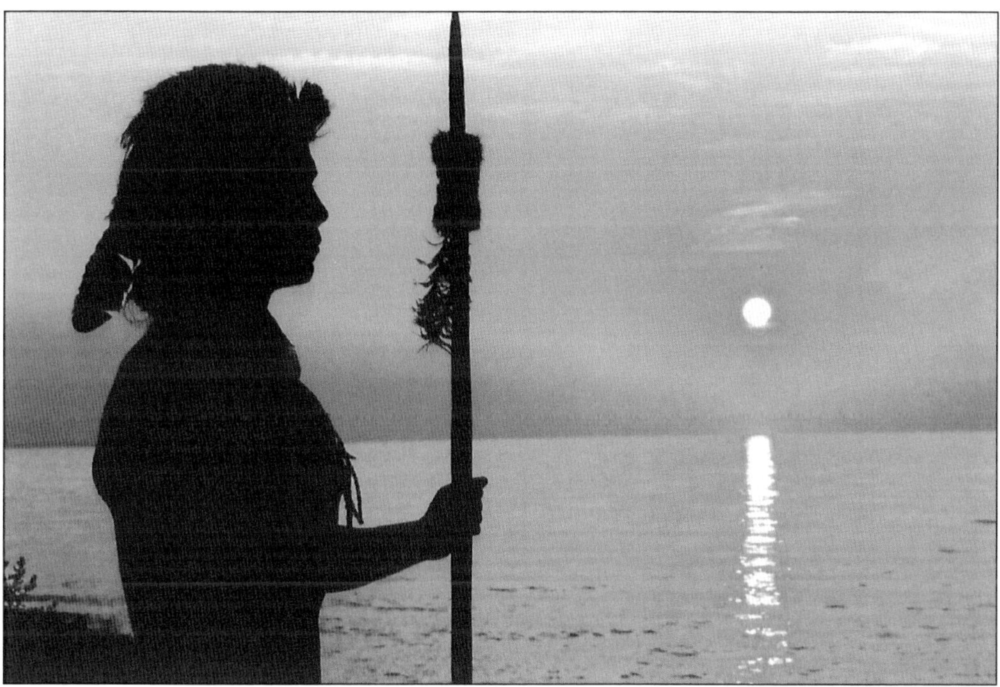

Evidence of Native American tribes, the earliest inhabitants of the Outer Banks and Down East barrier islands, can be traced to over 1,000 years ago. Early European explorers arrived in the 1500s. During the 18th and 19th centuries, descendants of those native tribes and European settlers claimed the lands of the Outer Banks. Many of them were farmers and harvesters of the sea, and they maintained a great deal of self-sufficiency in order to survive the harsh conditions found on this windswept and isolated coastal area. The indigenous population in the late 1500s was made up of Algonquian people. Separate groups were named the Croatan, who lived on Roanoke and Hatteras Islands, the Woccocock on Ocracoke Island, and the Corre tribe, which occupied the Harkers Island area of eastern North Carolina. (Courtesy of the Roanoke Island Historical Association.)

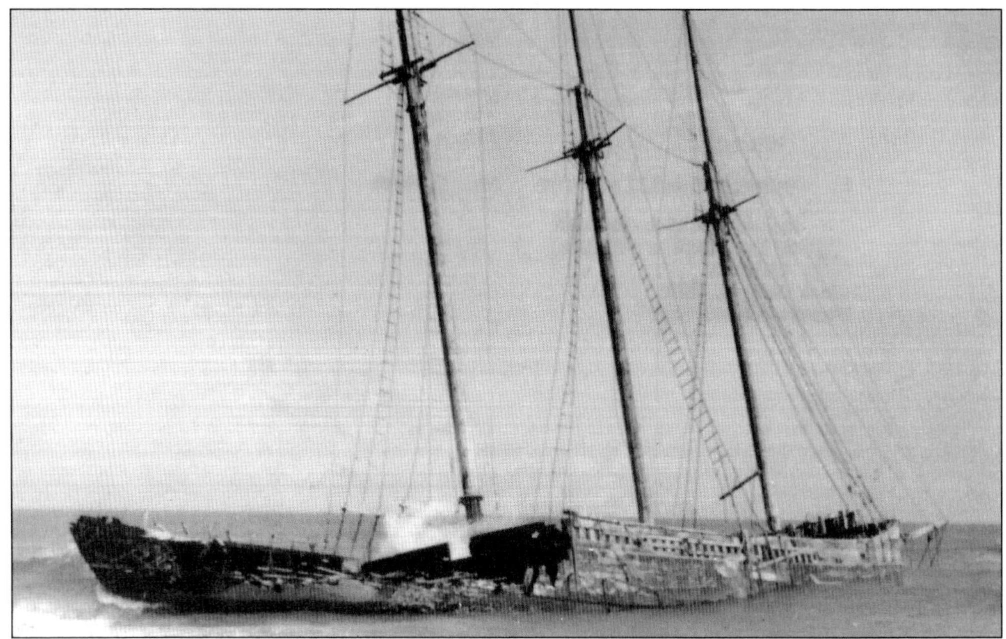

The Spanish explored much of the North Carolina coast before the English arrived. The history of the Outer Banks is rich in shipwreck and pirate stories. Three ships of a 1750 Spanish fleet met their fate in a hurricane, which washed them ashore on the beaches of the Outer Banks. Treasure hunters have long since sought the remains and treasures lost from the El Salvador fleet near Cape Lookout. The photograph is of an unknown shipwreck on Ocracoke Island. (Courtesy of the Cape Hatteras National Seashore.)

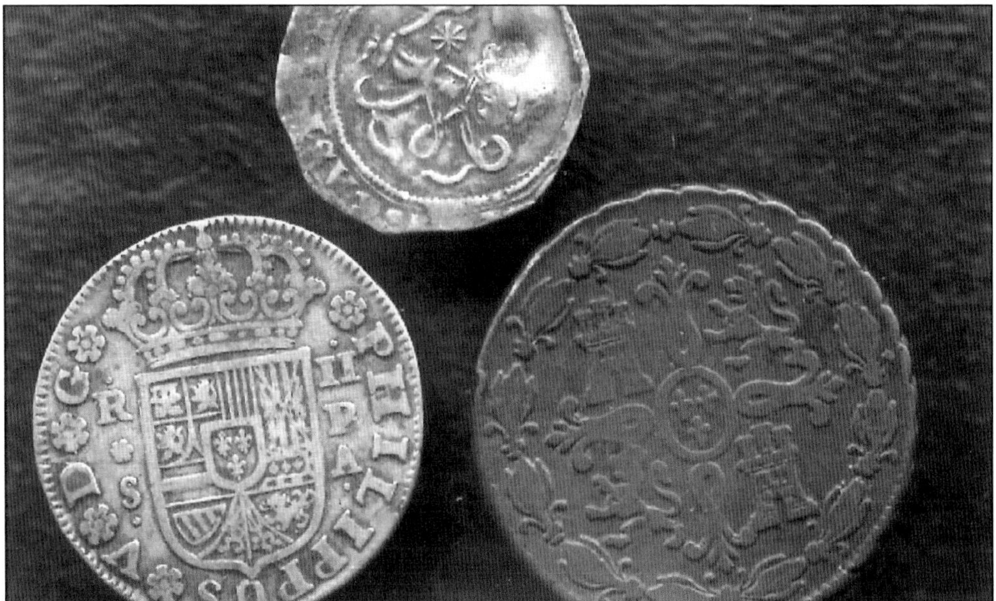

In the past, more shipwrecks were visible onshore than are seen today. Storm events are constantly covering and uncovering the remains of these old ships. Today, artifacts such as Spanish coins and olive jars continue to wash ashore. Pictured here in 2003 are examples of Spanish coins found after a hurricane. (Courtesy of the Cape Lookout National Seashore.)

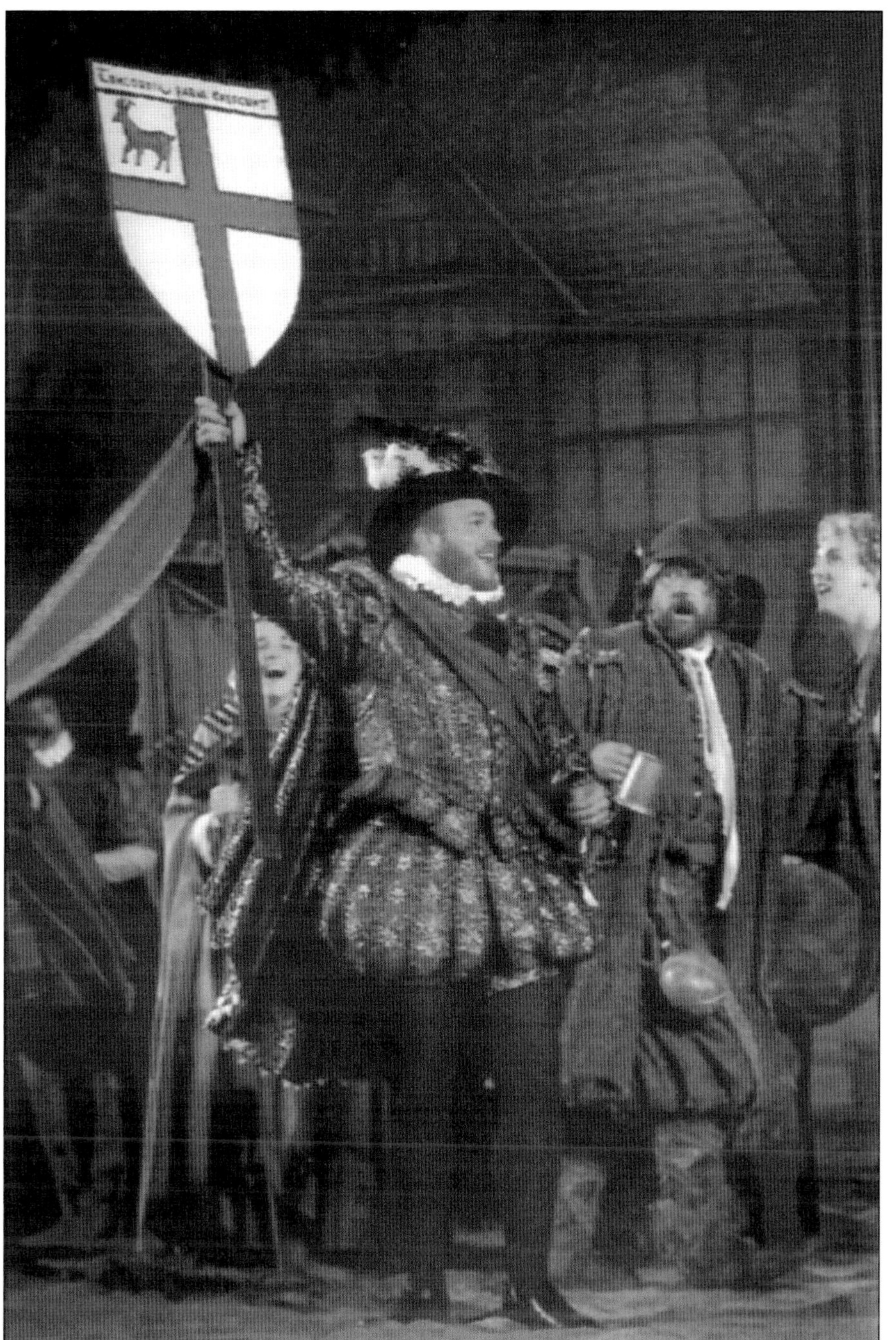

This is a 1980 photograph of *The Lost Colony* outdoor drama. The annual drama depicts the first (16th century) English colonists' attempt to settle the New World. In 1587, the English, with Capt. John White and 116 colonists, explored the surrounding waters of the Outer Banks, where they encountered friendly natives. Their first attempt at settlement occurred on Roanoke Island. White departed for England to bring back supplies and to carry the news of this new colony. When he returned in 1590, all of the 116 colonists had disappeared. (Courtesy of the Roanoke Island Historical Association.)

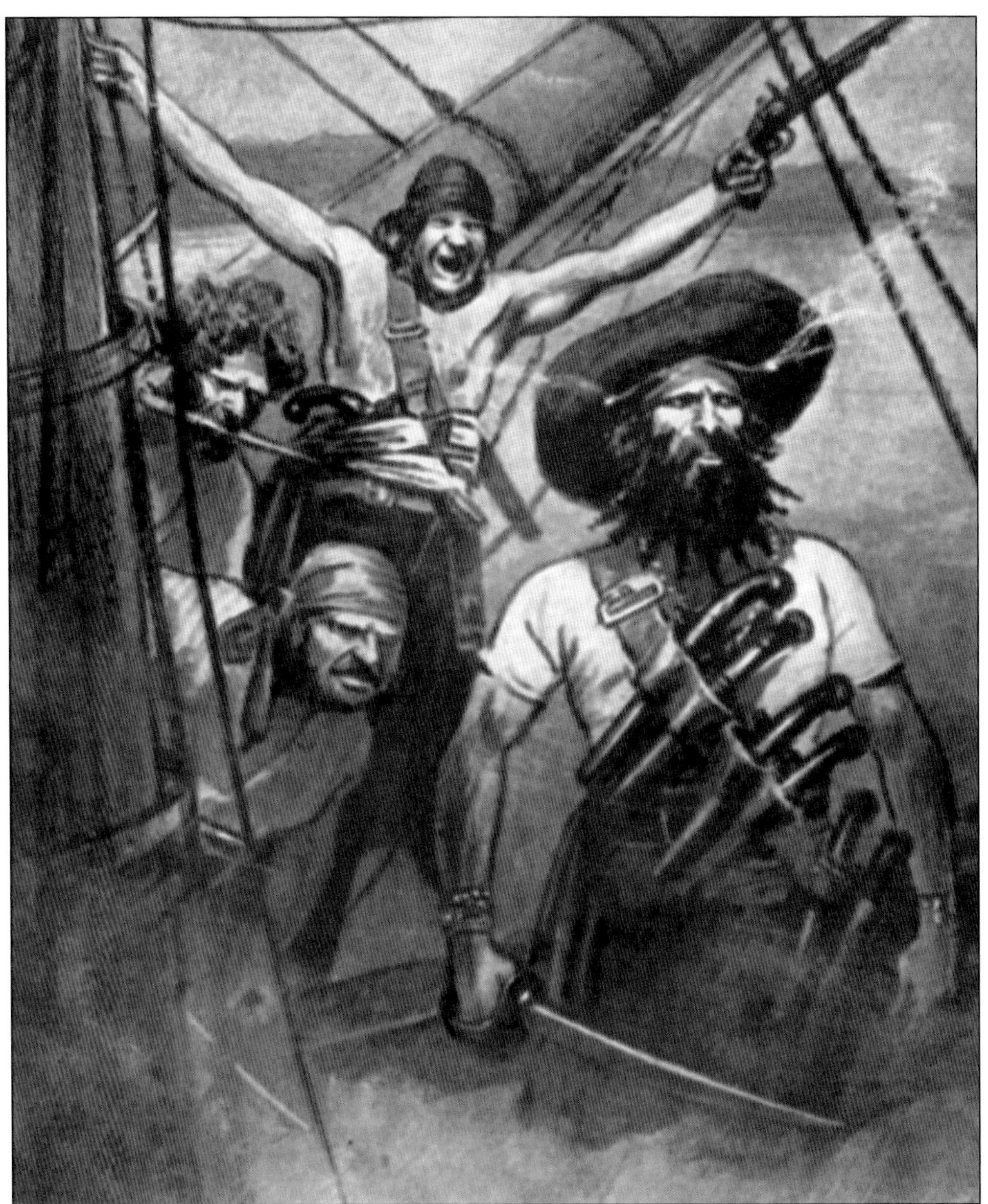

One of the most fearsome and infamous pirates of the time was Edward Teach, known as Blackbeard. In 1717, after stealing a ship from a plundering episode, he began his reign of terror in the new ship, which he named *Queen Anne's Revenge*. He outfitted her for pirating with 300 men and 40 cannons. He sailed the Caribbean and the Atlantic along coastal waters of the newly formed American colonies, torturing merchant ships and stealing cargo. Blackbeard was killed near Ocracoke, North Carolina, in 1718. (Courtesy of the North Carolina Department of Archives and History.)

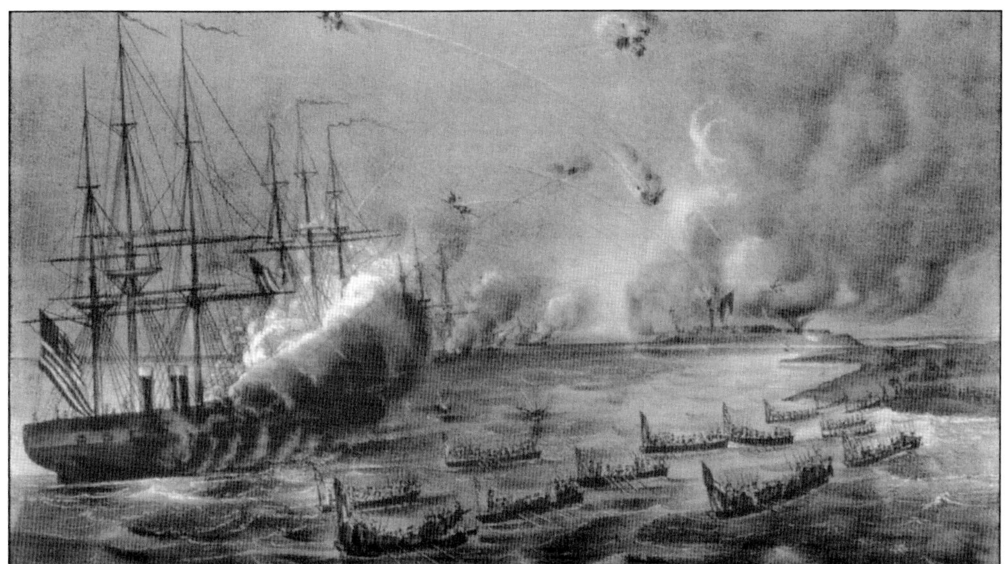

Both sides recognized the importance of controlling Hatteras Inlet as a strategic advantage to control the sounds, rivers, and seaports of North Carolina. In 1861, Confederate troops quickly erected both Fort Hatteras and Fort Clark to protect the inlet. The capture of the steamer *Fanny*, the sinking of the US troop transport *Oriental*, the loss of the USS *Monitor* offshore Cape Hatteras, and building Hotel De Afrique, the first safe haven for freed slaves in North Carolina, are examples of Civil War events that occurred on or offshore Hatteras Island. Camp Washington was established by Confederate troops on Core Banks in the spring of 1861. The areas of Back Sound and Straits were protected by two Confederate camps located on Harkers Island. (Courtesy of the Cape Hatteras National Seashore.)

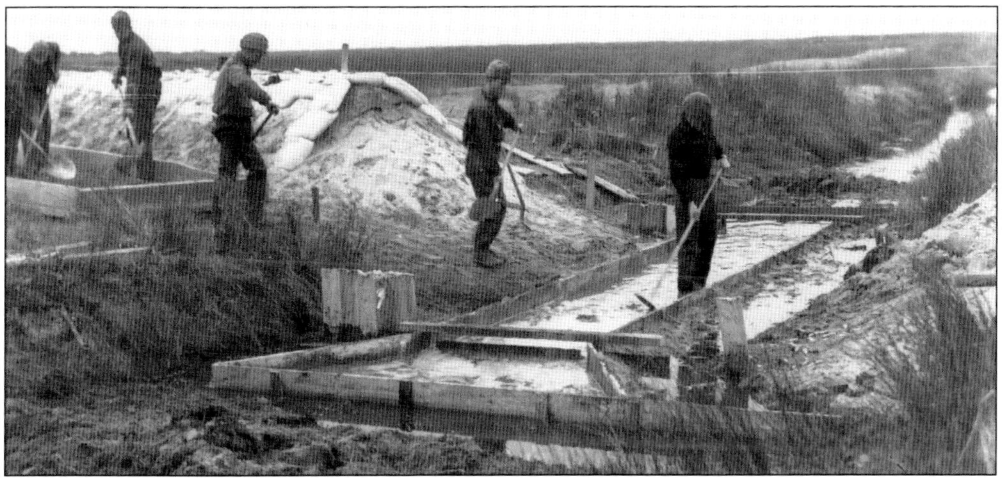

In the 1930s, Civilian Conservation Corps (CCC) workers constructed drainage and dunes near Buxton. The 1933 Roosevelt inauguration of work-relief projects and congressional legislation authorizing a new national park were vital in the establishment of Cape Hatteras National Seashore. With initial legislation on August 11, 1937, Congress established America's first national seashore, but it would be years before the park was officially dedicated, on April 24, 1958. To protect the new seashore, the CCC and the Works Progress Administration (WPA) set about building a protective barrier of dunes along the oceanfront. (Courtesy of the Cape Hatteras National Seashore.)

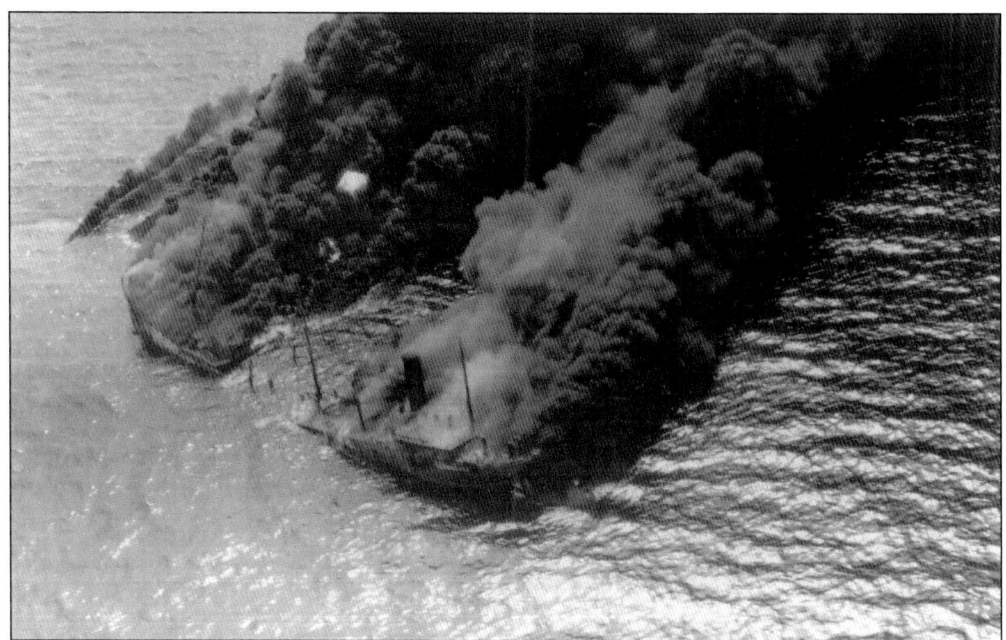

The Outer Banks played a crucial role in World Wars I and II. German submarines (U-boats) crossed the Atlantic and operated off the North Carolina coast, spying and causing great damage to East Coast shipping lanes. Today, the remains of many of those sunken ships and U-boats lie just offshore. The waters east of the Cape Hatteras and Cape Lookout, nicknamed "Torpedo Junction" during this era, became a watery grave for countless soldiers during the world wars. Pictured here is an attack on one of the tankers in 1942. (Courtesy of the Outer Banks History Center.)

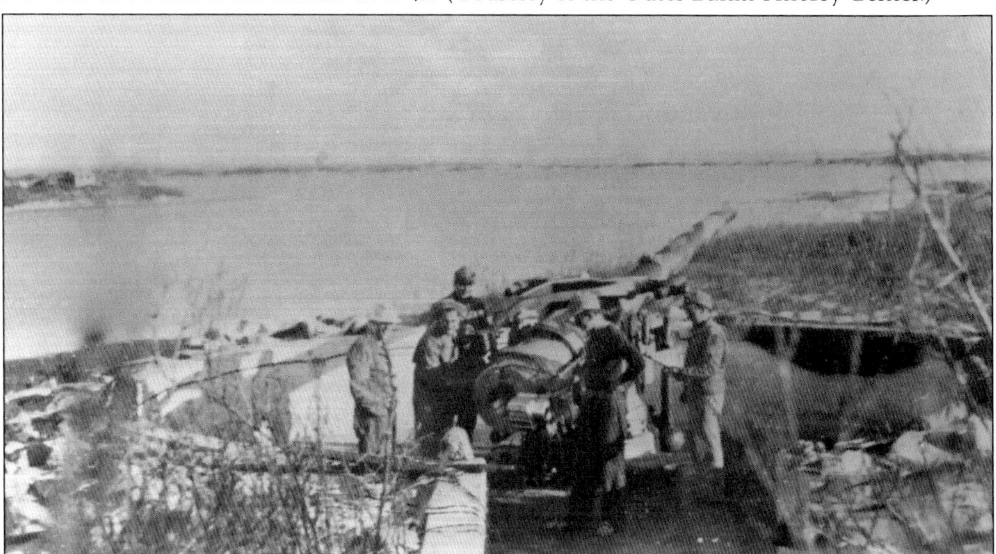

In 1942, while the nation's attention was diverted to Pearl Harbor and the frontline battles in the Pacific, U-boats prowled the waters off North Carolina's coast, wreaking havoc with maritime shipping lanes. Because of the threat to the crucial Morehead City Port, the Cape Lookout area was fortified. Battery Cape Lookout (1942) had multiple artillery guns mounted on concrete encasements. Pictured here is the battery that was constructed near the old Coast Guard station; these concrete supports are still visible today. (Courtesy of the Cape Lookout National Seashore.)

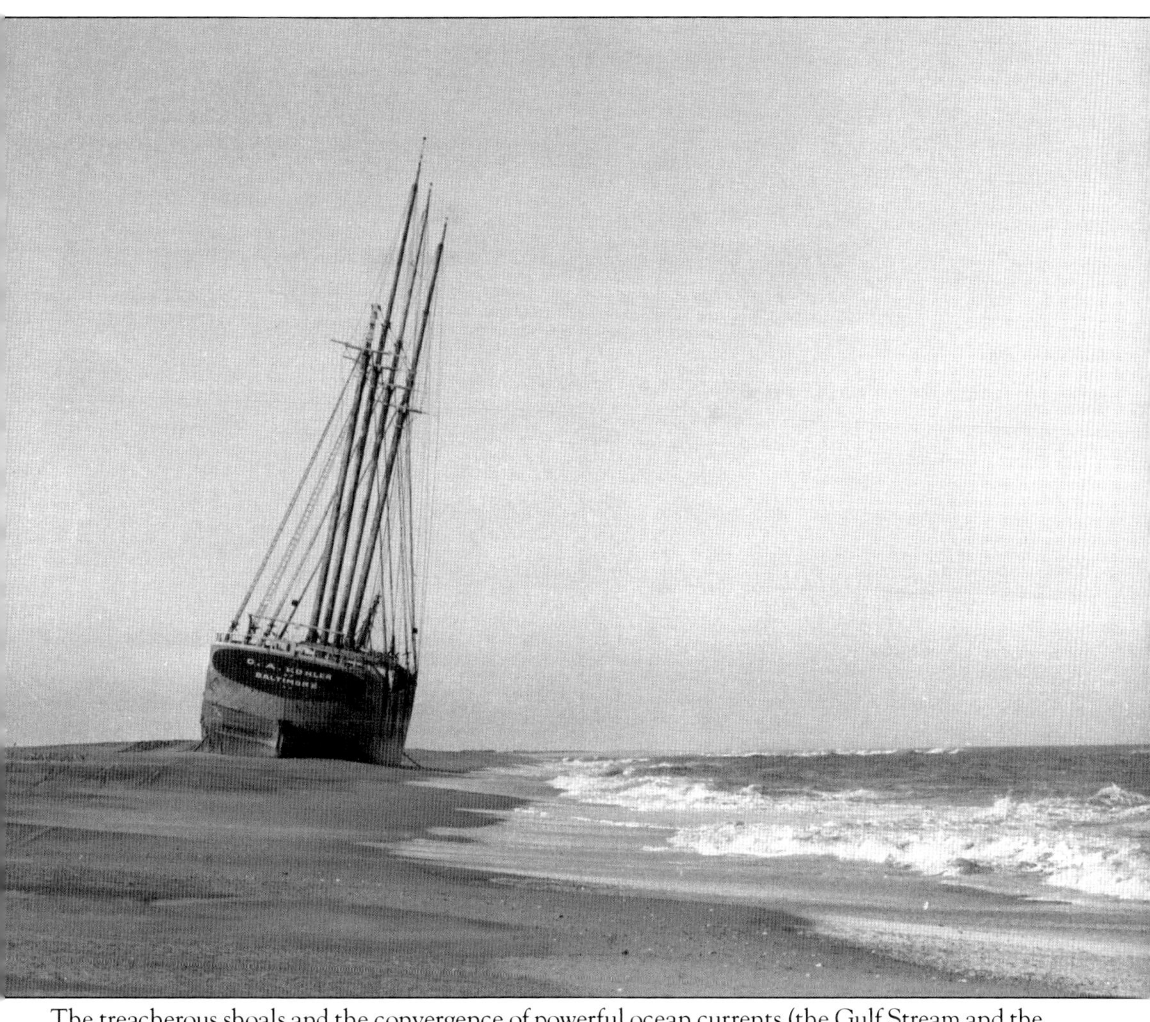

The treacherous shoals and the convergence of powerful ocean currents (the Gulf Stream and the Labrador Current) off the Outer Banks prove challenging and have endangered mariners since at least the 17th century. History reveals that hundreds of ships have fallen prey to formidable currents, fierce storms, and shifting shoals in what is known as the "Graveyard of the Atlantic." The construction of lighthouses on the Outer Banks was crucial to protect both lives and commerce from the hazards of the sea. Three tall coastal lights—Bodie Island, Cape Hatteras, and Cape Lookout—were built to warn ships traveling along the Outer Banks of the dangerous shoals. Pictured here in 1934 is the schooner *George A. Kohler*, from Baltimore, which was sailing to Haiti when it encountered the infamous August 1933 hurricane just offshore Cape Hatteras. (Courtesy of the Cape Hatteras National Seashore.)

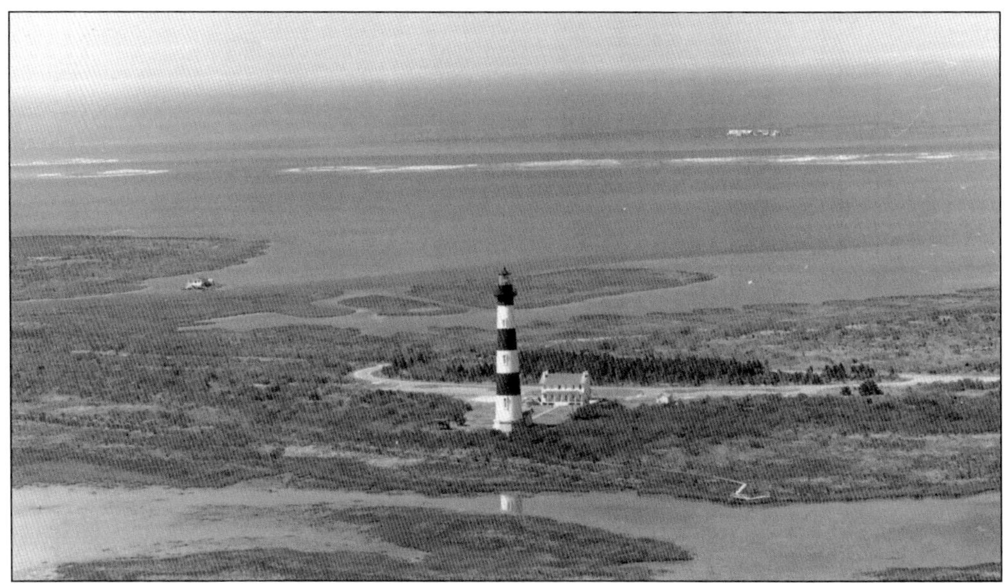

This 1970 photograph of the Bodie Island Lighthouse (pronounced "body") was completed in 1872. Standing 156 feet tall and equipped with an original, unique first-order Fresnel lens, the lighthouse is one of three found in Cape Hatteras National Seashore. The double keepers' quarters, located immediately west of the lighthouse, served as the living quarters for the lighthouse keeper and his family. (Courtesy of the Cape Hatteras National Seashore.)

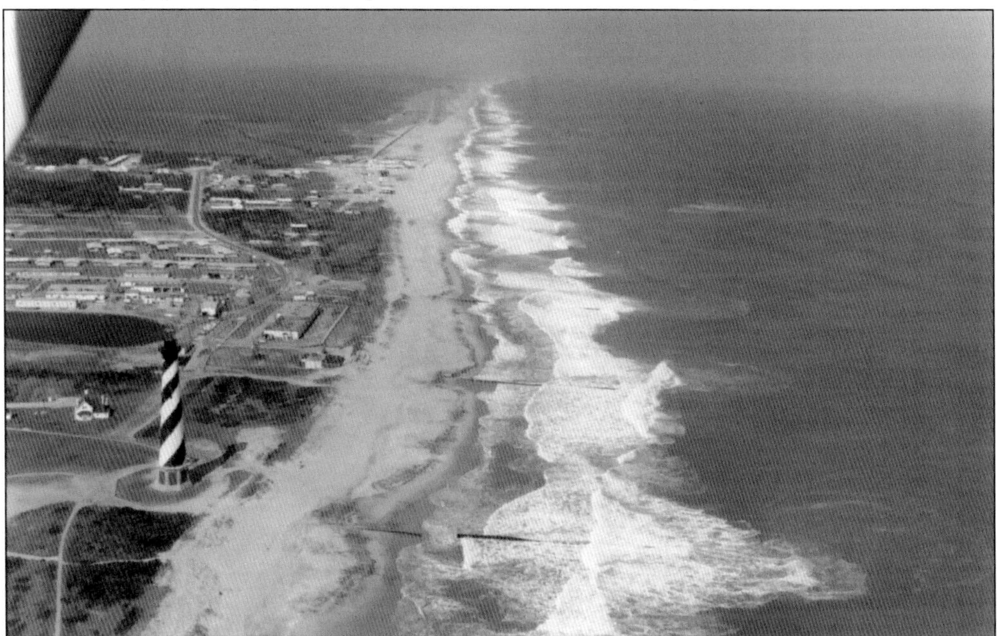

The Cape Hatteras Lighthouse, built in 1870, is located in Buxton, North Carolina. The beam of light can be seen 20 miles into the ocean, protecting one of the most treacherous stretches of the Outer Banks. The 208-foot-tall lighthouse stands as the world's tallest brick lighthouse. In 1999, to protect the lighthouse from the ravages of the Atlantic Ocean and the eroding shoreline, the National Park Service contracted to have the light station, including all outbuildings, moved 2,900 feet inland to a safer location. (Courtesy of the Cape Hatteras National Seashore.)

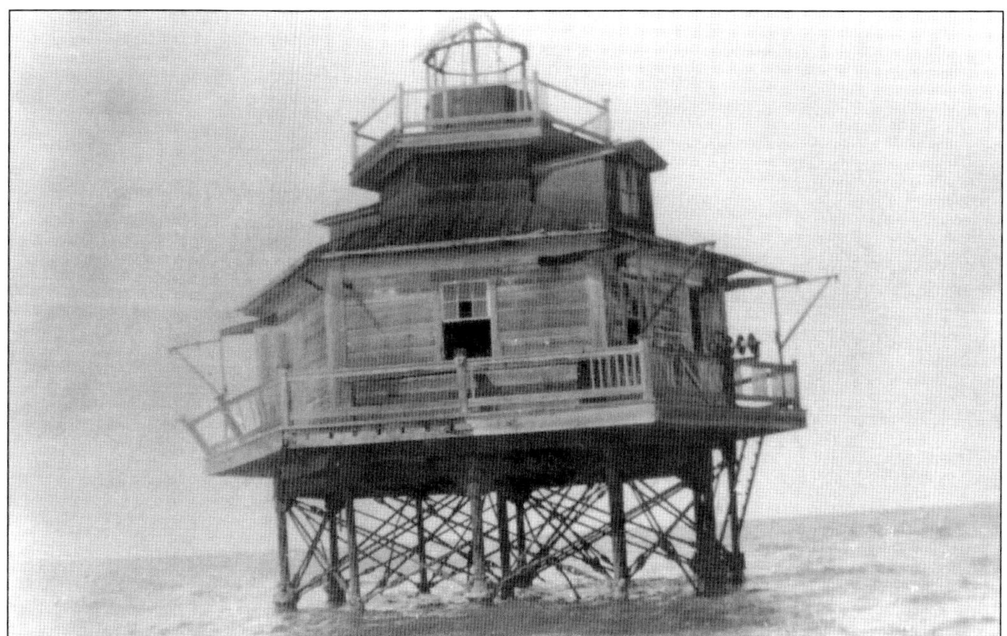

The 1922 Northwest Point Light, near Ocracoke, was a screwpile lighthouse, typical along the North Carolina sound waters. Installed in the years immediately after World War I, these beacons were built to guide mariners through Ocracoke Inlet, past Portsmouth Island, and across the Pamlico Sound. Today, this screwpile lighthouse design has been replaced with lighted channel markers and is no longer used. (Courtesy of the Outer Banks History Center.)

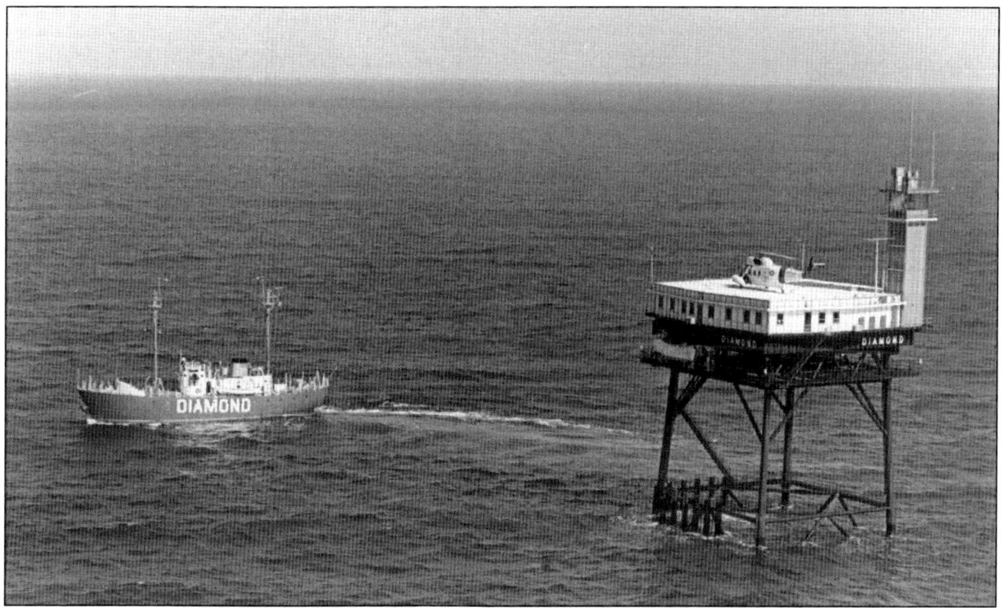

Pictured here in 1966, Diamond Shoals, offshore Cape Hatteras, is considered to be one of the most dangerous navigational areas on the Eastern Seaboard. Diamond Shoals Light was activated in 1966 and automated in 1977. The unmanned lighthouse suffered significant damage from Hurricane Fran in 1996. In October 2012, the tower was purchased at auction by a private citizen. (Courtesy of the Outer Banks History Center.)

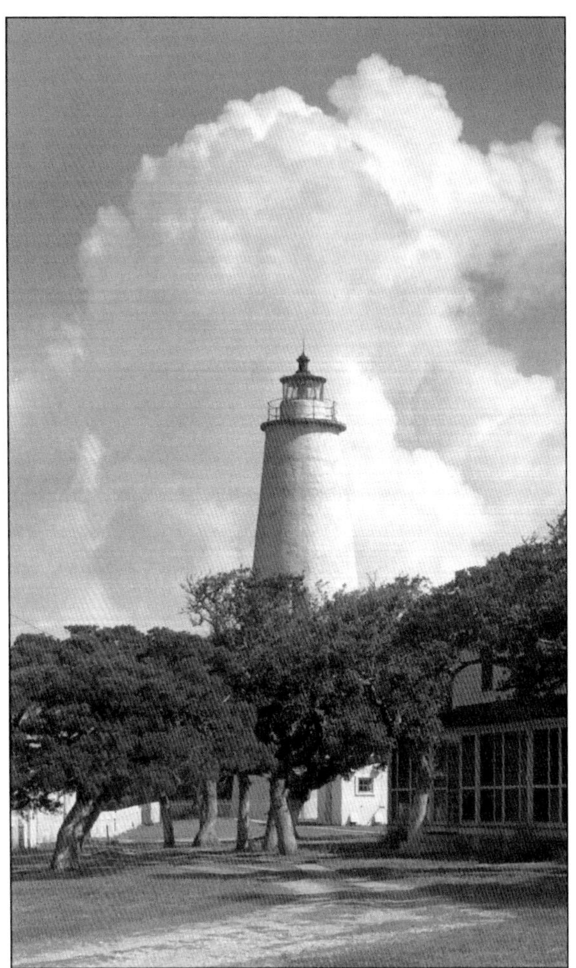

The Ocracoke Light Station, completed in 1823, is the oldest operating light station in North Carolina. Known as a harbor light marking Ocracoke Inlet and Silver Lake, the quaint solid-white lighthouse stands 77 feet tall, still has the original fourth-order Fresnel lens, and serves as an active aid to navigation. This 1960 photograph of the station shows multiple buildings, including the lighthouse and double keepers' quarters, the oil house, a shed, and the outhouse. (Courtesy of the Cape Hatteras National Seashore.)

The Cape Lookout Lighthouse, completed on November 1, 1859, stands 163 feet tall and is located in Cape Lookout National Seashore near Harkers Island, North Carolina. The Cape Lookout Lighthouse is the only such structure in the United States to bear the unique checkered pattern, intended not only for differentiation between similar light towers but also to show direction. The centers of the black diamonds point in a north-south direction, while the centers of the white diamonds point east-west. (Courtesy of the Cape Lookout National Seashore.)

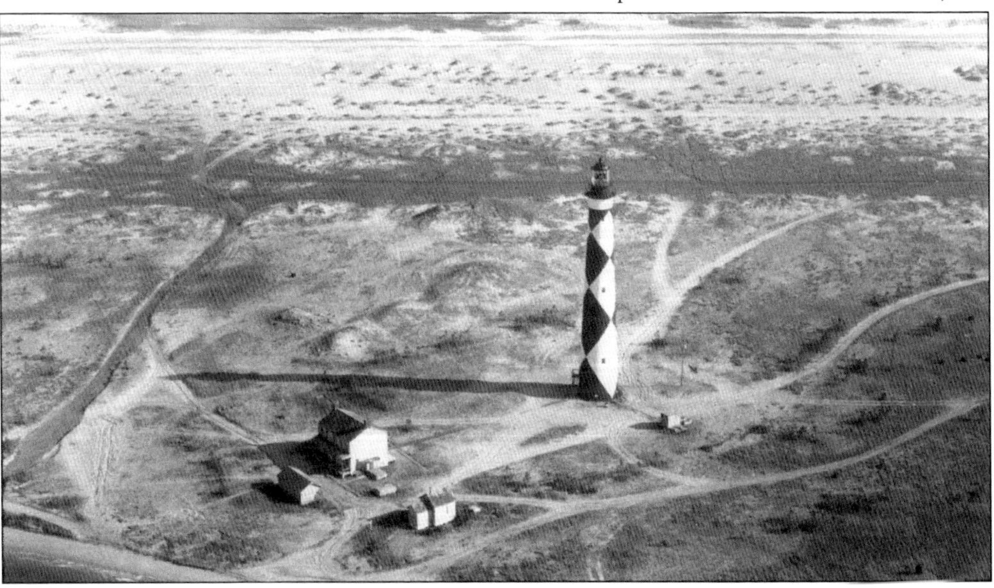

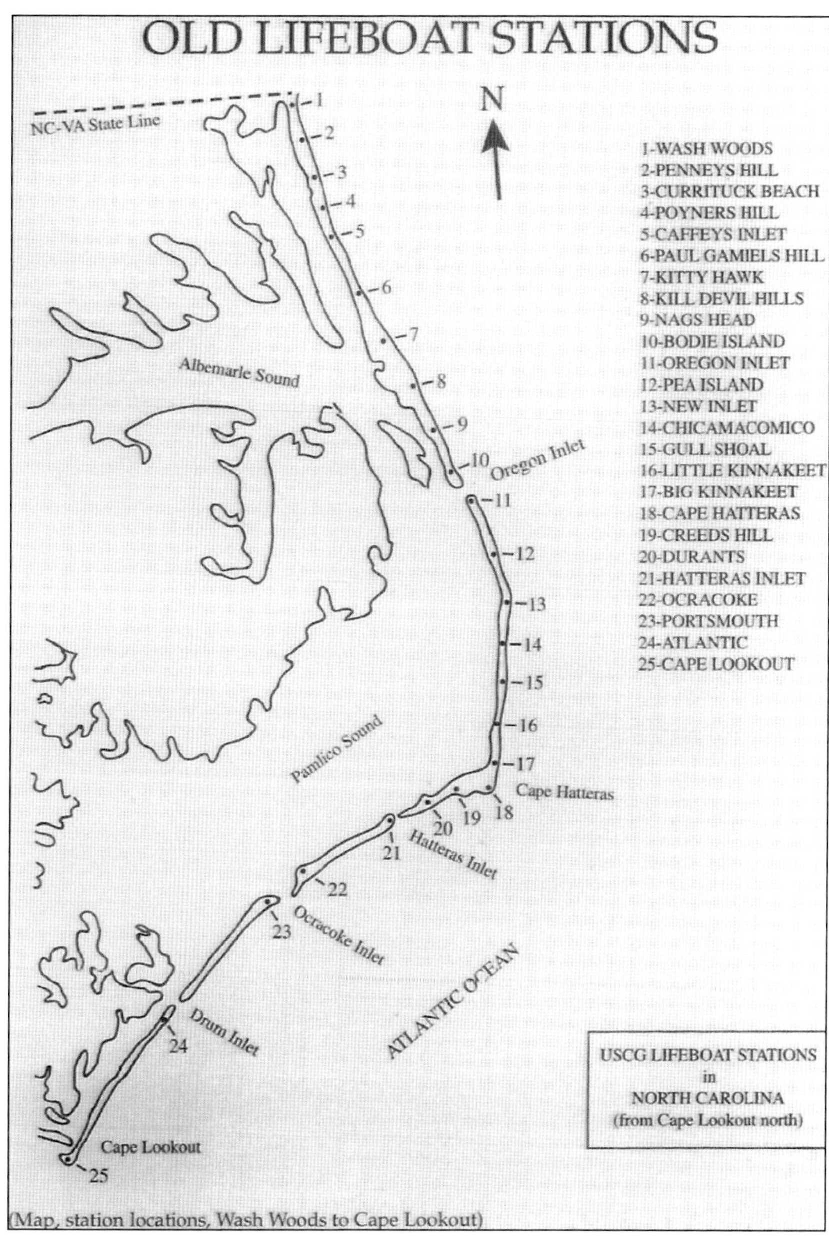

By 1918, despite the construction of and aid from lighthouses, shipwrecks were still happening in alarming numbers along the Outer Banks. In 1874, the first seven US Life-Saving Service stations were built along the North Carolina coast. Chicamacomico and Little Kinnakeet were the first two stations constructed. Later, more stations were added at various locations, including Bodie Island, Oregon Inlet, Pea Island, New Inlet, Gull Shoal, Big Kinnakeet, Cape Hatteras, Creed's Hill, and Durants (Hatteras Village). Three Life-Saving stations were built on Core Banks. These were Cape Lookout Life-Saving Station, Portsmouth Life-Saving Station, and Core Banks Station. In 1848, the US Life-Saving Service (USLSS), a precursor to today's the Coast Guard (USCG), was created out of private and local humanitarian efforts to save the lives of shipwrecked mariners and passengers. Ultimately, the service merged with the US Revenue Cutter Service to form the USCG on January 28, 1915. (Courtesy of the Cape Hatteras National Seashore.)

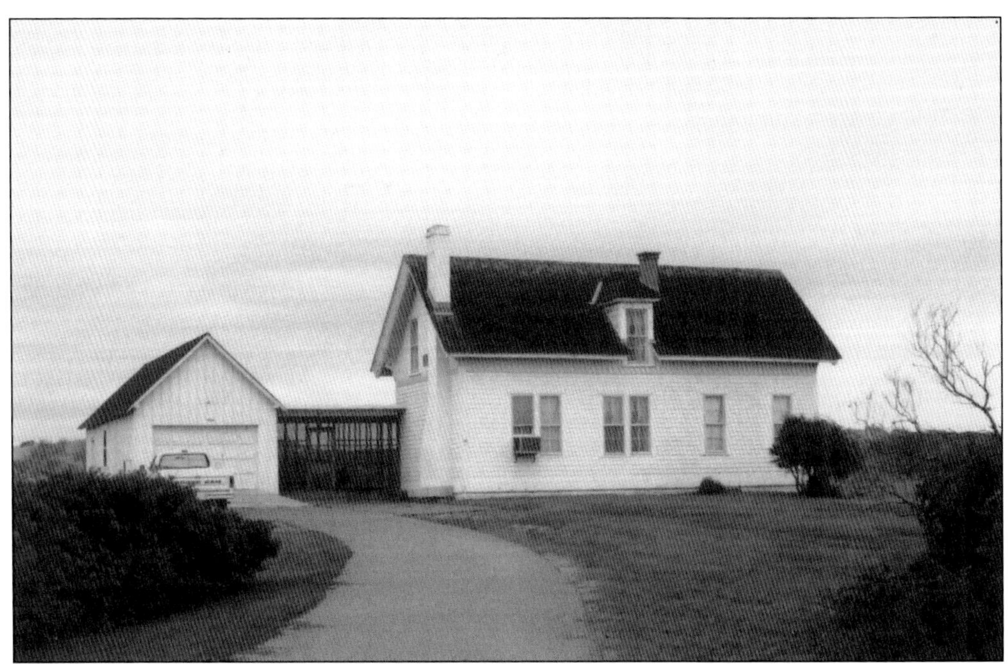

The 1878 Bodie Island Life-Saving Station (right), the 1916 boathouse (left), and the two-story 1925 Coast Guard station (below) comprised the Bodie Island Light Station Historic District. The structures were relocated in 2009 to the west side of NC Route 12, near Coquina Beach, due to shore line erosion on the oceanfront. They are visible from the road and the entrance to the current Bodie Island Light Station. The 1925 Bodie Island Coast Guard Station is indicative of a Chatham-type building. The structure was restored to its original condition and relocated in 2009. (Both, courtesy of the Cape Hatteras National Seashore.)

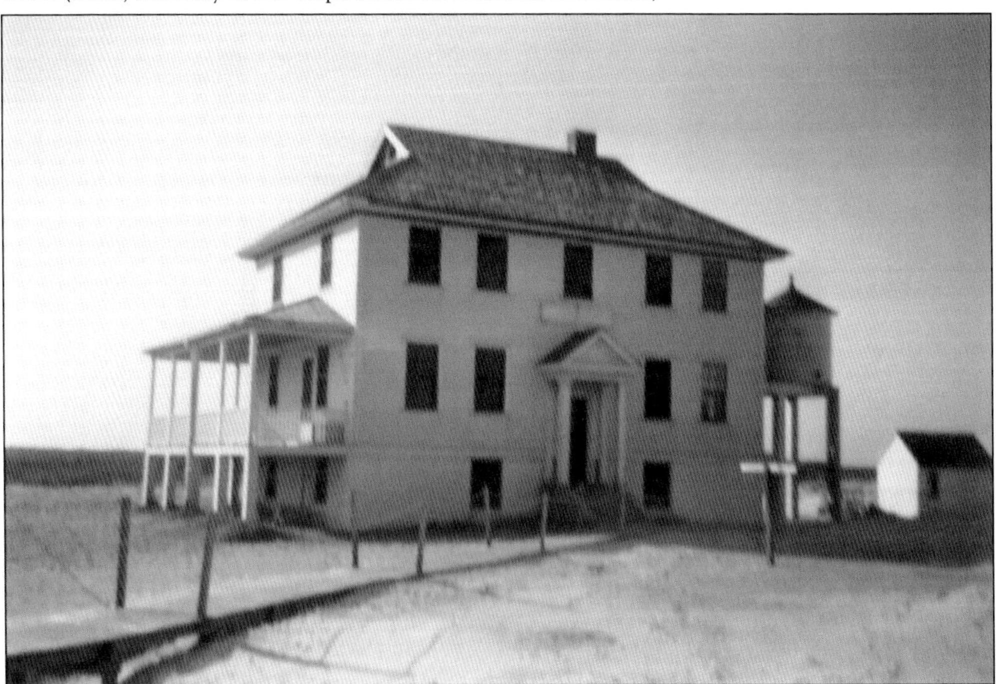

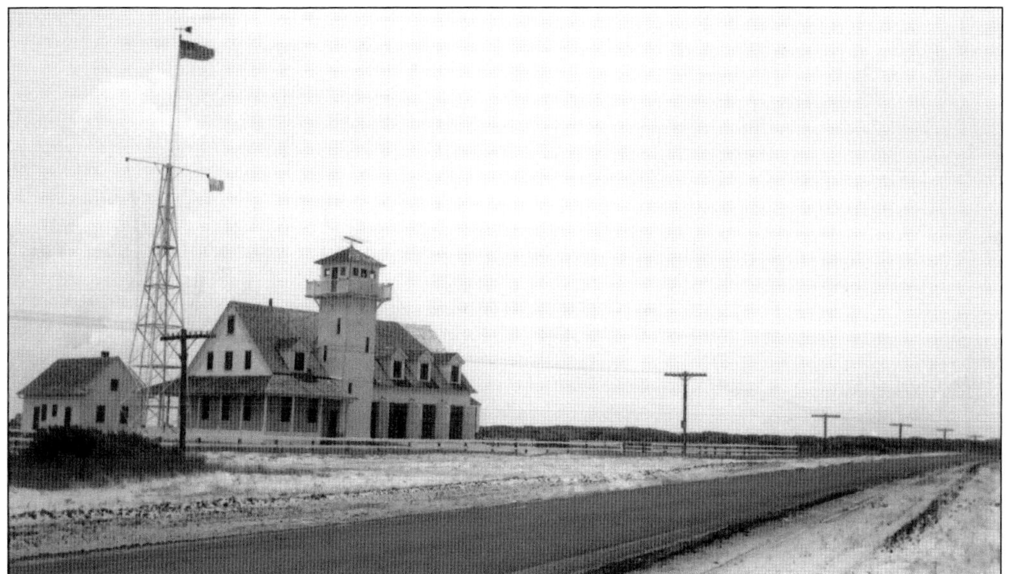

Pictured here in 1952 is the Oregon Inlet Life-Saving Station (active from 1897 to 1988). Note the newly paved NC Route 12 in the foreground, leading south to Pea Island. The USCG last occupied the station in 1988. The structure was restored in 2000 and is now maintained by the State of North Carolina. (Courtesy of the Cape Hatteras National Seashore.)

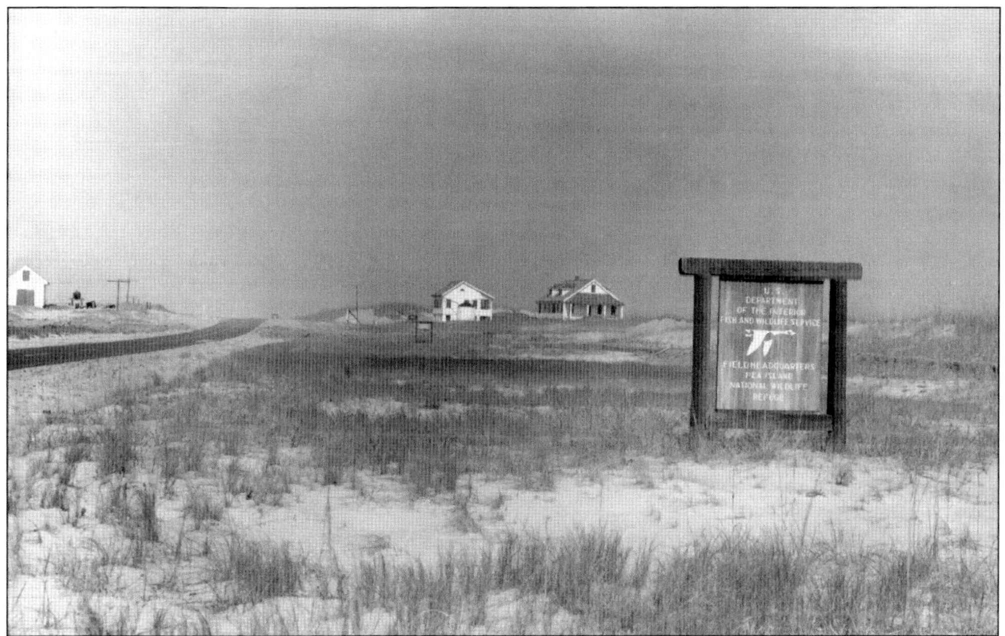

Pictured here in 1947, the Pea Island Life-Saving Station (active from 1878 to 1947) was once located opposite the current-day Pea Island National Wildlife Refuge Visitor Center. Today, the kitchen structure (center) has been moved to Manteo as a museum. The Pea Island Life-Saving Station boated the first all-black lifesaving crew in the country and included the first black commanding officer, Richard Etheridge. In 1996, the USCG awarded the Gold Life-Saving Medal posthumously to the late keeper and crew of the station for the rescue of the passengers and crew of the *E.S. Newman*. (Courtesy of the Cape Hatteras National Seashore.)

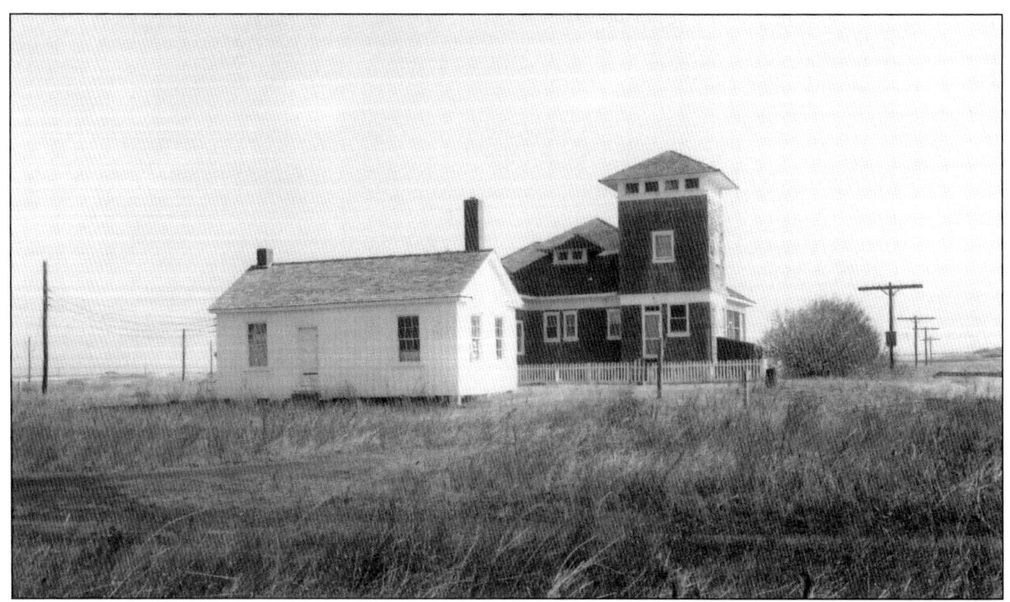

The historic Chicamacomico Life-Saving Station is located in Rodanthe, North Carolina (active as a Life-Saving and Coast Guard station from 1874 to 1954); decommissioned in 1954, it was transformed into a museum and opened to the public for tours. This station is best remembered for the famous 1918 rescue of the *Mirlo*, a British tanker carrying 42 crew members. Numerous accolades and awards were bestowed upon the six-man lifesaving team. (Courtesy of the Cape Hatteras National Seashore.)

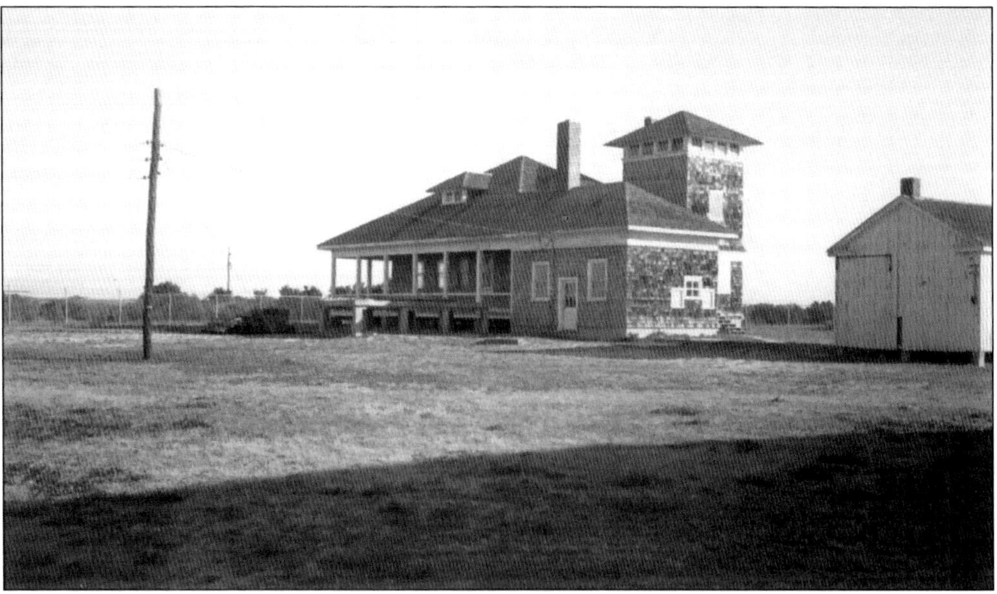

Little Kinnakeet Life-Saving Station is an excellent example of the type of stations constructed by the USLSS during its 44-year existence on the Outer Banks. Currently located north of the village of Avon within Cape Hatteras National Seashore, the original station building was among the first seven constructed on North Carolina's treacherous Outer Banks, in 1874. The site includes a main house, added in 1904, and the 1892 cookhouse. (Courtesy of the Cape Hatteras National Seashore.)

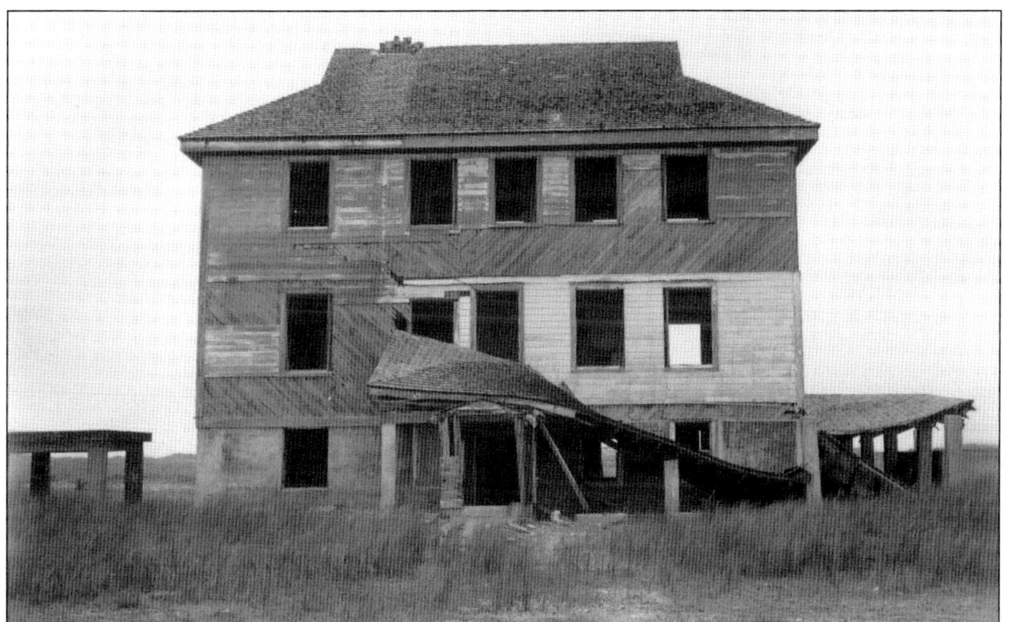

Big Kinnakeet Life-Saving Station (active from 1878 to 1929) was damaged in the 1944 hurricane and later demolished. Today, just the foundation remains south of Avon near Askins Creek. (Courtesy of the Cape Hatteras National Seashore.)

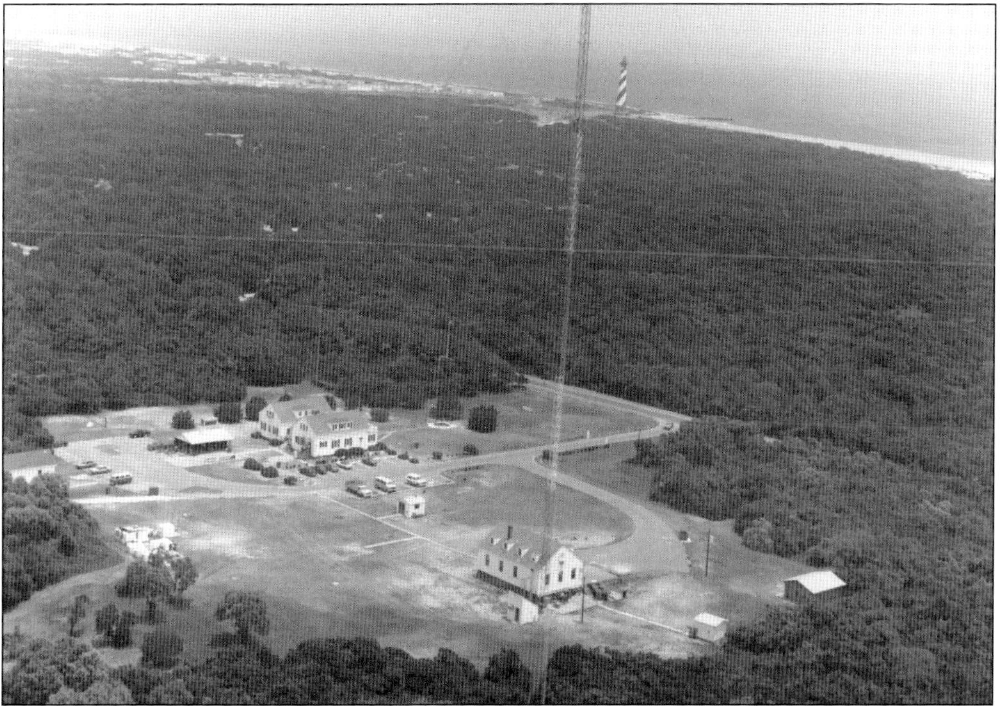

The former Cape Hatteras USCGS Buxton, North Carolina, consists of two buildings, which serve as an administrative offices and a garage for the National Park Service today. The station is located one mile south of the Cape Hatteras Lighthouse on Lighthouse Road, near Cape Point. (Courtesy of the Cape Hatteras National Seashore.)

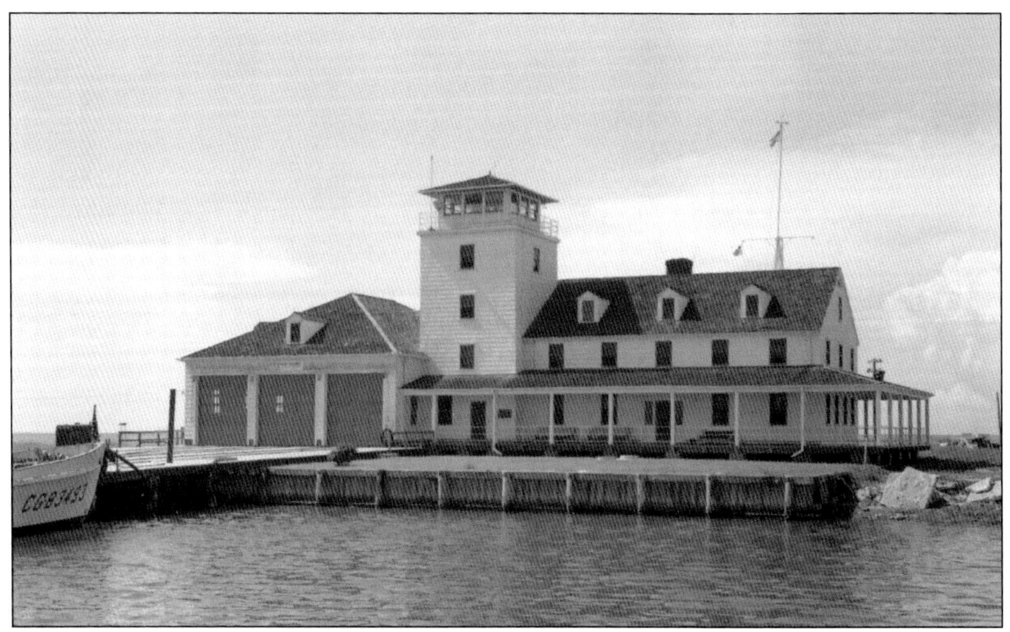

The Ocracoke Coast Guard Station, built in 1939–1940, was the 187th Coast Guard station to be constructed in the United States. In 2001, the federal government transferred the unused Coast Guard building to the State of North Carolina. Today, this historic building is a campus of the North Carolina Center for the Advancement of Teaching (NCCAT). (Courtesy of the Cape Hatteras National Seashore.)

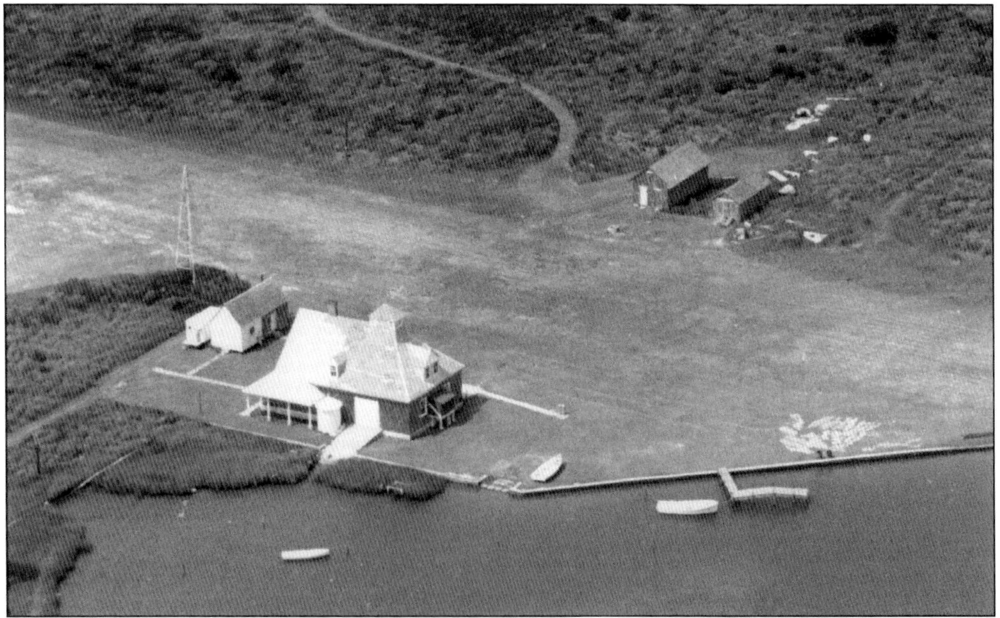

Portsmouth Life-Saving Station (active from 1894 to 1937) is accessible only by boat. Initially and until 1917, crews were employed seasonally from August 1 through May 31. On June 1, 1937, the Portsmouth Life-Saving Station was decommissioned from official duty, and it is now part of the Portsmouth Island Historic District in Cape Lookout National Seashore. (Courtesy of the Cape Lookout National Seashore.)

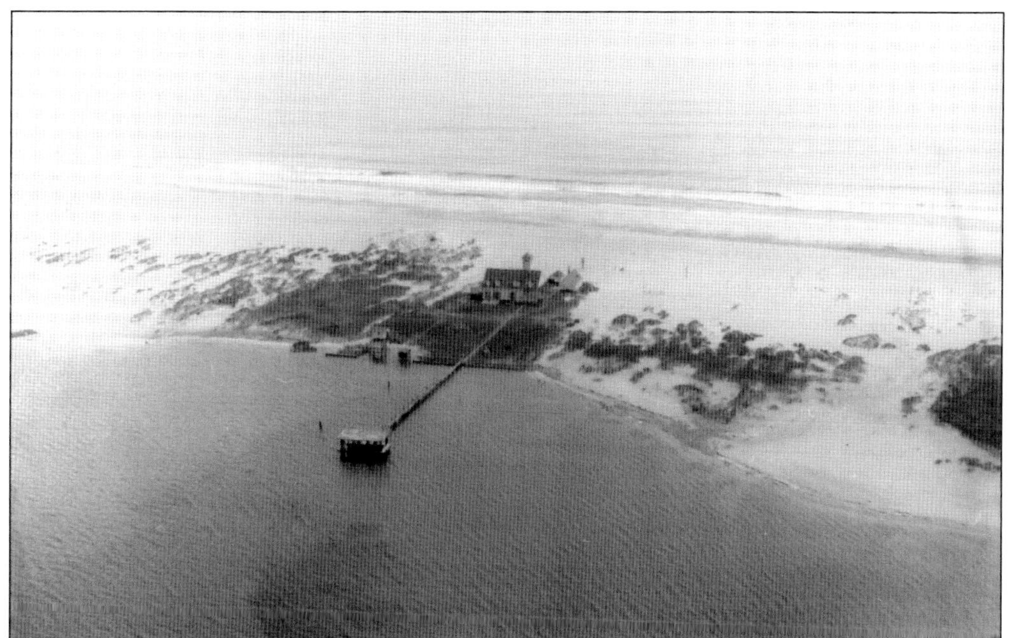

Old Drum Inlet Life-Saving Station (active from 1896 to the 1970s) was built in 1896 on the Core Banks in Cape Lookout National Seashore. The structure was destroyed in a fire in the 1970s. (Courtesy of the Cape Lookout National Seashore.)

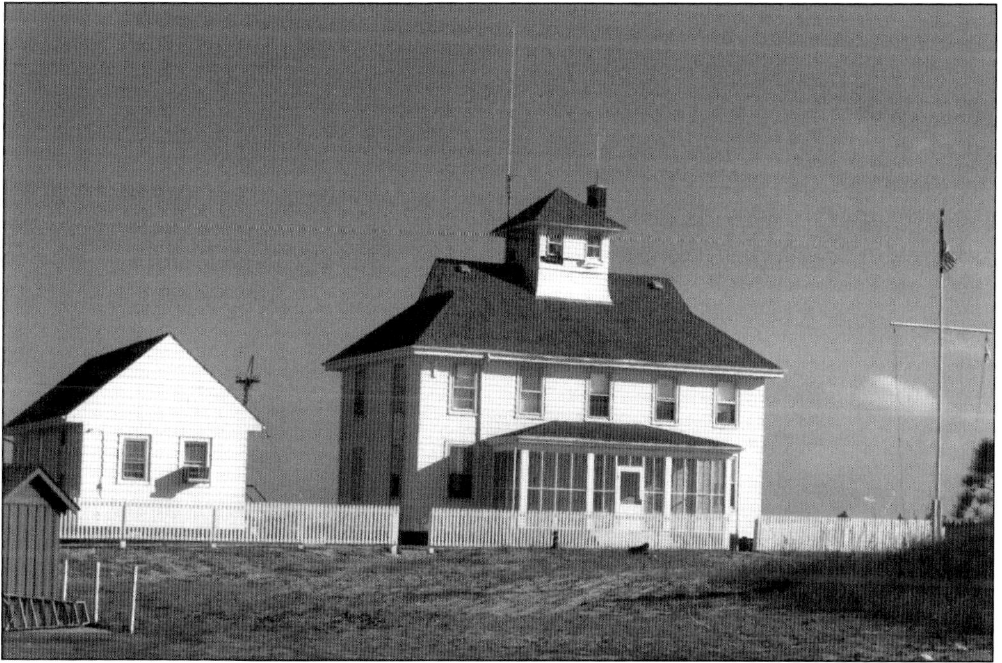

Cape Lookout Coast Guard Station (active from 1916 to 1982) is located on Core Banks, adjacent to the Cape Lookout Lighthouse. The station was built as a lifeboat station in 1916. The Cape Lookout Station was chiefly responsible for providing rescue services in the Cape Lookout Shoals, which extend 10 miles into the Atlantic Ocean from Core Banks. (Courtesy of the Cape Lookout National Seashore.)

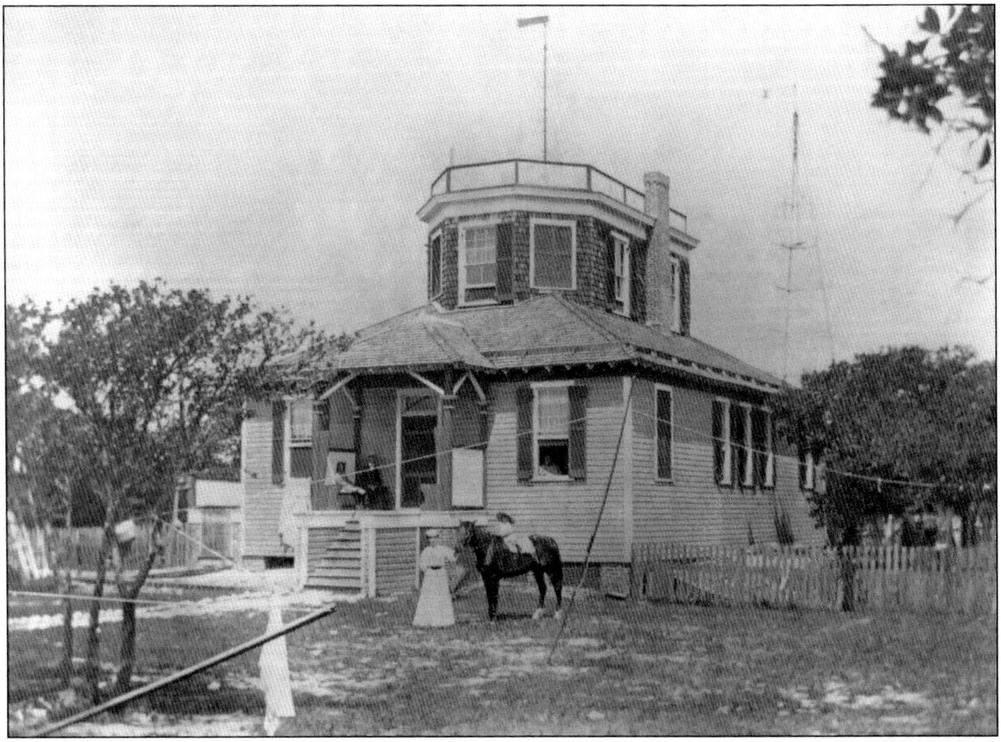

The Hatteras Weather Bureau Station was built in 1901. The remote location on the Outer Banks of North Carolina provided data on conditions in the Atlantic Ocean from a fixed location, which was extended farther into the ocean than any other location the Atlantic coast. The building served as a weather station from 1902 to 1946. (Courtesy of the Cape Hatteras National Seashore.)

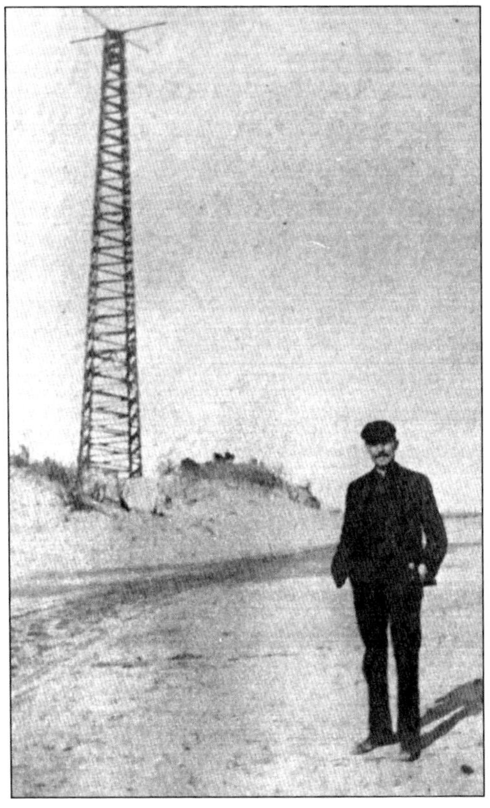

The origins of wireless communications began on the Outer Banks of North Carolina. Reginald Aubrey Fessenden (October 6, 1866–July 22, 1932) was a Canadian inventor who pioneered research and experiments in radio. His construction of efficient continuous-waves transmitters earned him the name of "Father of Voice Radio." By March 1902, working as a contractor for the Hatteras branch of the US Weather Bureau, Professor Fessenden conducted research that demonstrated the successful transmission and reception of voice with his devices. A 127-word voice message was sent from the Cape Hatteras transmitter tower to Roanoke Island, North Carolina. (Courtesy of the Outer Banks History Center.)

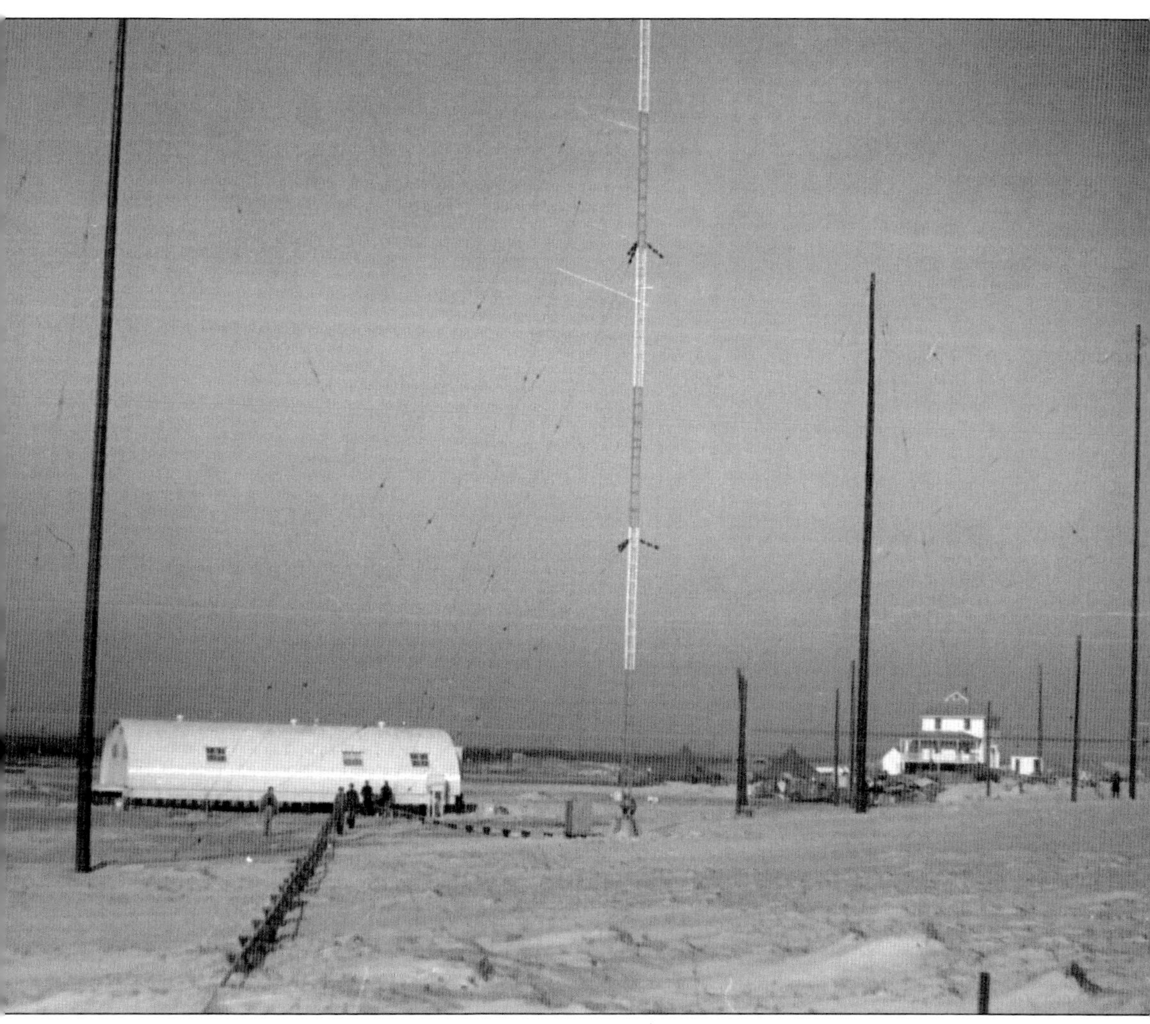

LORAN, an acronym for long-range navigation, was a radio navigation system developed in the United States during World War II that operated over long distances. The system was first used for ships crossing the Atlantic Ocean and later for long-range patrol aircraft. The Bodie Island LORAN station towers, constructed between 1944 and 1949, once dotted the landscape near the 1925 Bodie Island Coast Guard Station (seen in the background.) Synchronized pulses were transmitted from widely spaced radio stations to aircraft or shipping lanes. The arrival time of the pulses was used to determine the position of approaching ships or aircraft. (Courtesy of the Cape Hatteras National Seashore.)

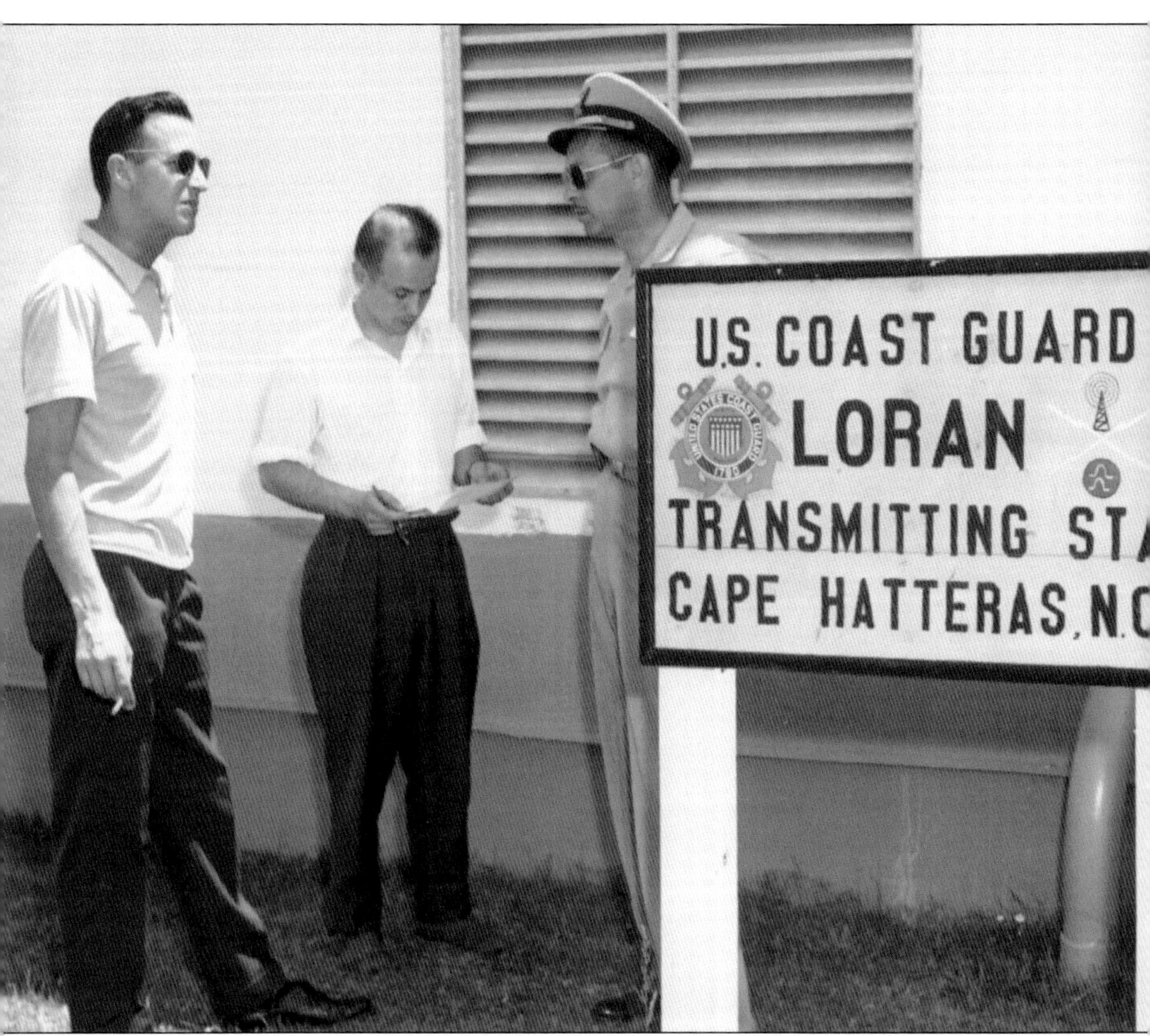

The Cape Hatteras LORAN Station was constructed in 1949. Two representatives of the French navy met with the USCG officials for a briefing on the LORAN construction and operation as the French were planning on building a LORAN station in France. From left to right are Lt. George Bouxin and civilian technician Jacques Grimonpret with the French navy and Lt. Comdr. E. Kopp, US Coast Guard. (Courtesy of the Cape Hatteras National Seashore.)

Three

Maritime Trades

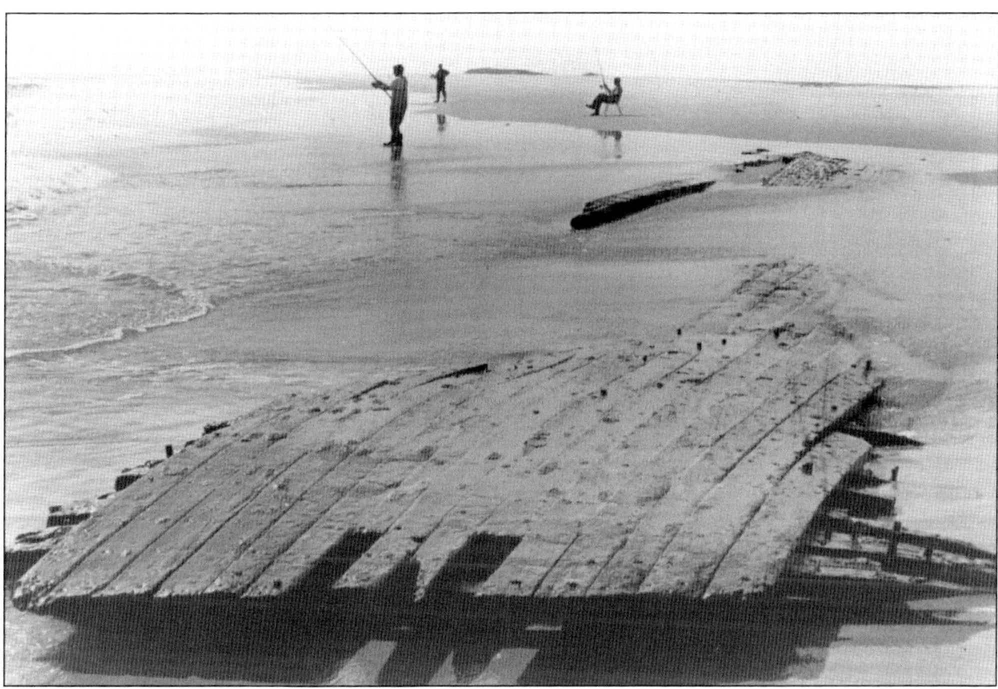

This 1975 photograph is of a shipwreck and surf fishermen on the beach of Portsmouth Island. In the late 1700s, shipwrecks were common off the North Carolina coastline. Two massive ocean currents, the cold northern Labrador Current and the warm southern Gulf Stream, collide offshore Cape Hatteras, creating waters so turbulent and dangerous to ships that they are referred to as the Graveyard of the Atlantic. Early residents of the Outer Banks were subsistence-living individuals who usually worked in some form of maritime trade. Many were commercial fishermen and waterfowl hunters who also worked in the shipping or boatbuilding industries, piloting, and lightering. Fishing not only put food on the family table but also was a source of income. Islanders fished with nets or hook and line, collected oysters, clams, scallops, sea turtles, whales, and porpoises, and harvested seaweed. (Courtesy of the Cape Lookout National Seashore.)

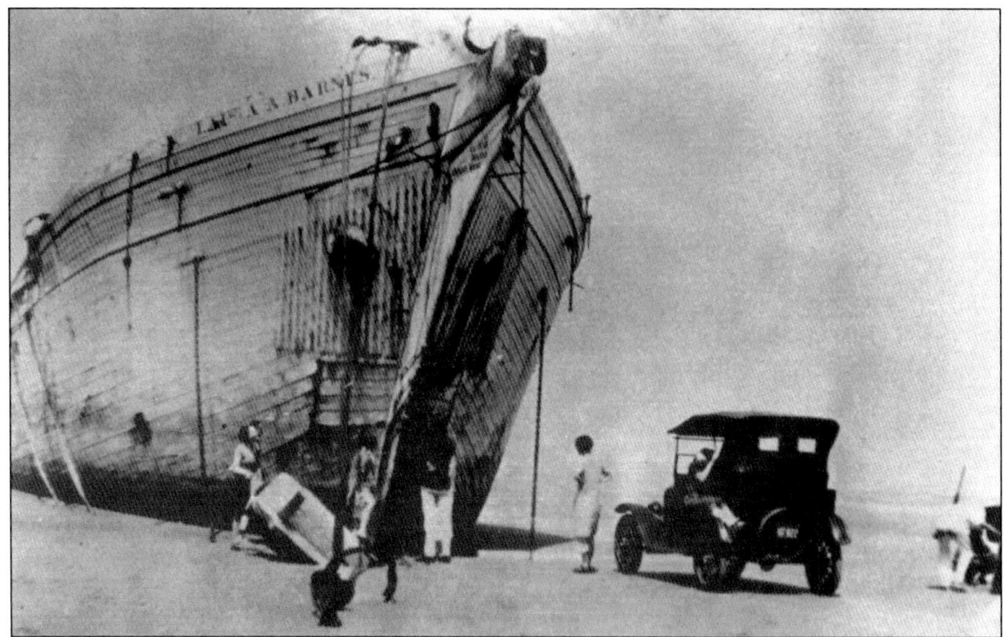

The *Laura A. Barnes* shipwreck is representative of boats from the wooden sailing ships era; many met their fates on the Outer Banks. Ships carried goods and passengers, keeping the young nation's economy and commerce afloat. The *Laura A. Barnes* was a four-masted schooner that came ashore in dense fog on the night of June 1, 1921. The crew was rescued by Coast Guardsmen from the nearby Bodie Island Station. The remnants of the hull remain buried in the dunes at Coquina Beach today. (Courtesy of the Cape Hatteras National Seashore.)

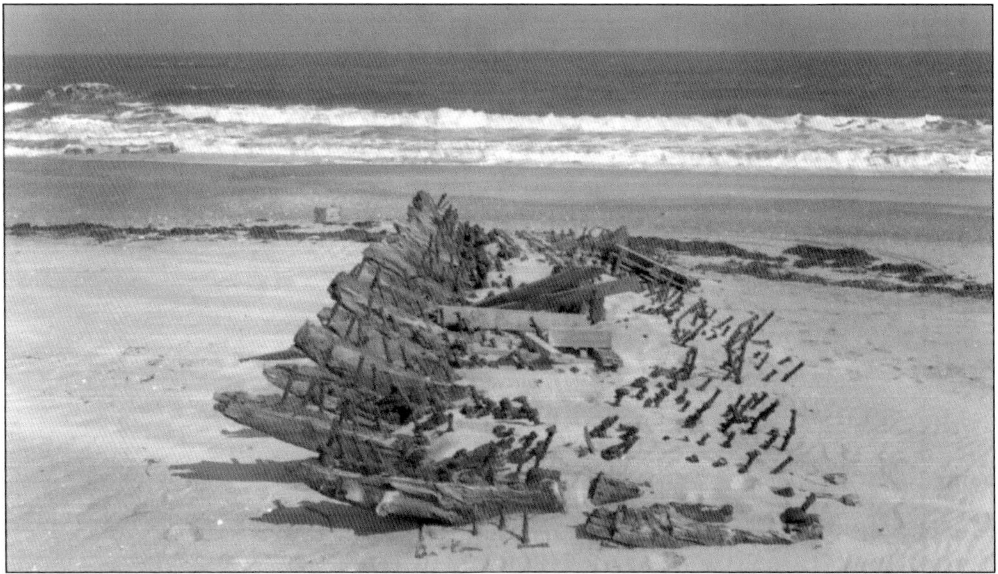

Here lie the unidentified wooden remains of a shipwreck on a Hatteras Island beach. Ships followed the coastal trade routes, and thousands of these vessels had to successfully navigate not only North Carolina's barrier islands, which jut out 30 miles into the sea from the mainland, but also Diamond Shoals, a treacherous, constantly shifting series of shallow underwater sandbars that extend eight miles seaward from Cape Hatteras. (Courtesy of the Cape Hatteras National Seashore.)

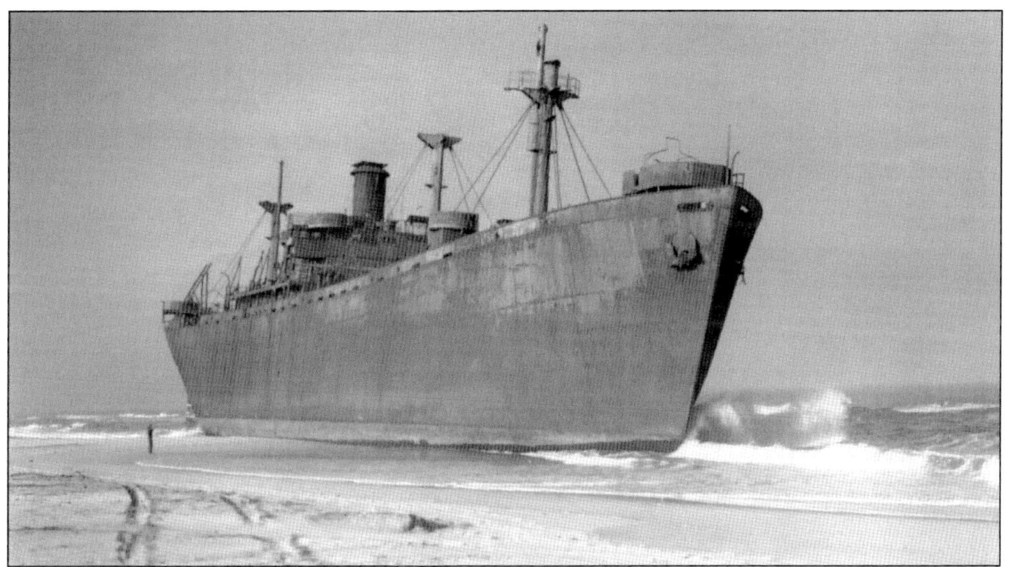

The *Antonin Dvrock* was a liberty ship that washed ashore near Little Kinnakeet after breaking away from tow tug at sea during a heavy storm. It was later salvaged and scrapped for metal. At one time, the Outer Banks had so many shipwrecks that salvaging the beach for loot was a viable occupation. Unlike the pirates of days gone by, there was a pecking order established among the salvagers. Wreck districts were established to keep track of the number of wrecks, and vendue (public auction) masters were hired to handle the sale of salvageable goods. (Courtesy of the Cape Hatteras National Seashore.)

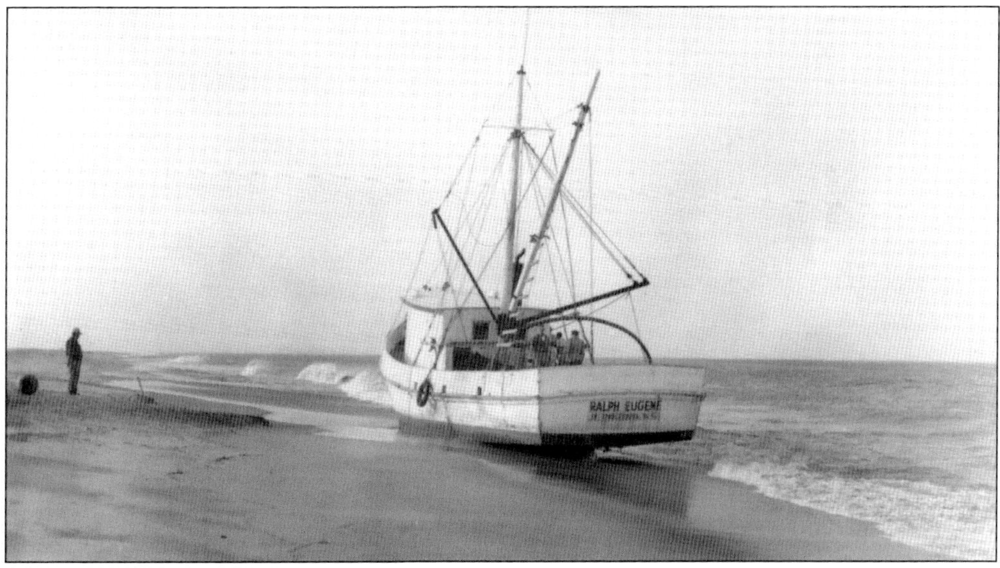

The beached trawler *Ralph Eugene* fell victim to the treacherous waters offshore of Cape Hatteras. In today's world, shipwrecks and buried treasure are a rare occurrence. After all, modern ships are equipped with sophisticated radar navigation systems and traversing the oceans is reasonably safe. In 2006, a cargo container that apparently fell from a ship during rough conditions later washed up on Hatteras Island, spilling thousands of bags of Doritos-brand tortilla chips on the beach. Like modern-day pirates, the beachcombers scrambled to collect the chips and helped to clean up the beaches. (Courtesy of the Cape Hatteras National Seashore.)

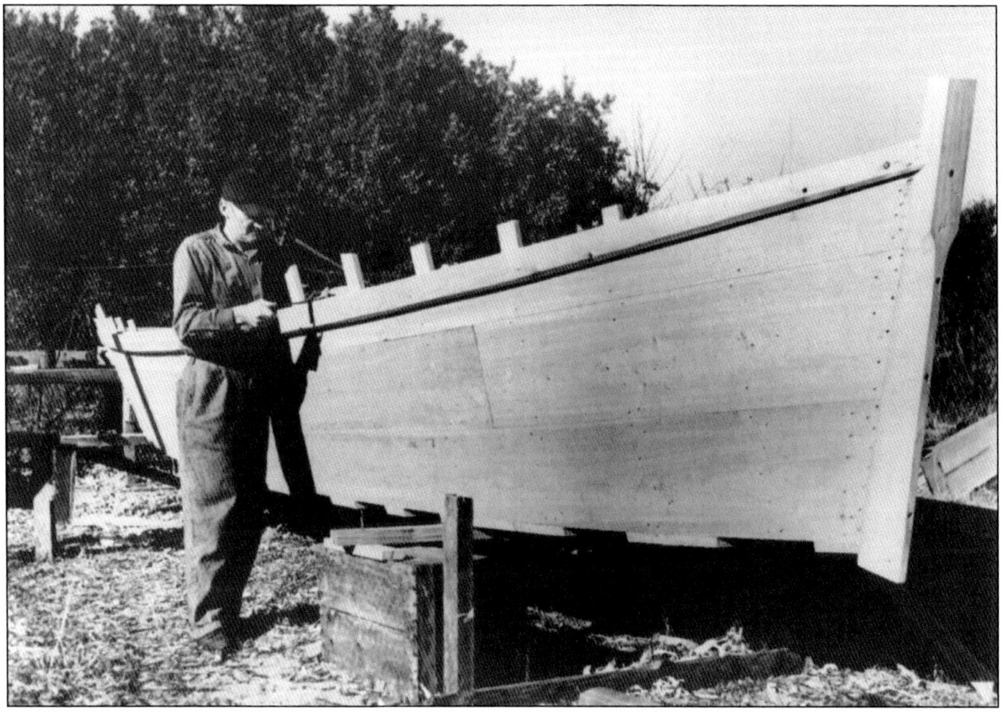

The backyard boatbuilder, like the man shown here, was the earliest form of and an important precursor to North Carolina's rich boatbuilding industry on the Outer Banks. The shad boat, a 20-to-30-foot round-bottomed boat with a wide midsection to hold nets and fish, was used to fish pound nets during the spring American and hickory shad runs. These shallow-draft boats were capable of fast travel in the expansive, shallow sound waters. Over time, the design was adjusted to a V-bottom hull, which was easier and cheaper to build. Gasoline-powered engines replaced sails, and the shad boat became one of the most versatile commercial fishing vessels used along the coast. (Courtesy of the North Carolina Maritime Museum.)

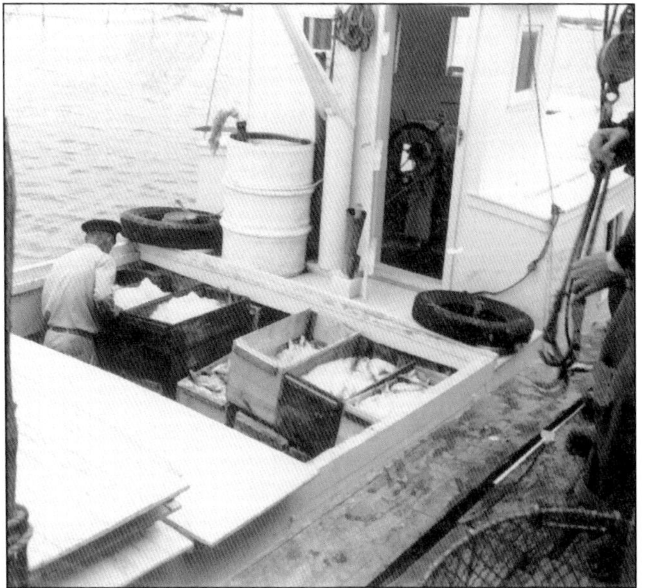

The photograph shows a fishing vessel hauled out for repairs on Ocracoke Island. The boats built on the northern and southern Down East Outer Banks are a reflection of the region as well as the individual local craftsmen who built them. Strong bonds existed between early charter boat captains and commercial fishermen, many of whom were boatbuilders during the winter months. These sturdy boats were designed to take the high ocean waves directly head-on at Oregon, Hatteras, and Ocracoke Inlets. (Courtesy of the Cape Hatteras National Seashore.)

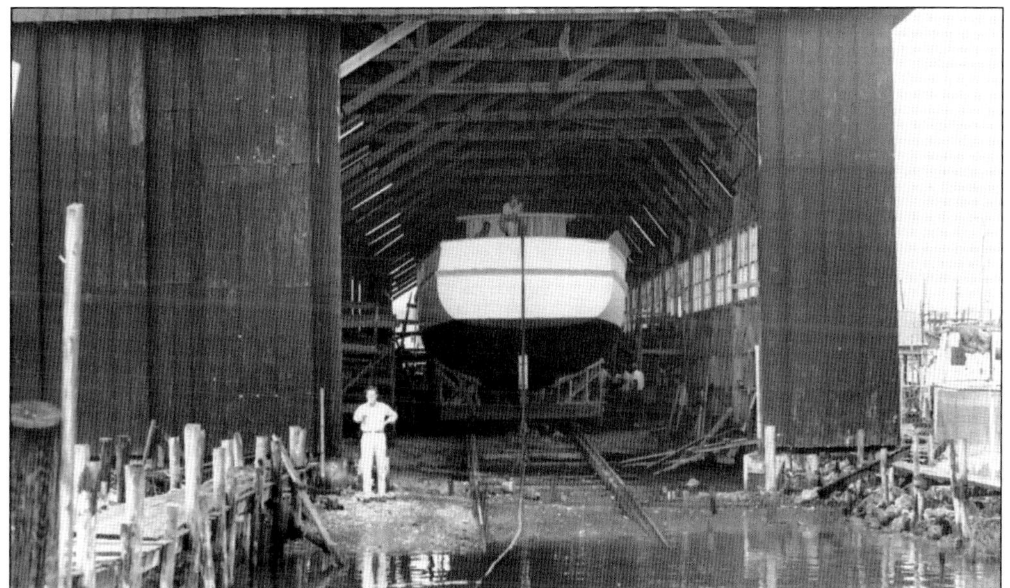

Pictured here is a Down East boatyard with a vessel ready to be launched. The backyard boatbuilders of the Core Sound region had a thriving industry. Once the operation of modern-day gasoline engines was perfected, this boat type could operate at speeds of 30 miles per hour or better and allowed for trips to the Gulf Stream for deep-sea fishing expeditions. The offshore charter boat industry became a popular excursion for the hearty fishermen and women of the time. (Courtesy of the North Carolina Maritime Museum.)

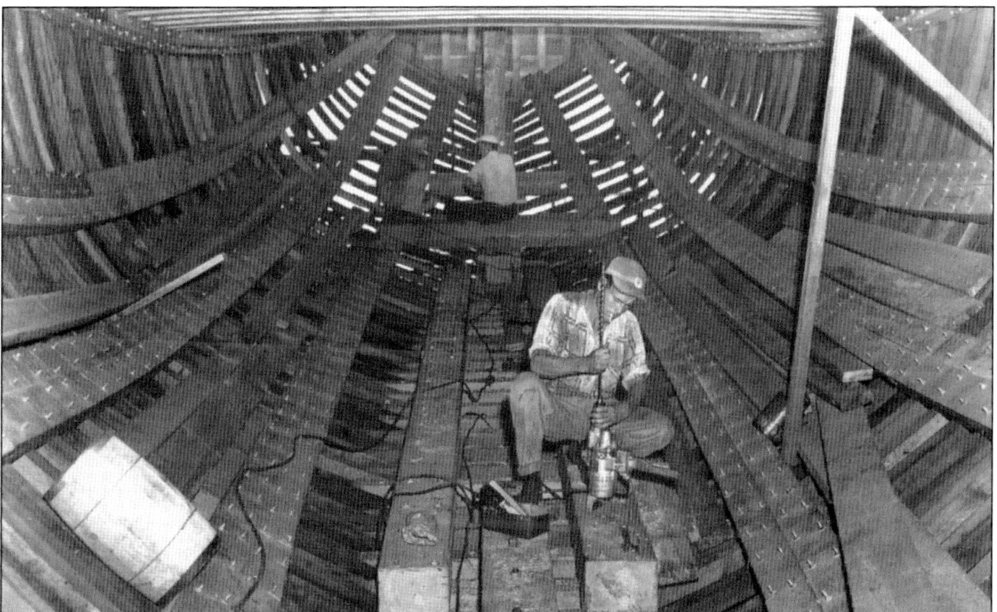

Many boatbuilders in the Core Sound area are recognized for the Harkers Island flare. This unique boat style was well adapted to the local maritime environment of the Carolina sounds; the wide flared bow threw water away from the hull at high speeds in the choppy waters. Today, the region is known for its prolific boatbuilding and sportfishing heritage and rich maritime history. (Courtesy of the North Carolina Maritime Museum.)

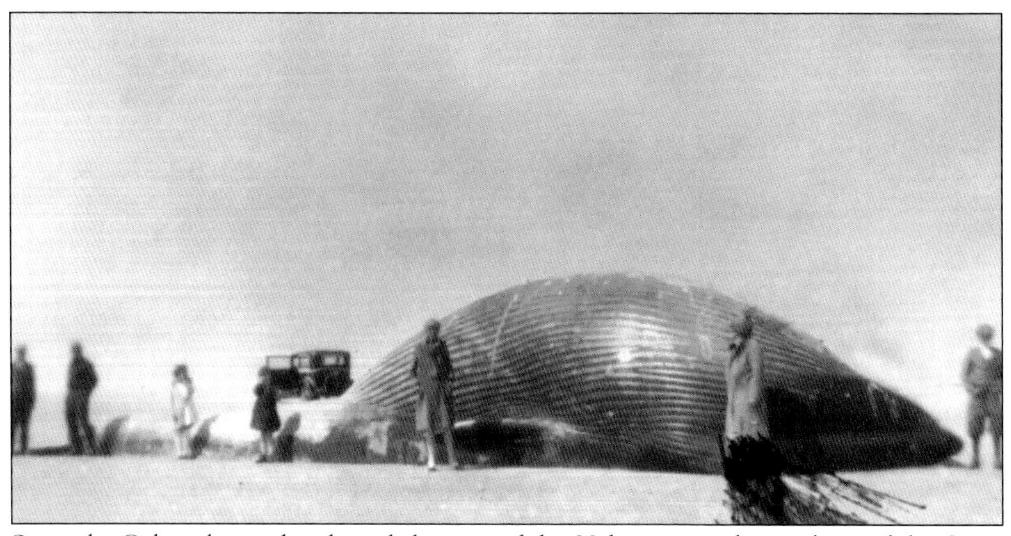

Since the Colonial period and until the turn of the 20th century, the residents of the Outer Banks hunted whales. Each spring, native fishermen kept their eyes on the horizon of the sea and waited for migrating whales to pass the Outer Banks. As the call of "Whales!" was heard, they launched boats from shore in pursuit of these marine mammals. Oil was the main product sought from whales; it was used to lubricate machinery and provide illumination. (Courtesy of the Cape Lookout National Seashore.)

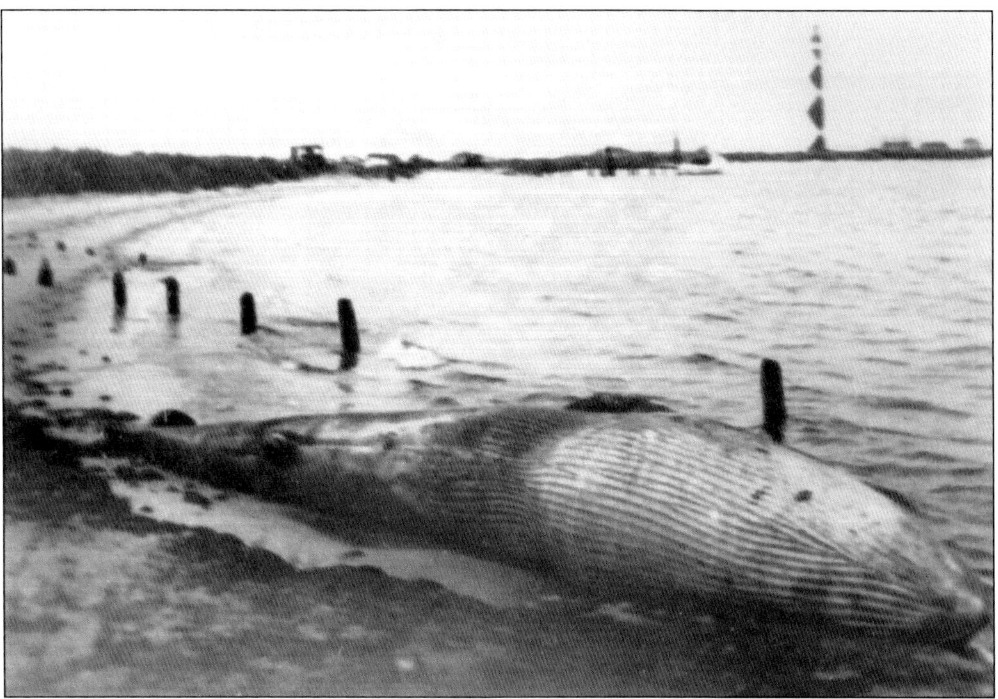

Pictured here is a beached whale with the Cape Lookout Lighthouse in the background. Whaling was a seasonal occupation at Cape Lookout, limited almost entirely to the months of February, March, and April. The shore-based whalers were also engaged in mullet fishing and a few operated porpoise oil (bottlenose dolphins) rendering plants in both Core Banks area as well as Hatteras Village and Frisco from 1885 to 1891. (Courtesy of the Cape Lookout National Seashore.)

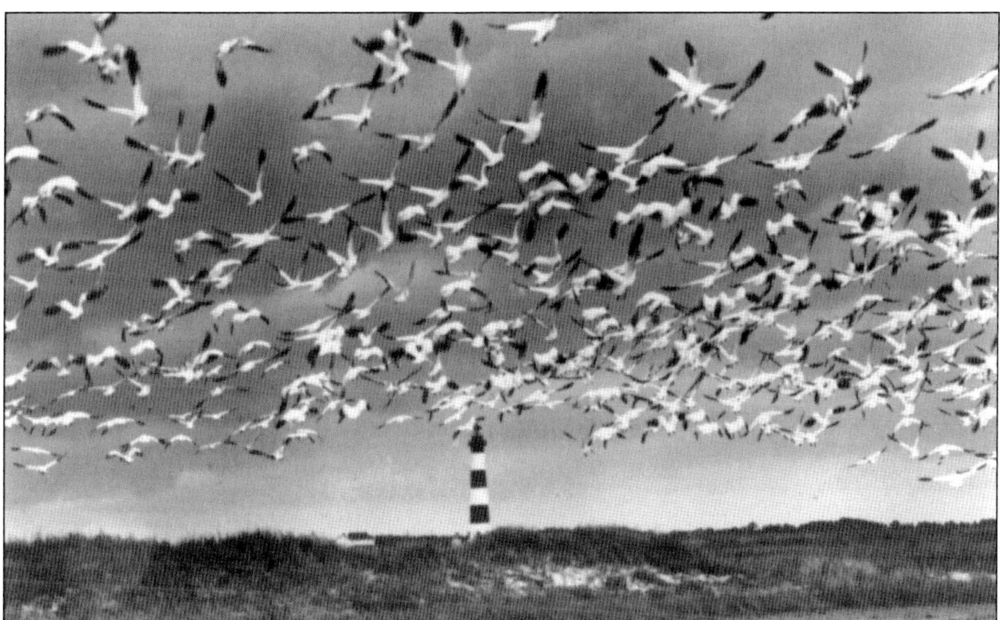

From the 1930s through the 1950s, North Carolina's northern and southern Outer Banks provided some of the best duck hunting on the Eastern Seaboard. Puddle ducks, divers, snow geese, swans, or brant could be found on any given day by hunters in boats and duck blinds, which dotted the Carolina sound waters. Today, in Cape Hatteras National Seashore, waterfowl hunting is legal during the fall duck-hunting season. In the Bodie Island District, the park offers a lottery system for prospective hunters. (Courtesy of the Cape Hatteras National Seashore.)

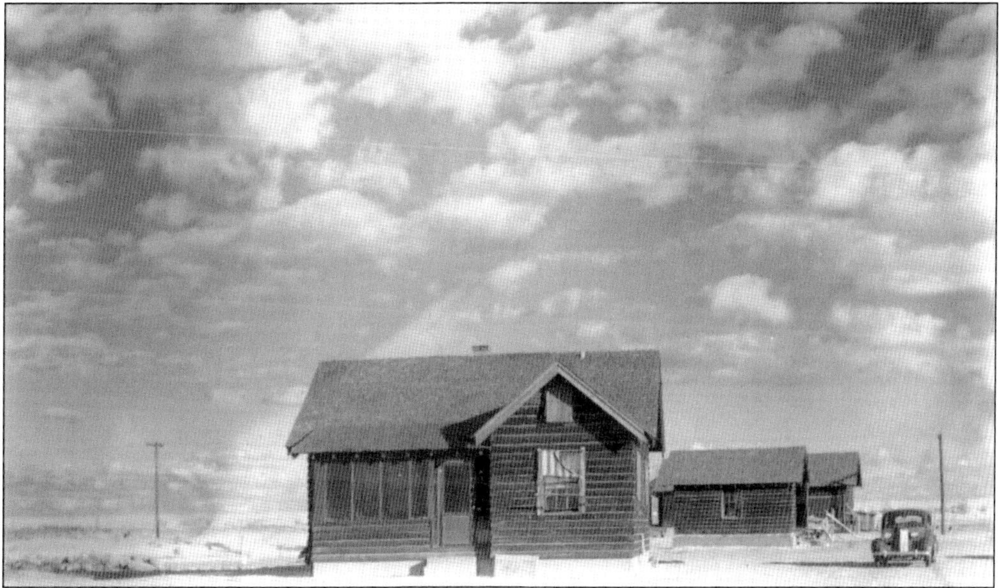

In the early 1900s, many of the native residents were market hunters, selling their plentiful harvest of waterfowl to New York City markets. When wealthy sportsmen discovered the bountiful hunting opportunities in the area, they built hunt clubs along the barrier islands. This photograph of the 1938 Buxton Hunt and Fishing Club is representative of those early clubs. (Courtesy of the Cape Hatteras National Seashore.)

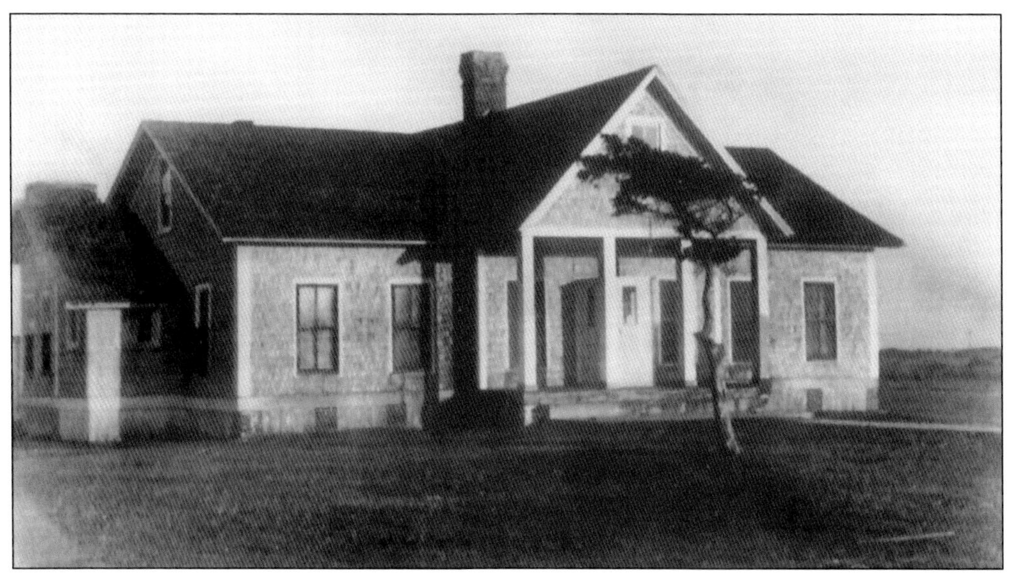

Today, a few family-owned vacation home retreats are all that remain of the old traditional hunt clubs. These homes are scattered along the sound side the length of the barrier islands. Today's hunters use state-permitted hunting blinds, which can be seen dotting the Carolina sound waters in the fall and winter months. Pictured here is the former Carteret Gun & Rod Club near Cedar Island, North Carolina. (Courtesy of the North Carolina Maritime Museum.)

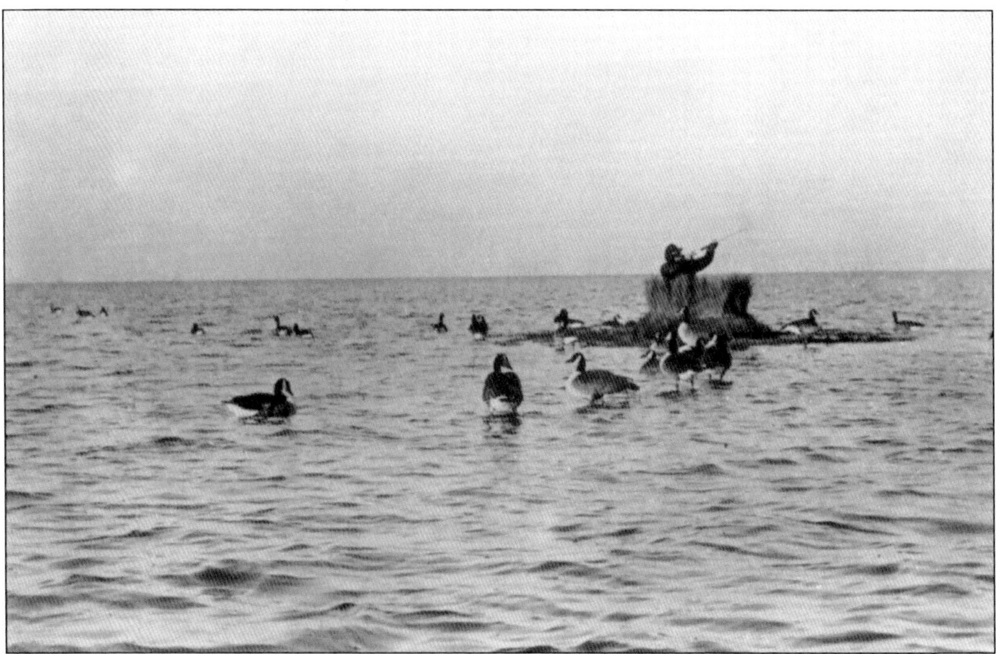

Duck hunters sometimes placed live decoys in the water surrounding their blinds to lure wild waterfowl to within shooting range. This duck blind was photographed Down East near Cedar Island, North Carolina. This same method of waterfowl hunting can be seen today during the fall months. Waterfowl still flock to the region during the winter months. Pea Island and Cedar Island National Wildlife Refuges are great places to view this impressive gathering of waterfowl and wading birds. (Courtesy of the Cape Lookout National Seashore.)

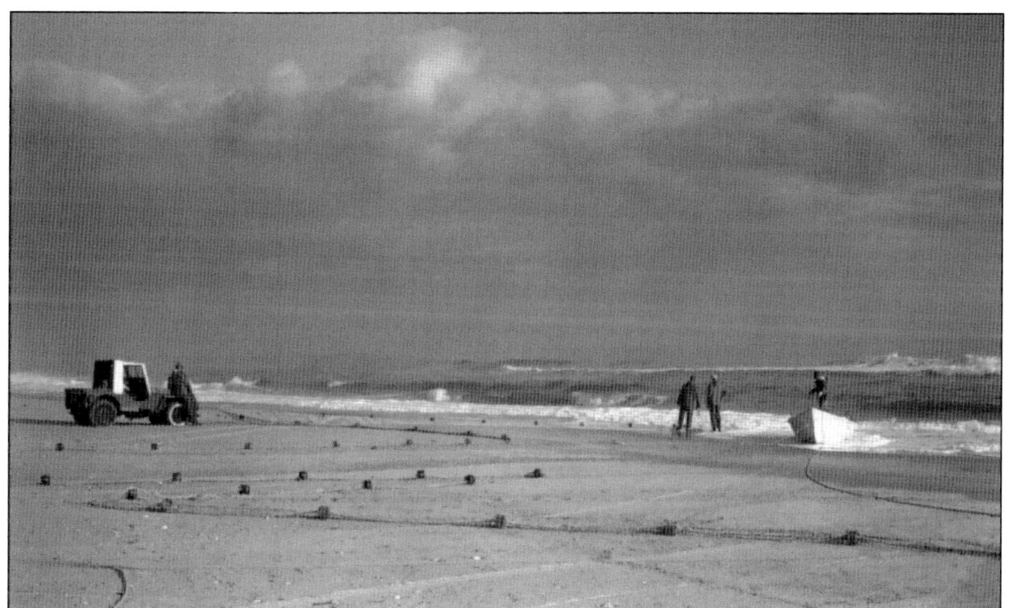

Traditional seine netting was conducted on many of the Outer Banks beaches. The dory, a small wooden boat, is launched from the beach through the surf zone, carrying the bulk of the net, while one end of the net is secured by crewman onshore. Once offshore, the fishermen feed the net into the ocean. A seine fishing net hangs vertically in the water with its bottom edge held down by weights and its top edge buoyed by floats. After a period of time, the net is hauled back onto the beach by wrenching it in with a sand buggy or truck. (Courtesy of the Cape Hatteras National Seashore.)

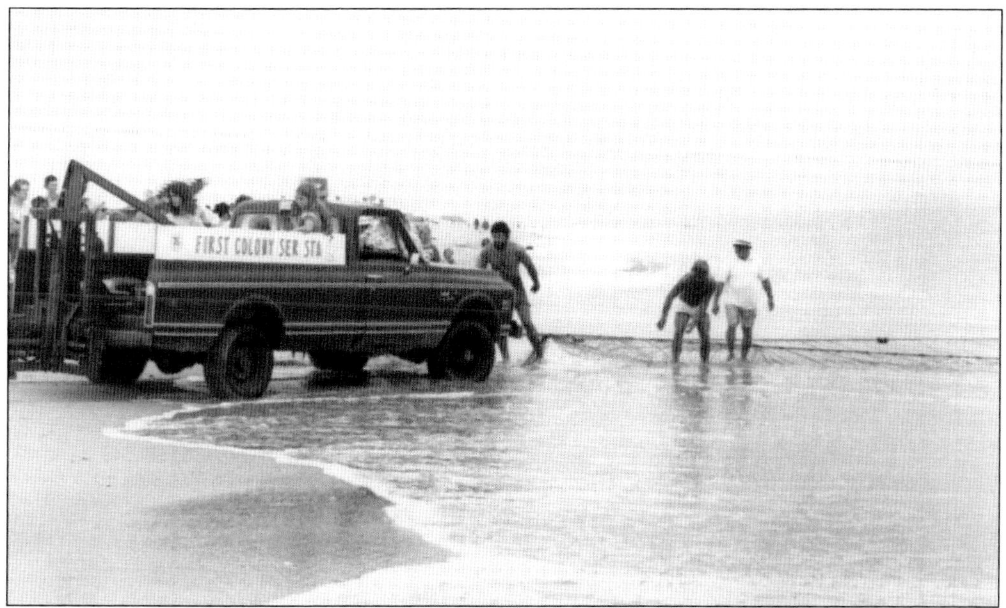

A seine is being pulled to shore on Hatteras Island in 1960. The beach seine–haul fishery is one of the oldest North Carolina fisheries and is still practiced today. Commercial fishermen spread nets out in long lines on the hard-packed sand, checking for tears and tangles. (Courtesy of the Cape Hatteras National Seashore.)

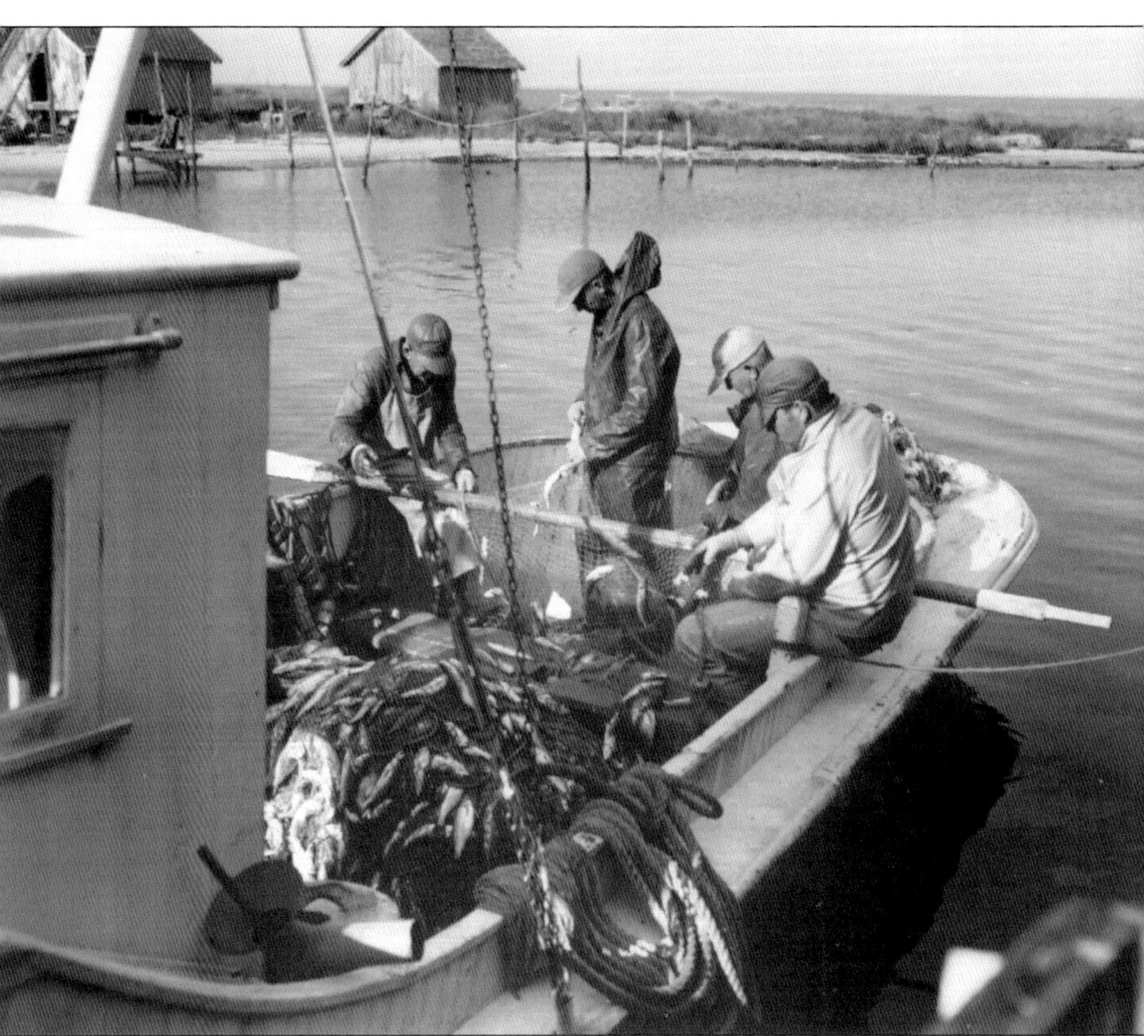

These fishermen, on board the *Jackie Fay*, called the fishing village in Hatteras homeport and brought a bountiful gillnet catch of sea trout to market. North Carolina's maritime history has long been linked to the small community fishermen and their harbors dotting the shorelines. Fishing the sea and the Carolina sounds is a way of life for many. The traditional waterman must possess determination, dedication, and understanding of the resource to maintain a sustainable way of life. (Courtesy of the Cape Hatteras National Seashore.)

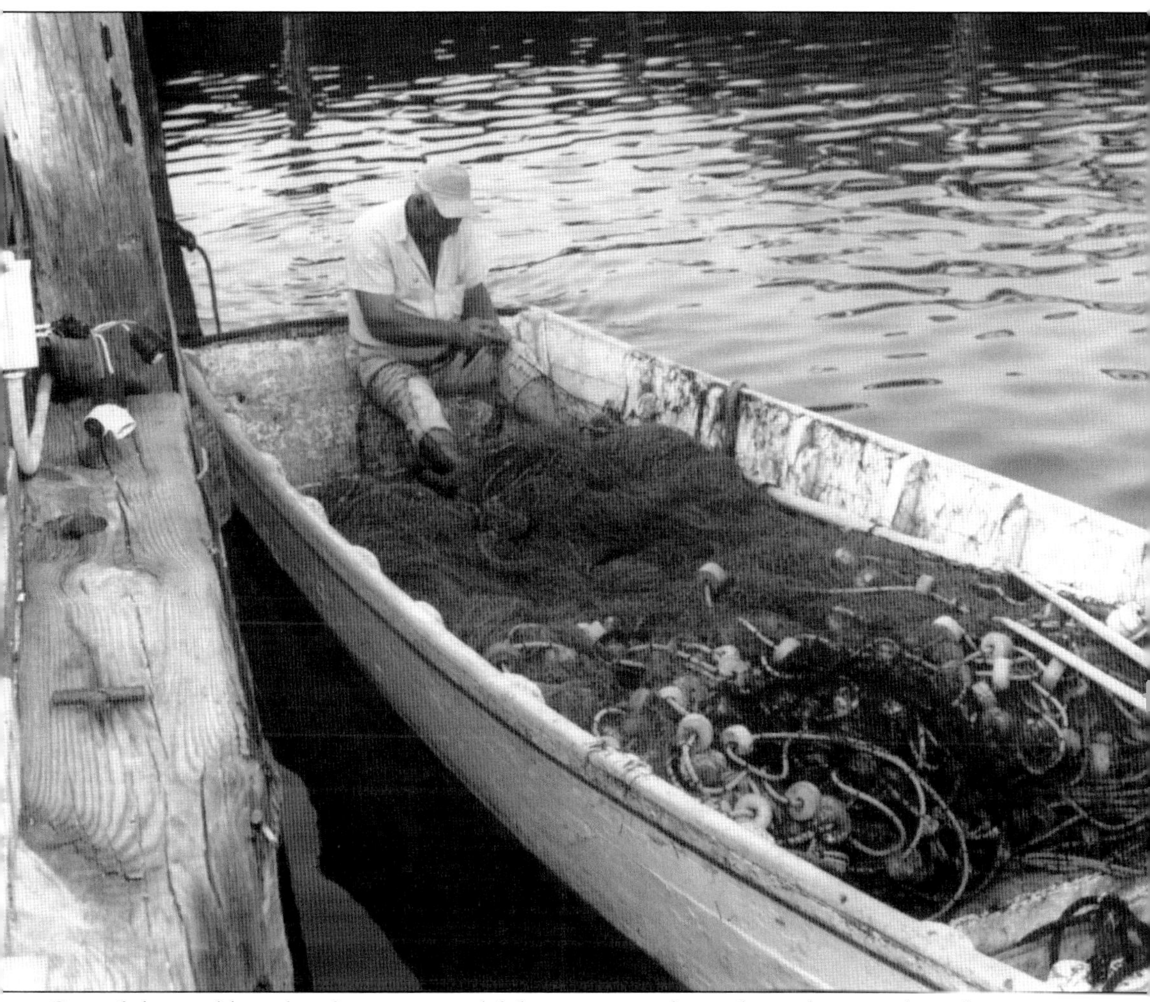

One of the weekly tasks of a commercial fishermen is to dry and mend nets such as this one photographed on Hatteras Island. Commercial fishing became a profitable occupation, as natives began exporting their catches to markets as far north as New York City's famous Fulton Fish Market. (Courtesy of the Cape Hatteras National Seashore.)

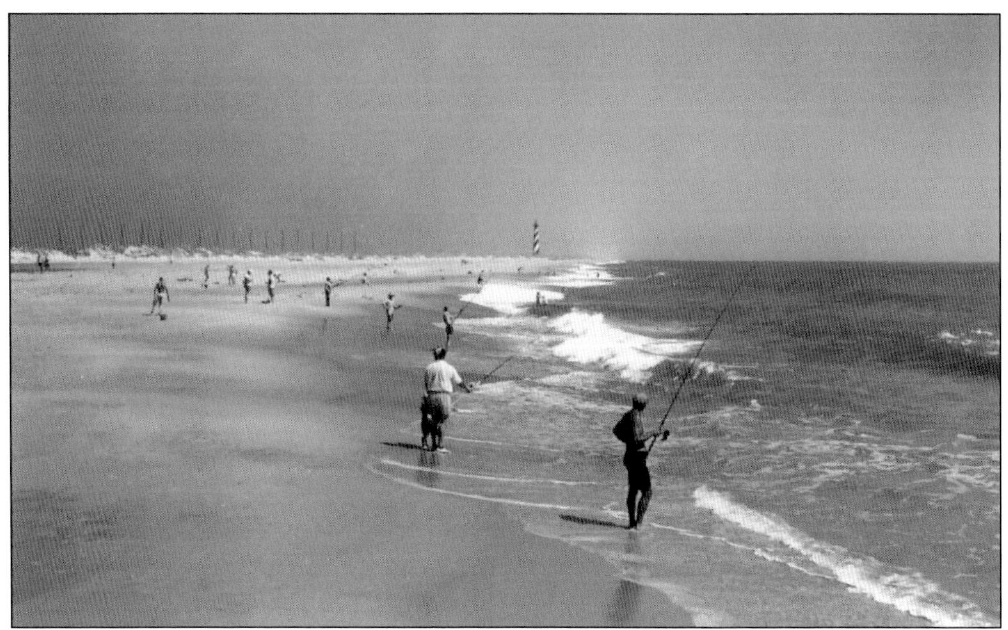

Surf fishing in Buxton, with the Cape Hatteras Lighthouse in the background, is a popular recreational pastime. Surf fishing gained in popularity in the latter half of the 20th century. The Cape Hatteras Anglers Club began a surf-fishing tournament in 1958, and in 1960 Hatteras village women formed the Hatteras Gulls, one of the first women's surf-fishing teams. (Courtesy of the Cape Hatteras National Seashore.)

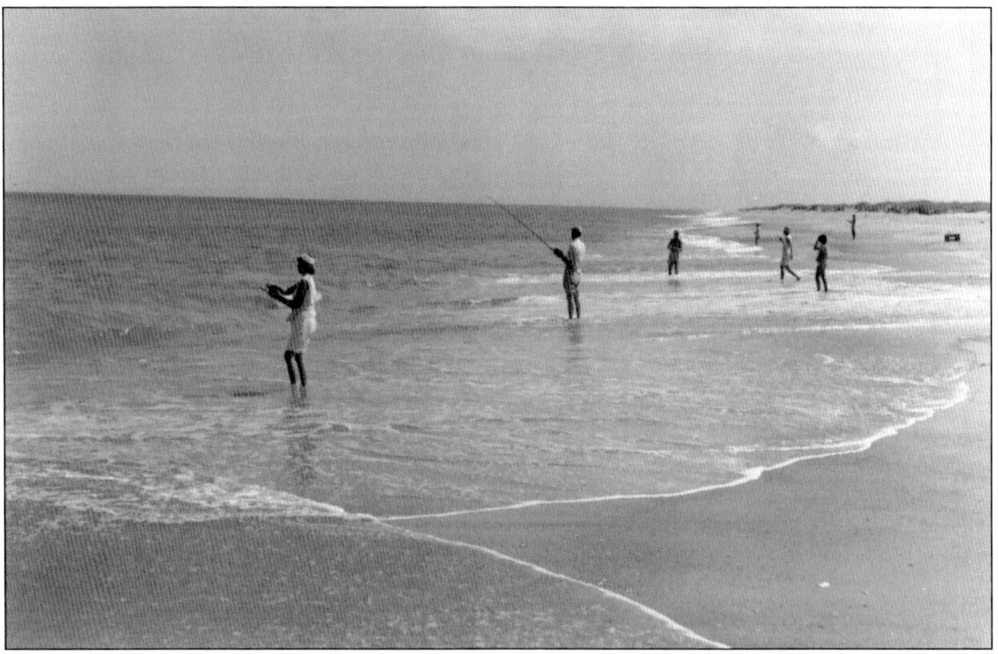

With the establishment of Cape Hatteras National Seashore and Cape Lookout National Seashore, surf fishing with hook and line became a popular recreational sport as part of the overall increase in park visitation during the 1960s and 1970s. (Courtesy of the Cape Hatteras National Seashore.)

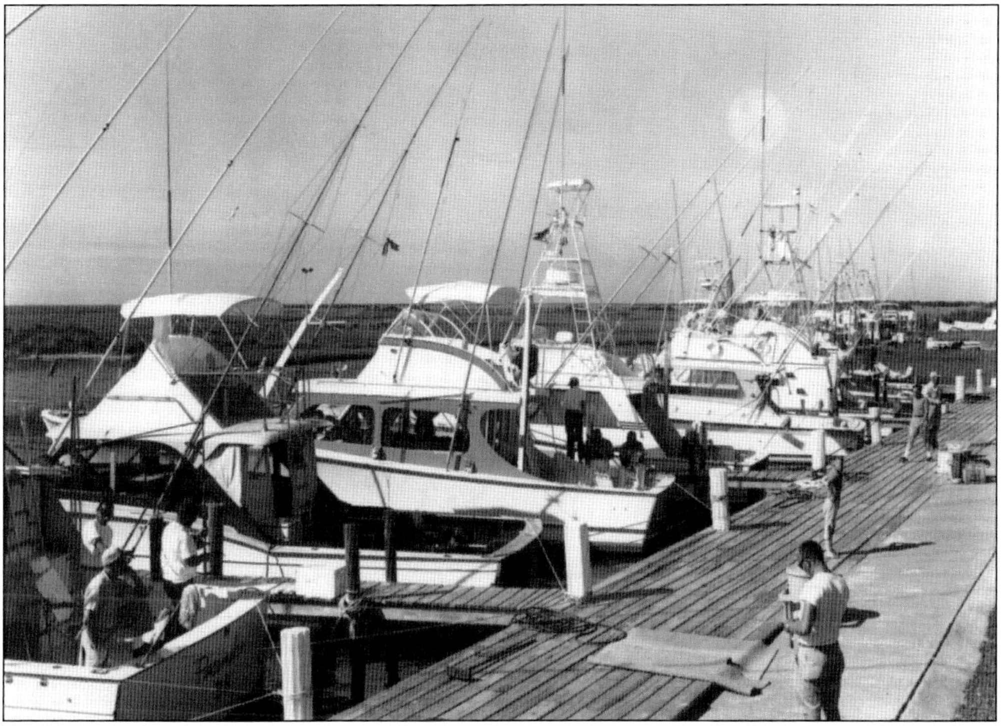

Oregon Inlet Fishing Center is a premier marina facility with an impressive fleet of charter boats for offshore Gulf Stream fishing. The landmark Oregon Inlet is one of the most dynamic inlets on the byway. Charter boats take daily fishing parties offshore to catch the big ones—blue marlin, sailfish, and tuna—as well as fish to take home for supper. (Courtesy of the Cape Hatteras National Seashore.)

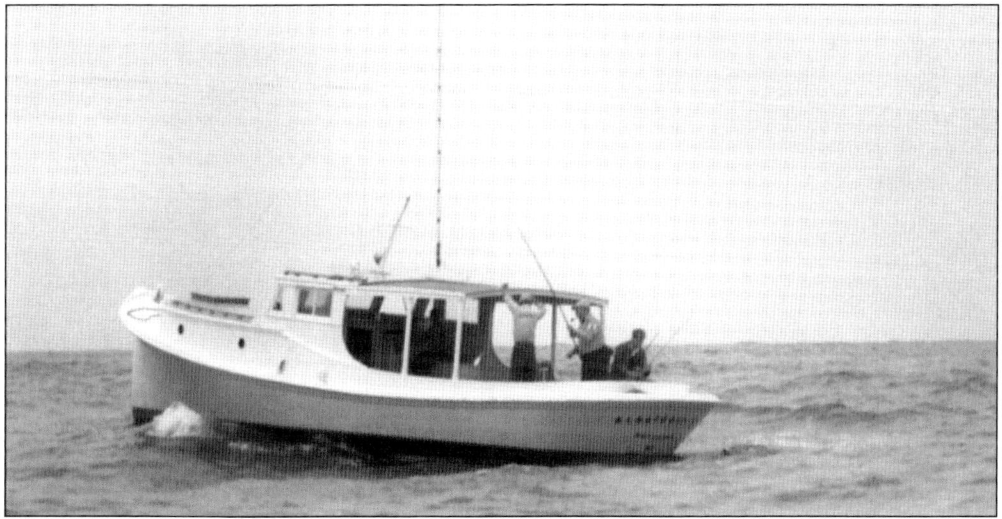

Anglers can fish the wrecks and artificial reefs offshore or try their luck in the calmer sound waters nearby. On an offshore deep-sea Gulf Stream fishing trip, anglers may find abundant game fish such as marlin, sailfish, tuna, dolphin, and wahoo. Closer to port and the marina, one may find speckled trout, flounder, striped bass, and red drum. (Courtesy of the Cape Hatteras National Seashore.)

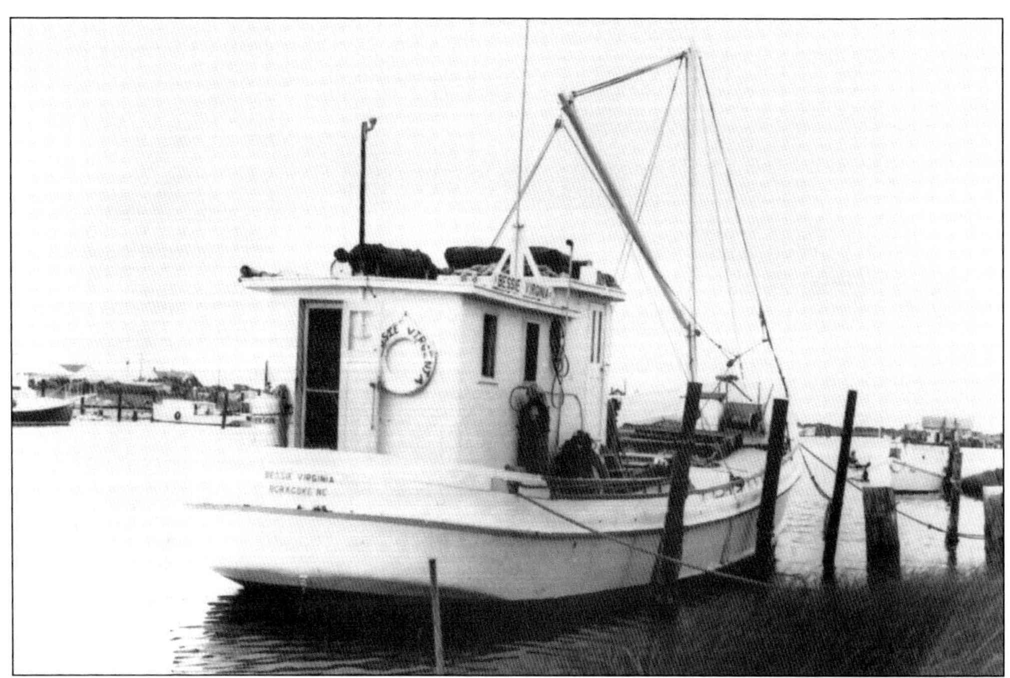

Pictured here is Silver Lake Dock on Ocracoke Island during the village's shrimping heyday. Outer Banks fishermen were among the last to join the shrimp fishery. Hatteras and Ocracoke Islands are home to some of the oldest charter fishing fleets on the East Coast. Note the former US Coast Guard station in the background of the photograph. (Courtesy of the Cape Hatteras National Seashore.)

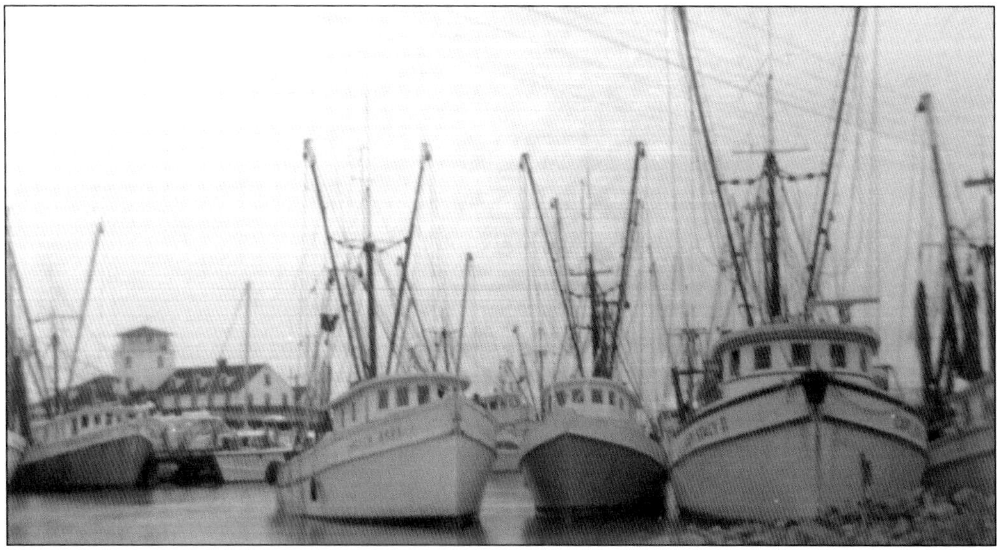

The variety of coastal working skiffs and commercial fishing boats on the northern and southern Outer Banks is unique to each region. The boats evolved to adapt to the varied water conditions, depth of the water, type of fish normally sought, and exposure to ocean currents. The names of many of the backyard boatbuilders' work boats go by various names, including shad boat, mullet skiff, flounder boat, beach dory, menhaden, shrimp trawler, sharpie, set-net boats, and crab-pot boats. (Courtesy of the Cape Hatteras National Seashore.)

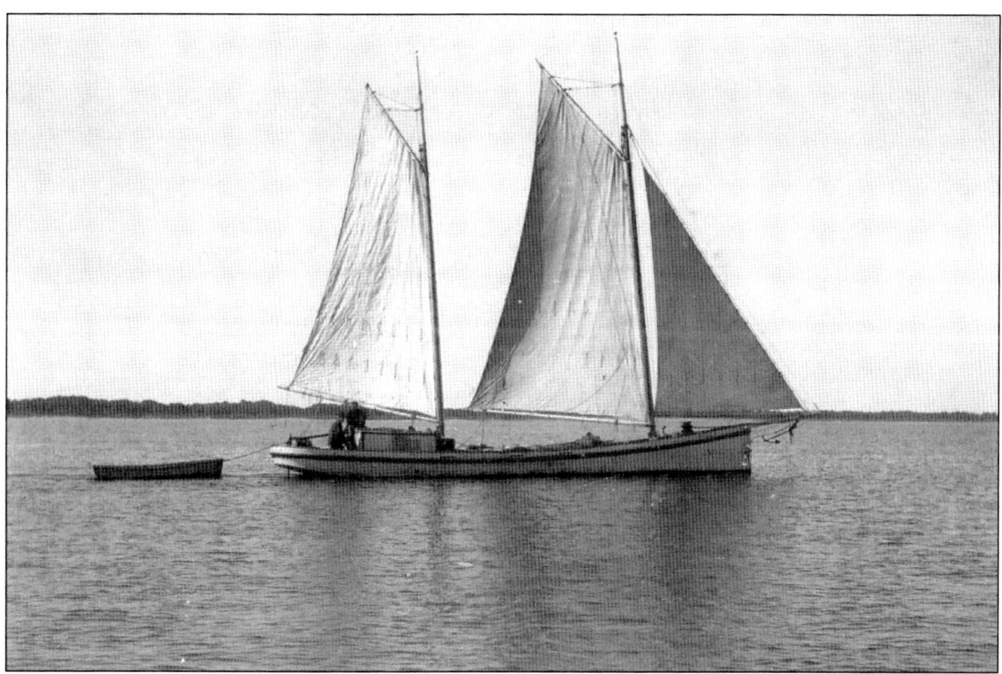

A sharpie, pictured here off Marshallberg, North Carolina, was a type of hard-chained sailboat with a flat bottom, extremely shallow draft, centerboards, and straight flaring sides. Sharpies were traditional fishing boats used to harvest oysters. The photograph below shows a mound of oysters on a sharpie along the Core Banks on the Pamlico Sound. (Both, courtesy of the North Carolina Maritime Museum.)

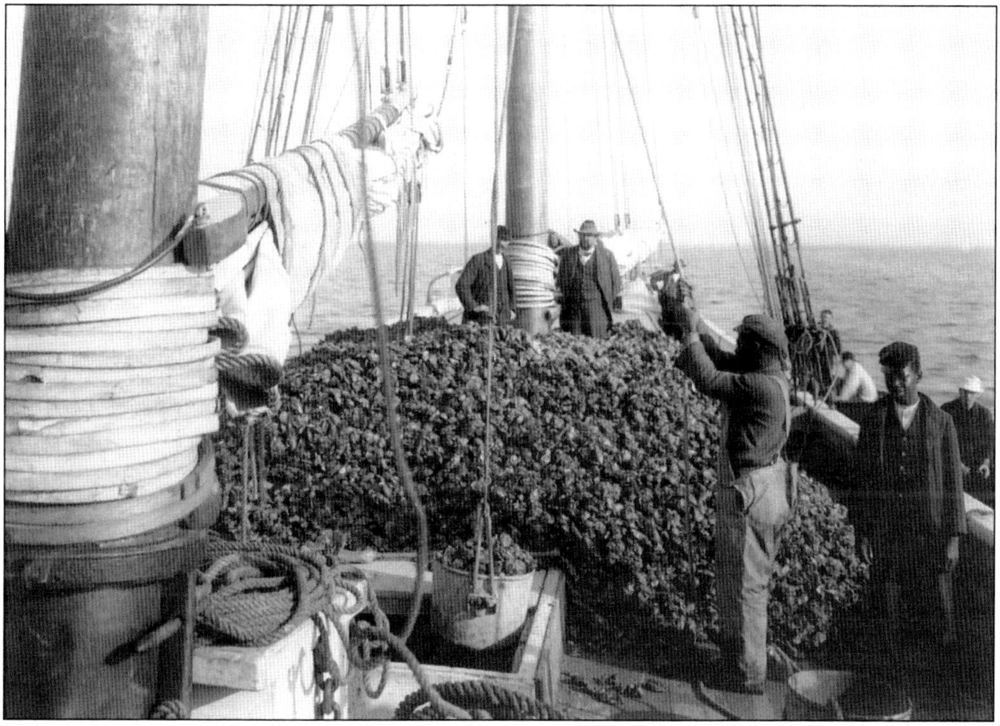

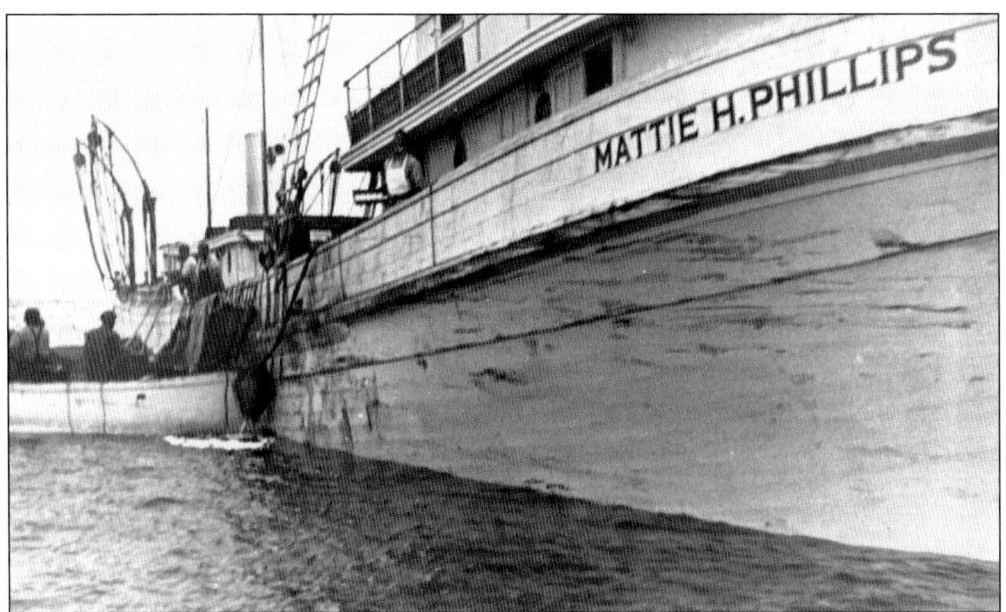

Menhaden, a type of fish, swim near the surface of the water in schools as large as a football field. A small striker boat locates the school of menhaden in the sound while the big vessel drops two smaller purse seine boats into the water. Menhaden, too oily and bony to eat, are caught and sold as bait or processed into an oil used in printing ink, plastics, building materials, and animal feed. Pictured below in 1945 is a menhaden harvest. (Both, courtesy of the North Carolina Maritime Museum.)

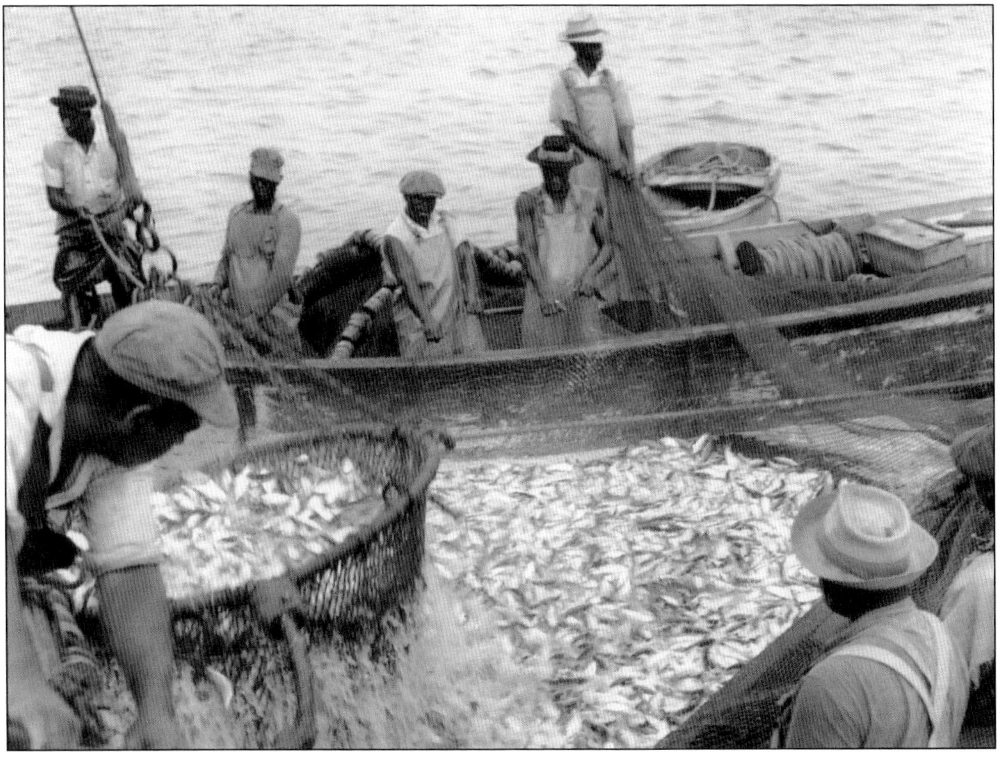

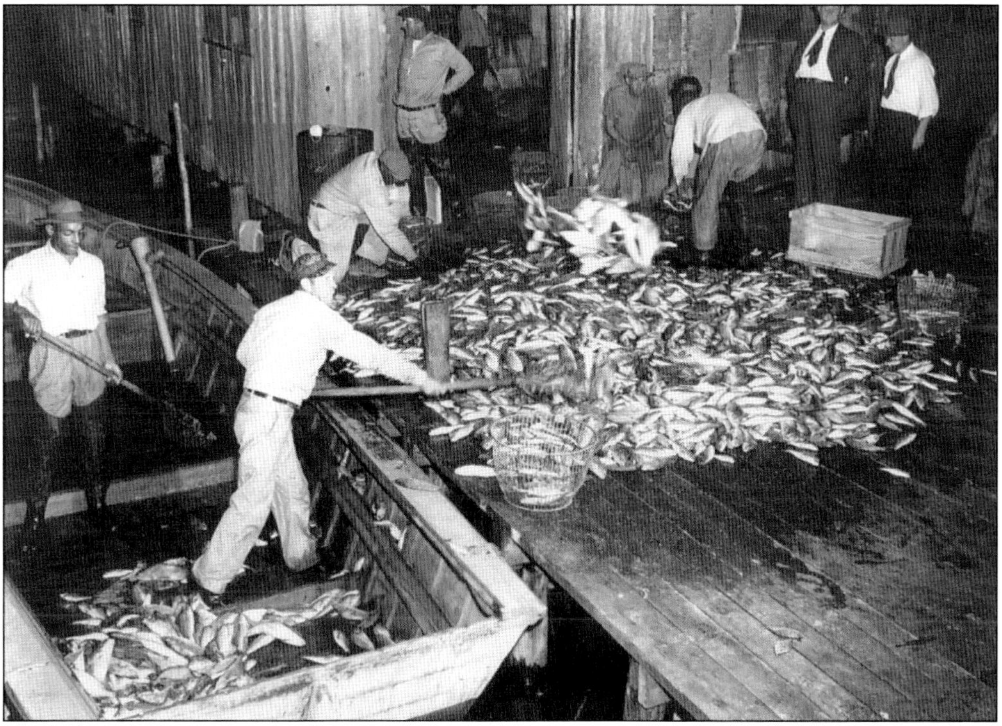

The unloading and sorting of fish took place along the docks of Core Sound working waterfronts. Note the cat catching the marl fresh off the boat below. In the early 1940s–1950s, fish on the Outer Banks were plentiful. (Both, courtesy of the North Carolina Maritime Museum.)

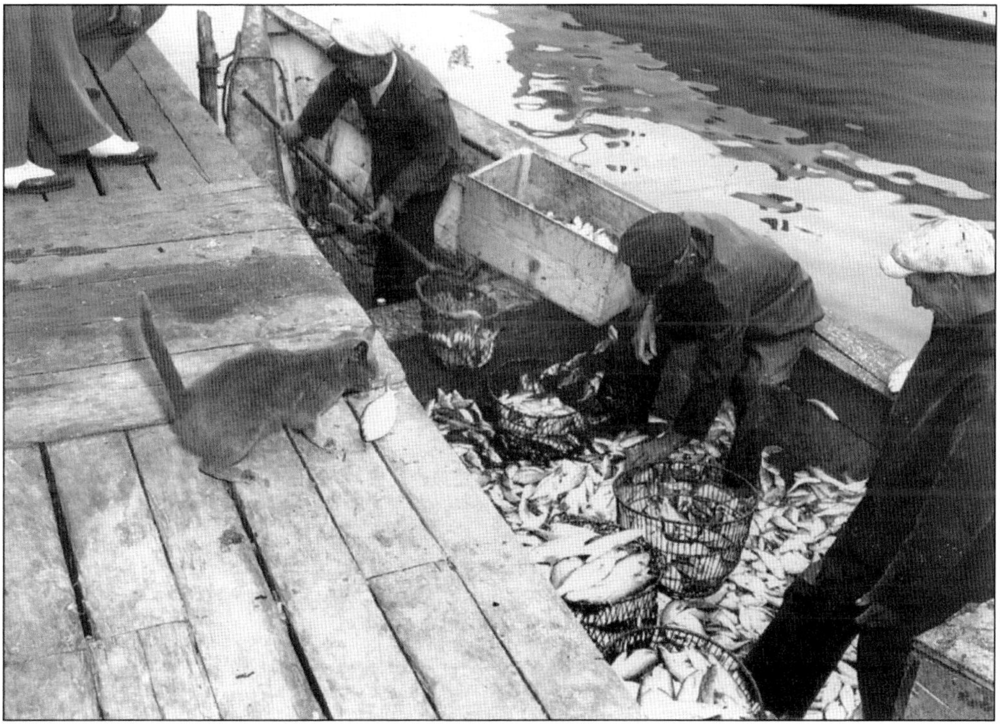

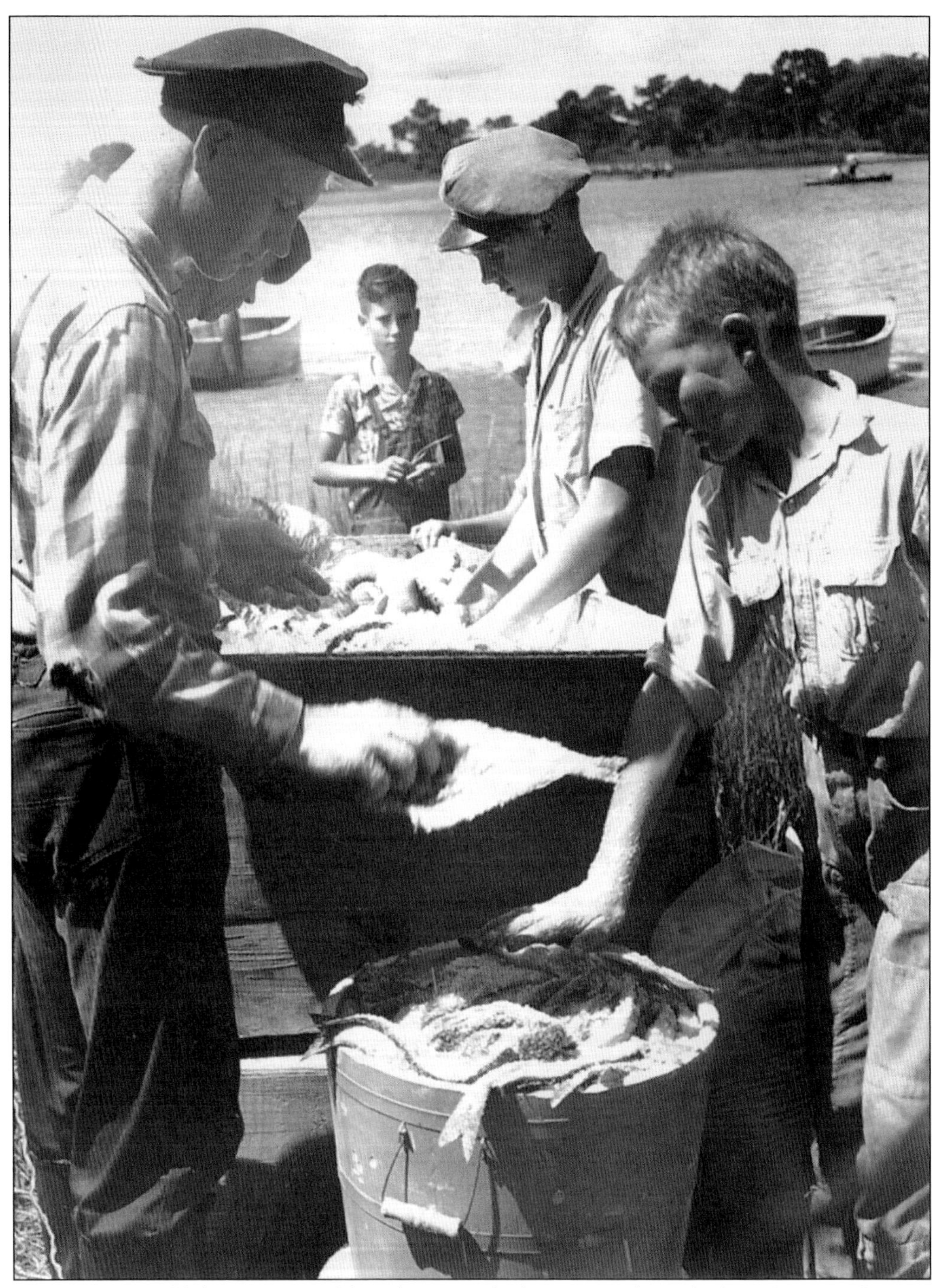

Mullet, a type of fish, are pictured here being packed at a waterfront dock in Carteret County. They generally inhabit salt water or brackish water and frequent shallow inshore areas. Mullet commonly feed by grubbing about in the sand or mud for microscopic plants, small animals, and other food sources. (Courtesy of the North Carolina Maritime Museum.)

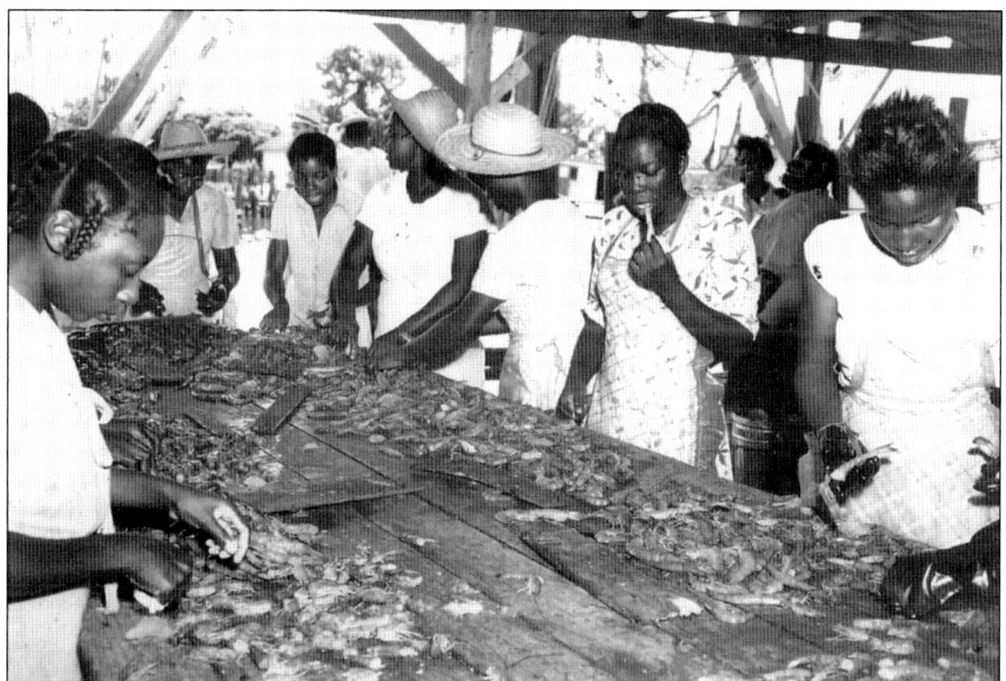

The working waterfronts have always employed local residents for processing local seafood. This photograph shows workers de-heading shrimp at fish house. (Courtesy of the North Carolina Maritime Museum.)

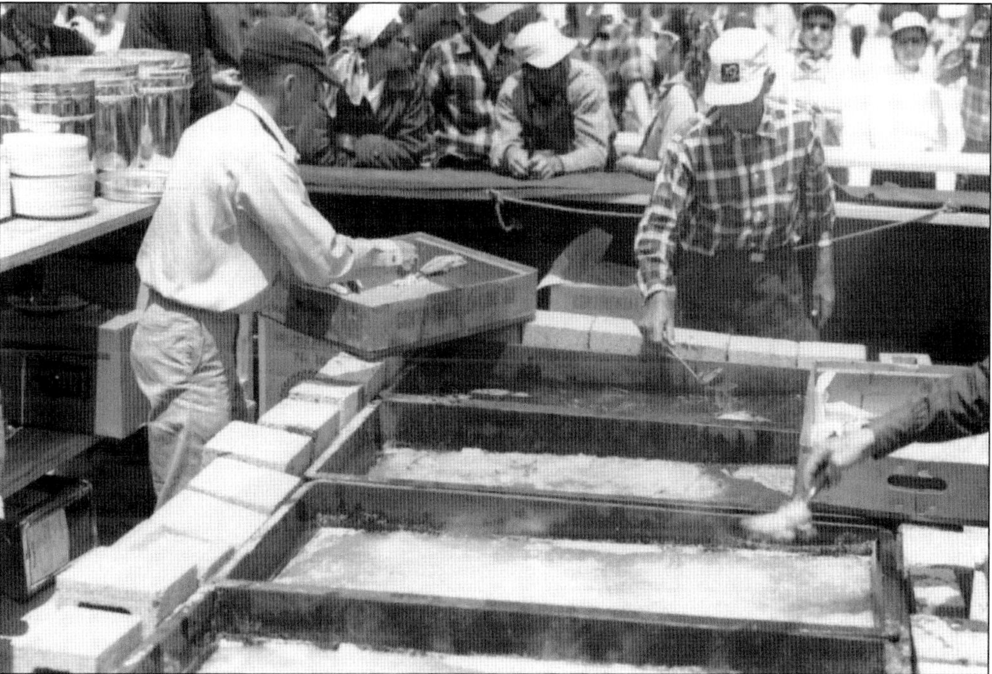

Pictured here in 1958 is a local fish fry, an opportunity for members of the local communities to gather. Today, fish fry events are held as fundraising activities for many churches and organizations. (Courtesy of the Cape Hatteras National Seashore.)

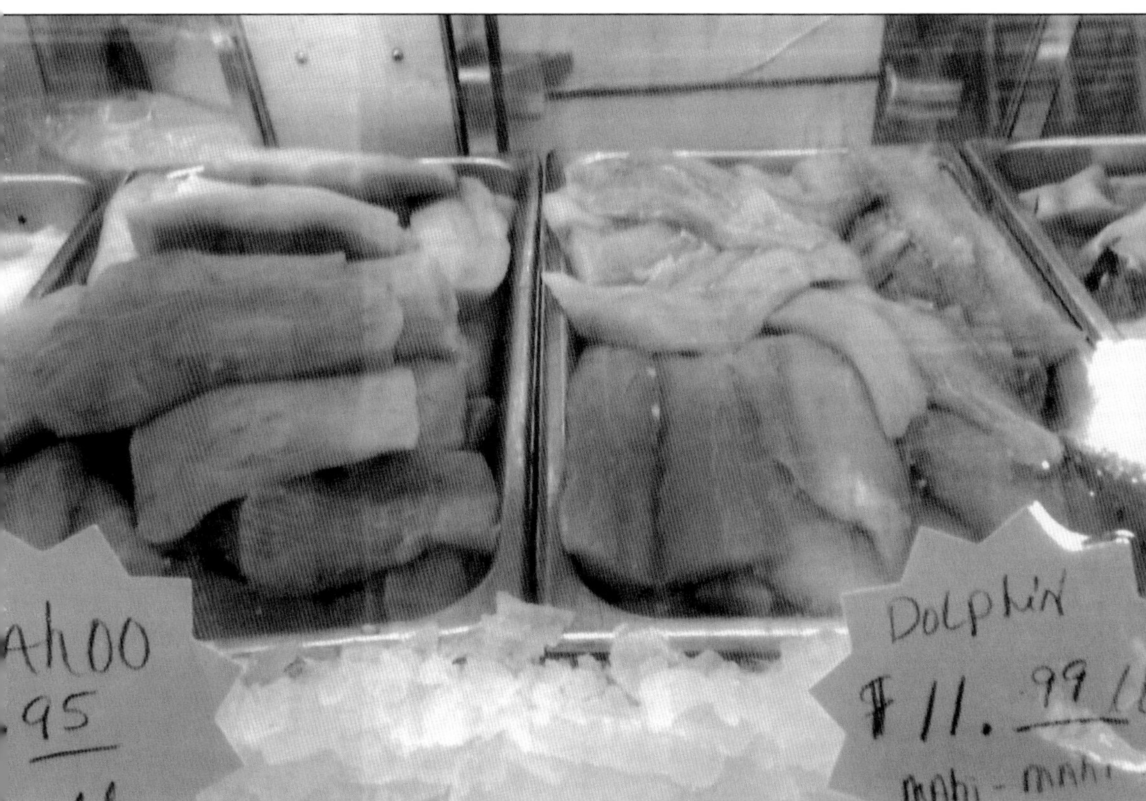

In recent times, NC Catch, a local catch partnership, was organized to strengthen the North Carolina seafood economy through promotion and education of buying locally caught seafood. The Outer Banks has a multigenerational community of commercial fishermen who earn their livings bringing fresh seafood to the market. (Courtesy of the Cape Hatteras National Seashore.)

Four

Village Traditions

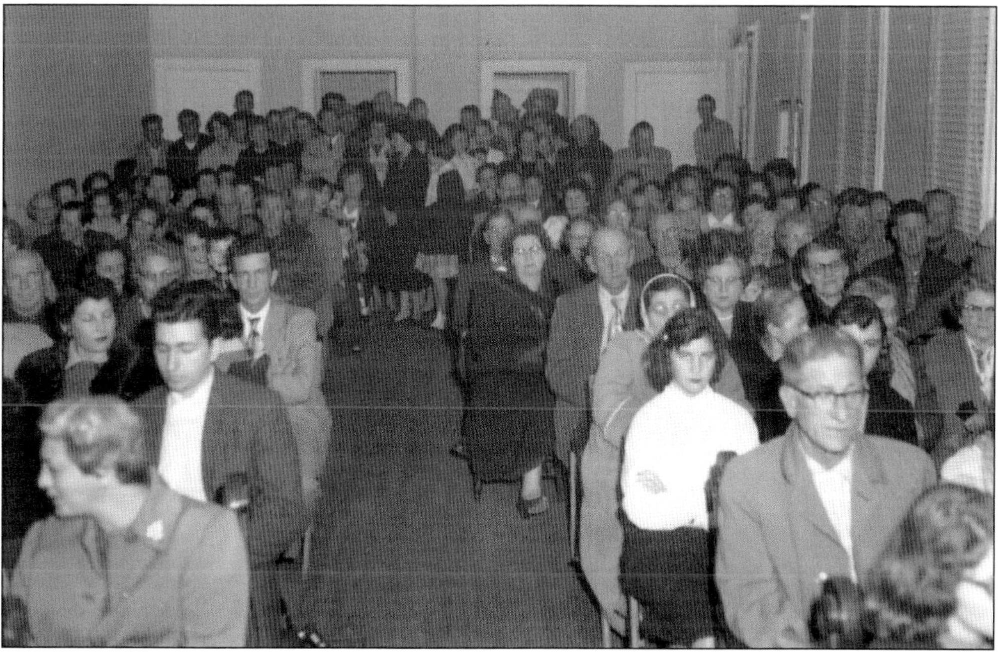

The highway meanders through 21 maritime communities, each with its own unique character and residents. They all have interesting histories and old salt tales to be enjoyed along with the natural beauty of the region. The native people were tenacious, skilled survivalists who lived off the land and sea and adapted to the changing winds and tides. The Atlantic Ocean and adjacent sound waters of this estuarine environment along the byway villages are rich in traditions, old buildings, landscapes, family cemeteries, churches, local stories and tales, music, and food. Many villagers celebrate their heritage with seasonal community events that relate to their earlier fishing, hunting, and boatbuilding way of life. Today, on Hatteras and Ocracoke Islands, travelers will see many beautiful beach vacation homes along with endless outdoor recreation opportunities. In contrast, the Down East region of the byway reveals the historical maritime culture with very little impact from modern-day tourism. (Courtesy of the Cape Hatteras National Seashore.)

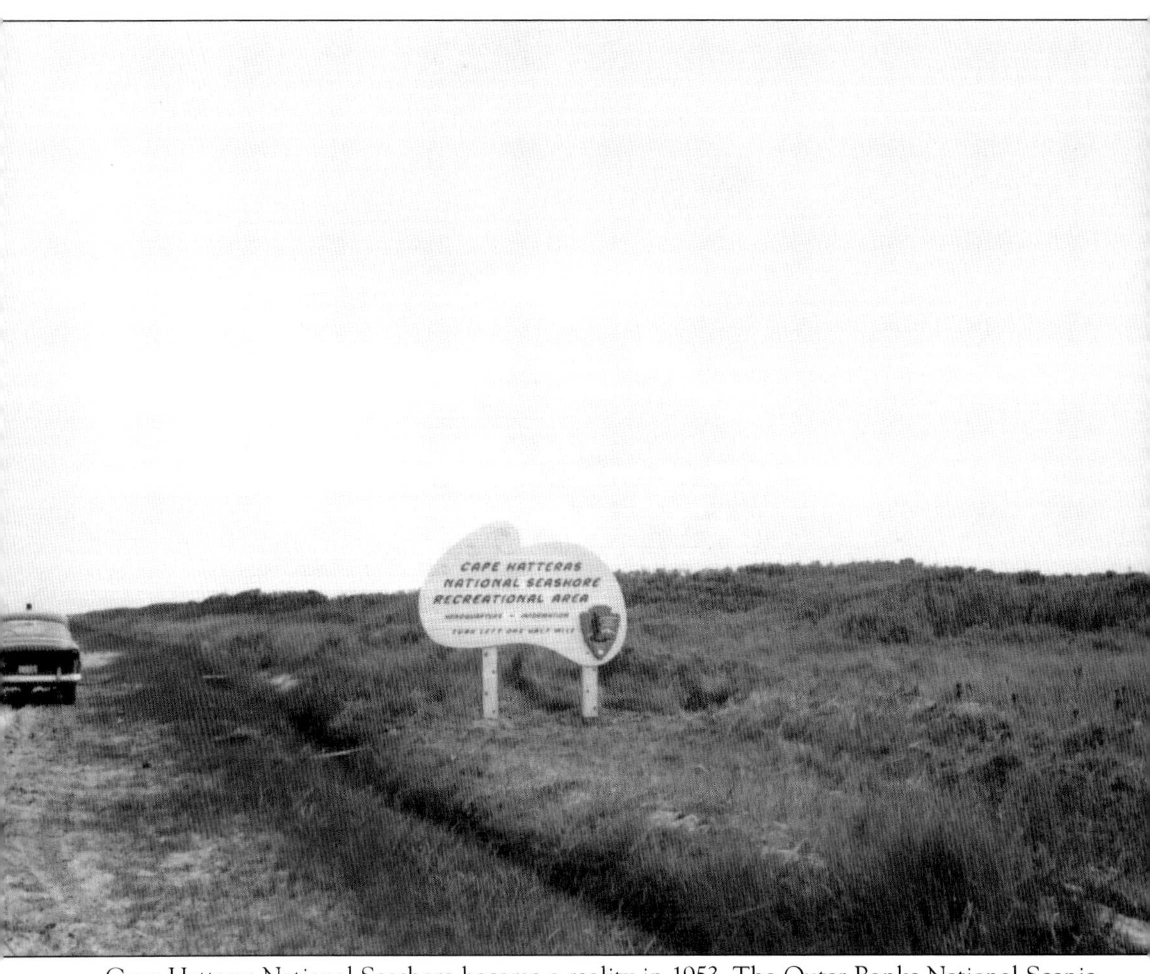

Cape Hatteras National Seashore became a reality in 1953. The Outer Banks National Scenic Byway northern entrance is located at Whalebone Junction. In the 1930s, local people nicknamed this area when Alexander Midgett hauled a 72-foot whale skeleton in the back of his Model T truck from nearby Pea Island and deposited the skeleton at what is today's junction of US 64-264, US 158, and NC Route 12 in Nags Head, North Carolina. Today, the northern entrance of the park consists of a small information center and restroom facility. An unmaintained trail just south of the restroom leads to the site of a granite US Coastal Survey Marker, the North Monument, set on Bodie Island in 1848. This marker commemorates one of the first official surveys of the Outer Banks region. Farther south, near the junction of South Old Oregon Inlet Road and NC Route 12, a state historical marker, titled Port Ferdinando Roanoke, explains the early colonial voyages of 1585–1590 to this region. (Courtesy of the Cape Hatteras National Seashore.)

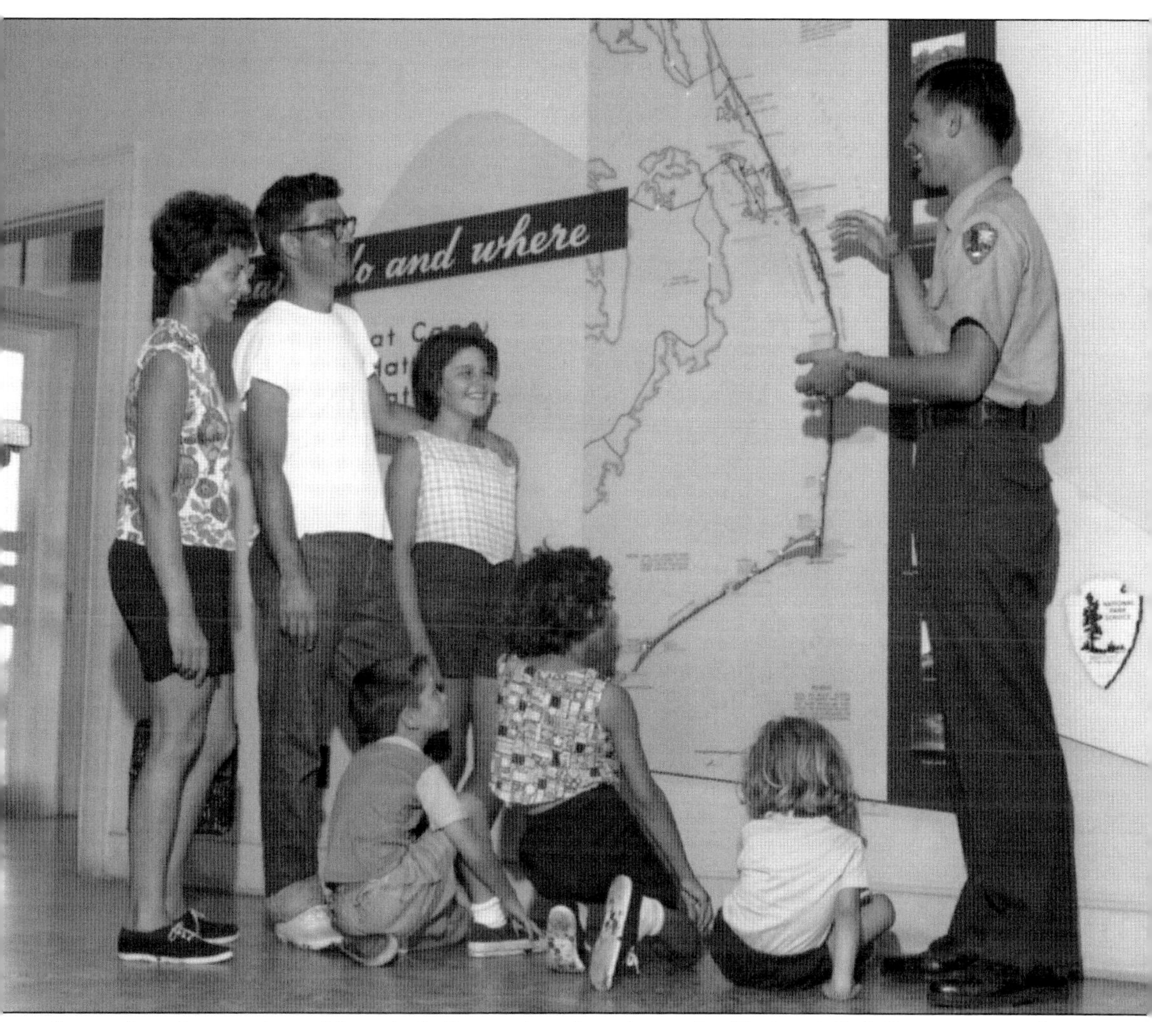

Soon after the creation of America's first national seashore, the National Park Service opened visitors; centers providing information at Bodie Island Light Station. Travelers on the byway can see two classic examples of the early influence of the USLSS on the Outer Banks with the beautifully designed and restored structures near the entrance to the Bodie Island Lighthouse: the Bodie Island Life-Saving Station and a later US Coast Guard station building. The buildings are still used by park staff today—a testament to their solid construction and ability to weather many storms. (Courtesy of the Cape Hatteras National Seashore.)

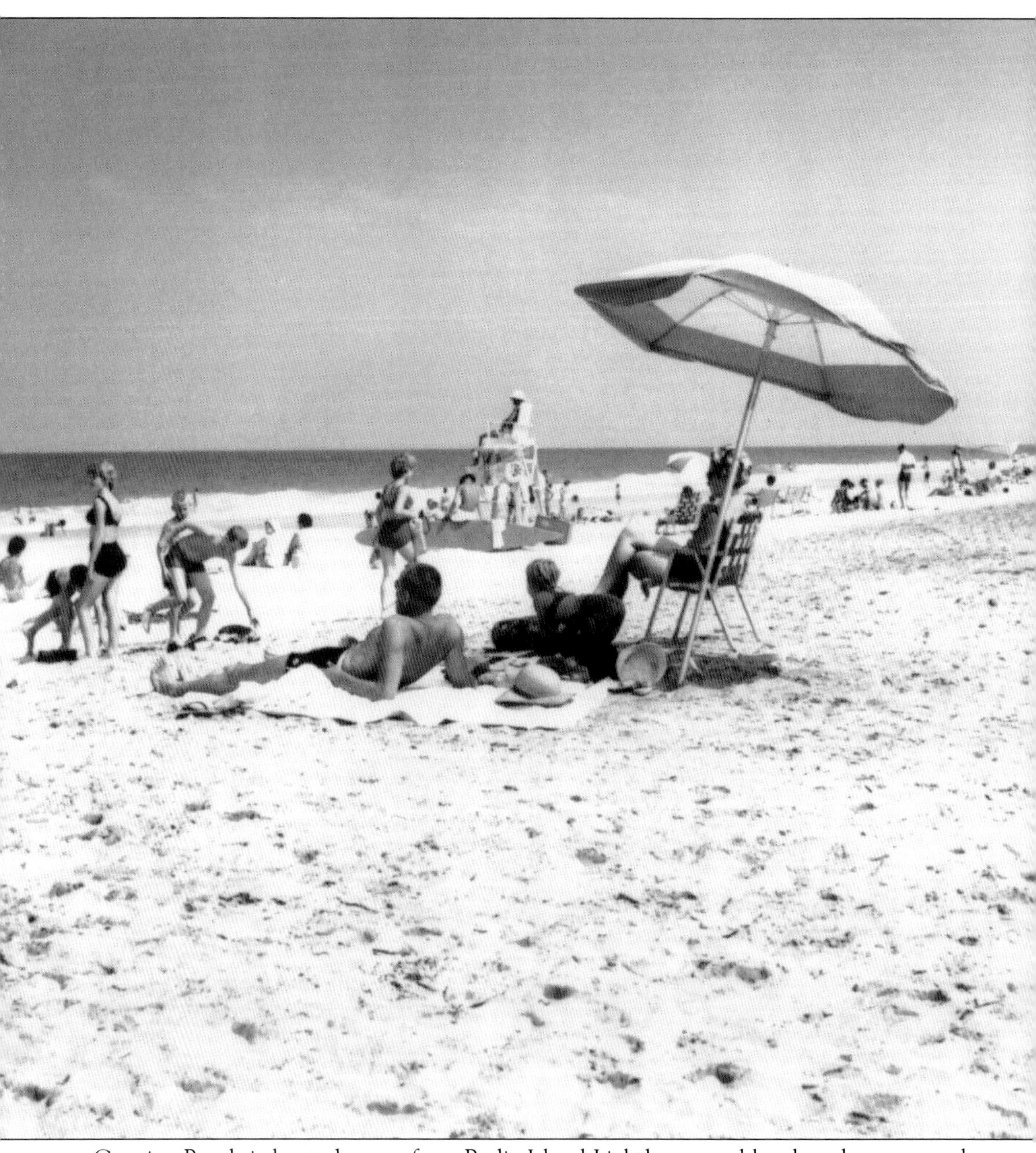

Coquina Beach is located across from Bodie Island Lighthouse and has long been a popular day-use beach area offering a bathhouse with outdoor showers, restrooms, and a boardwalk. This popular summertime swimming beach is named for the tiny coquina clams (*Donax variabilis*) that can frequently be found in the gravel wash of the surf zone. (Courtesy of the Cape Hatteras National Seashore.)

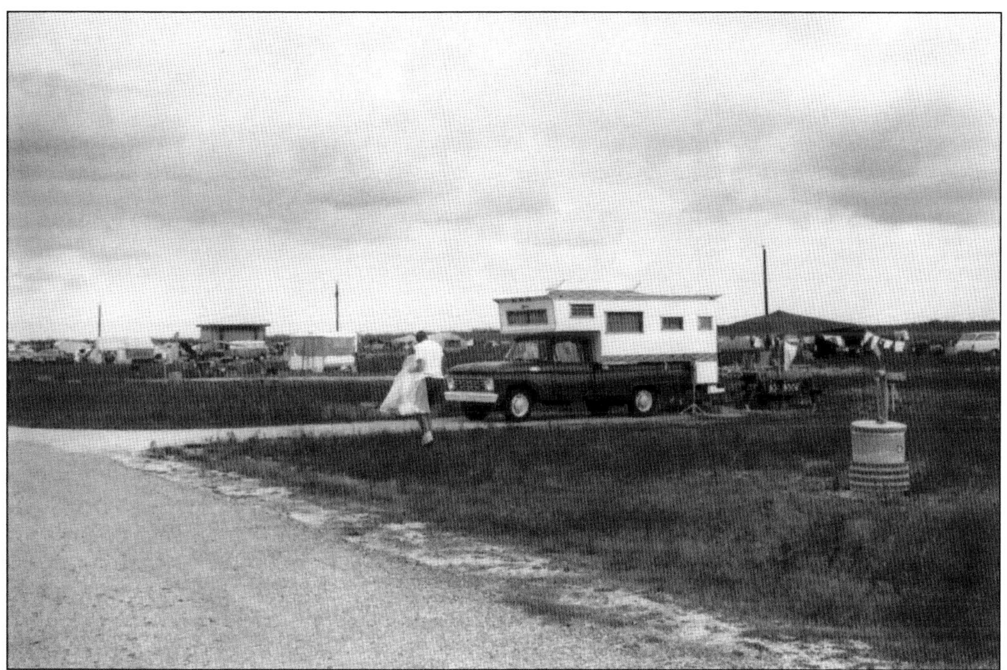

Oregon Inlet Campground is located on the east side of the barrier island where the sound of the Atlantic Ocean waves will lull campers to sleep—just a short walk through the sand dunes to the beach. (Courtesy of the Cape Hatteras National Seashore.)

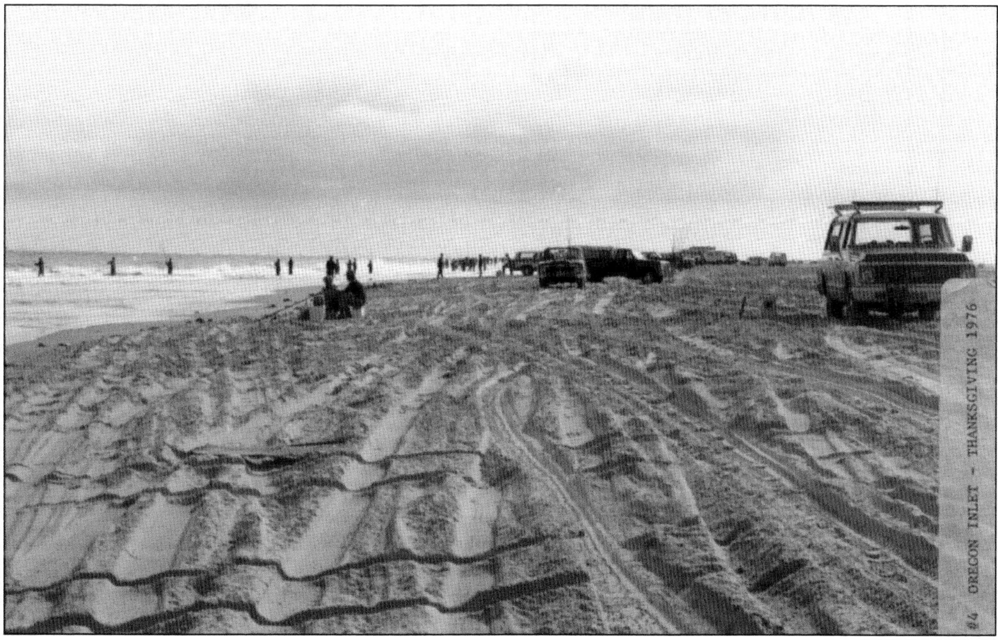

The beach south of Oregon Inlet Campground has one of many off-road-vehicle ramps that permit visitors to access and enjoy the ocean beaches and sound-side waters of Cape Hatteras National Seashore in four-wheel-drive vehicles. The National Park Service is managing ORV use with protection of important wildlife habitats and recreational interests in mind with a more balanced plan. (Courtesy of the Cape Hatteras National Seashore.)

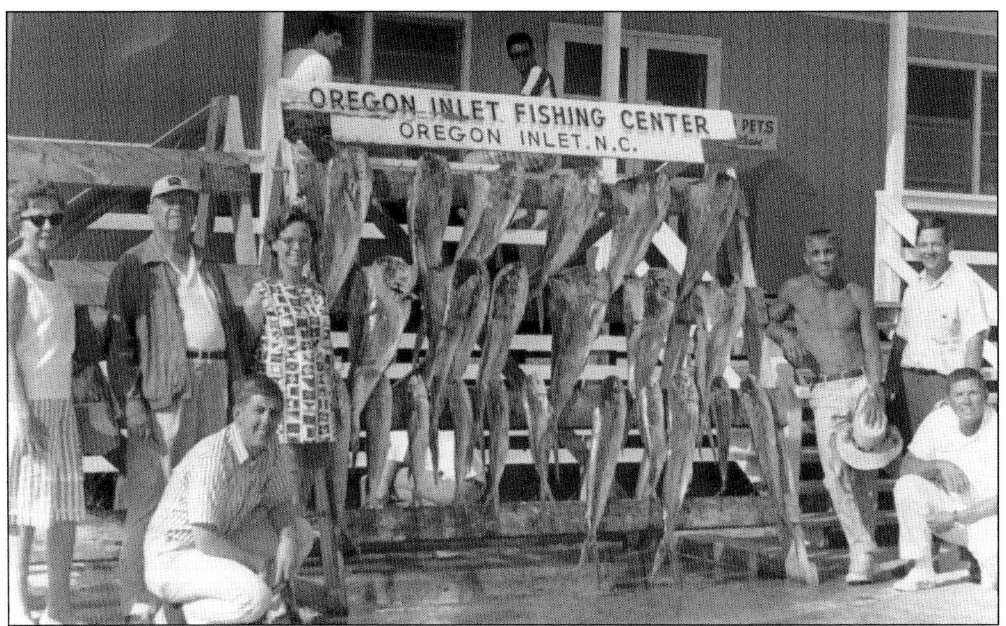

The Oregon Inlet Fishing Center is located across the highway from the campground. The fishing center is the home of the coast's largest and most modern fishing fleet, and offers a full-service marina as well as inshore and offshore charter fishing opportunities. On-site are the Oregon Inlet public boat ramps and current Bodie Island Coast Guard Station. (Courtesy of the Cape Hatteras National Seashore.)

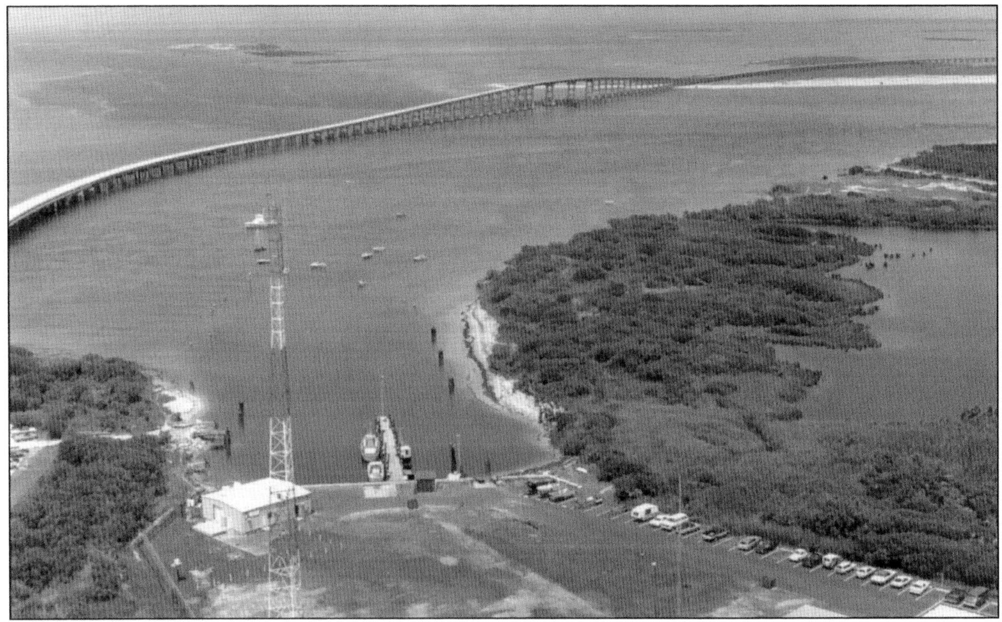
The channel for Oregon Inlet opened in 1846 during a hurricane, and travelers' only means of crossing was mainly by ferry until 1963, when the Herbert C. Bonner Bridge opened to vehicle traffic. The inlet joins the Pamlico Sound with the Atlantic Ocean and separates Bodie Island and Hatteras Island, which are connected by a 2.5-mile-long bridge spanning the inlet. In the foreground is the Oregon Inlet Fishing Center. (Courtesy of the Cape Hatteras National Seashore.)

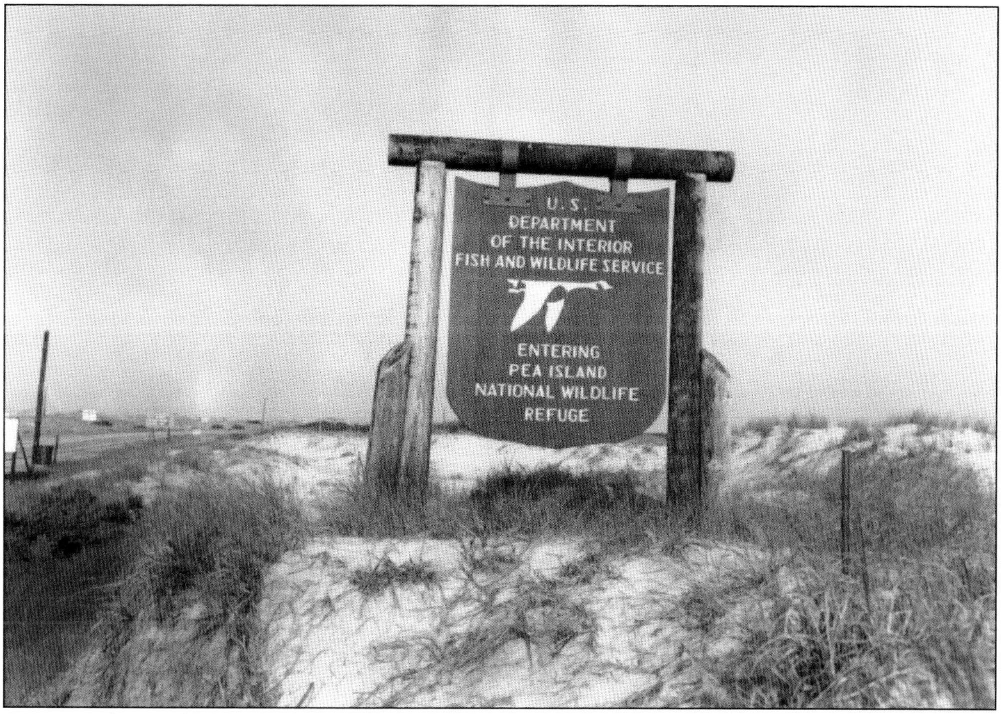

Crossing the Herbert C. Bonner Bridge, the traveler enters Pea Island National Wildlife Refuge and the northern end of Hatteras Island. The 5,834-acre refuge was established in 1938 to provide nesting, resting, and wintering habitat for migratory waterfowl. (Courtesy of the Cape Hatteras National Seashore.)

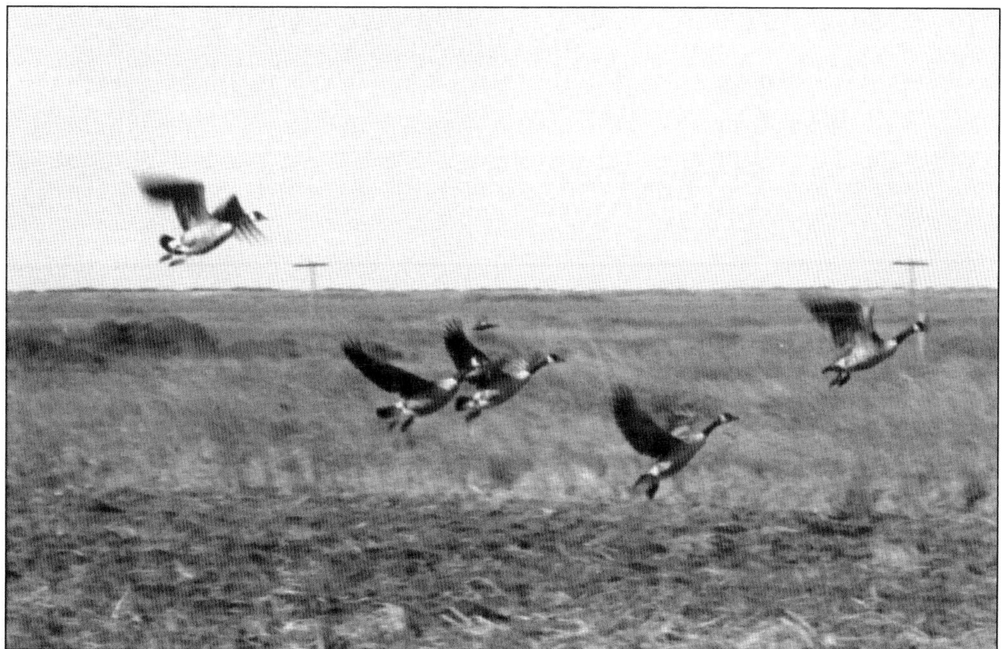

The refuge was created to protect breeding grounds for migratory birds such as Canada geese and other wildlife. (Courtesy of the Cape Hatteras National Seashore.)

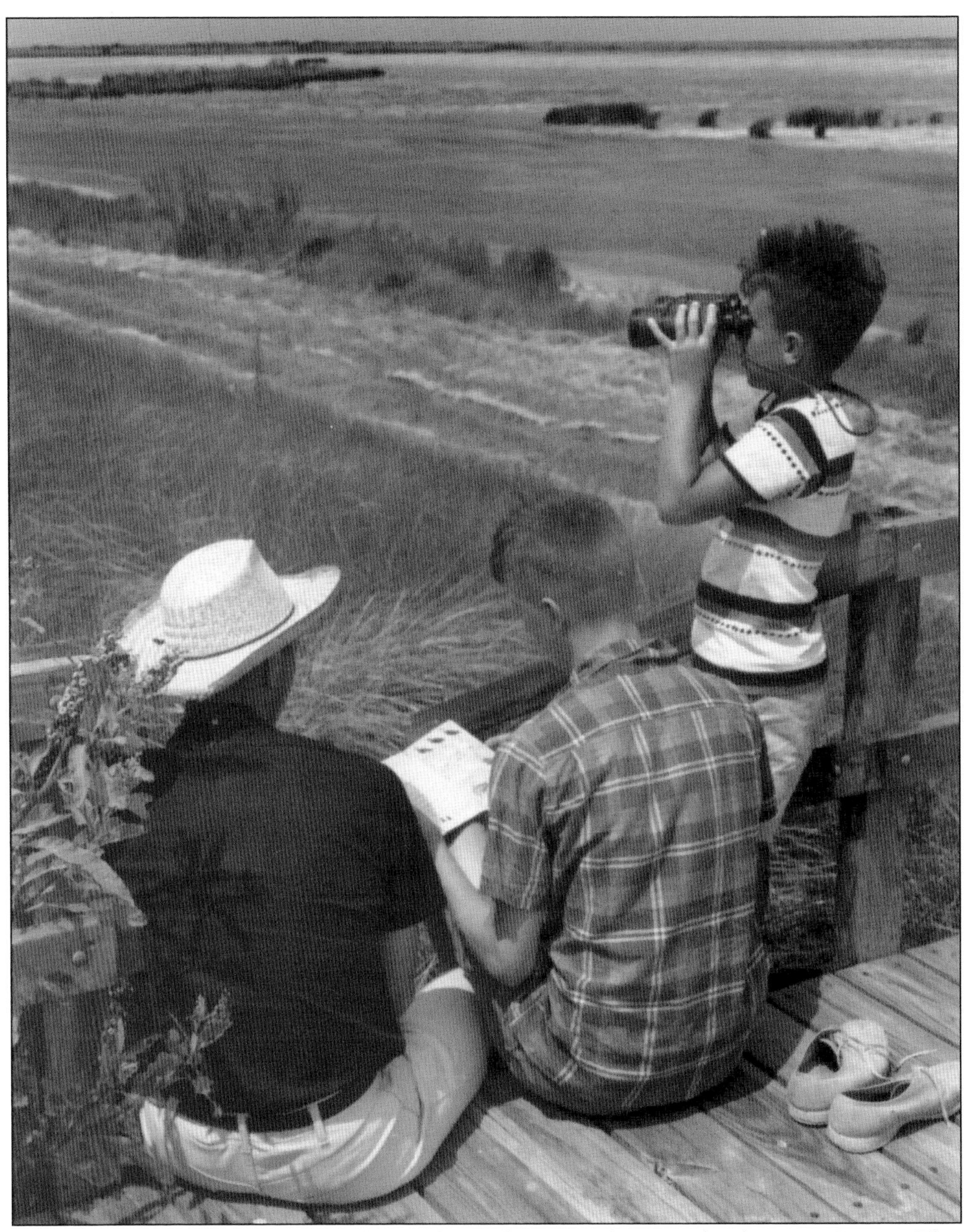

Refuge visitors enjoy the boardwalk trail located next to the Pea Island Visitor Center. This information center is filled with information on the trails, plants, and animals that one may see in the refuge, including butterflies, shorebirds, wintering waterfowl, snakes, turtles, and other wildlife that call this area home for the season. The refuge also consists of 13 miles of ocean beach, providing nesting habitat for sea turtles and several species of shorebirds. A state historical marker tells the story of the Pea Island Lifesavers. (Courtesy of the Cape Hatteras National Seashore.)

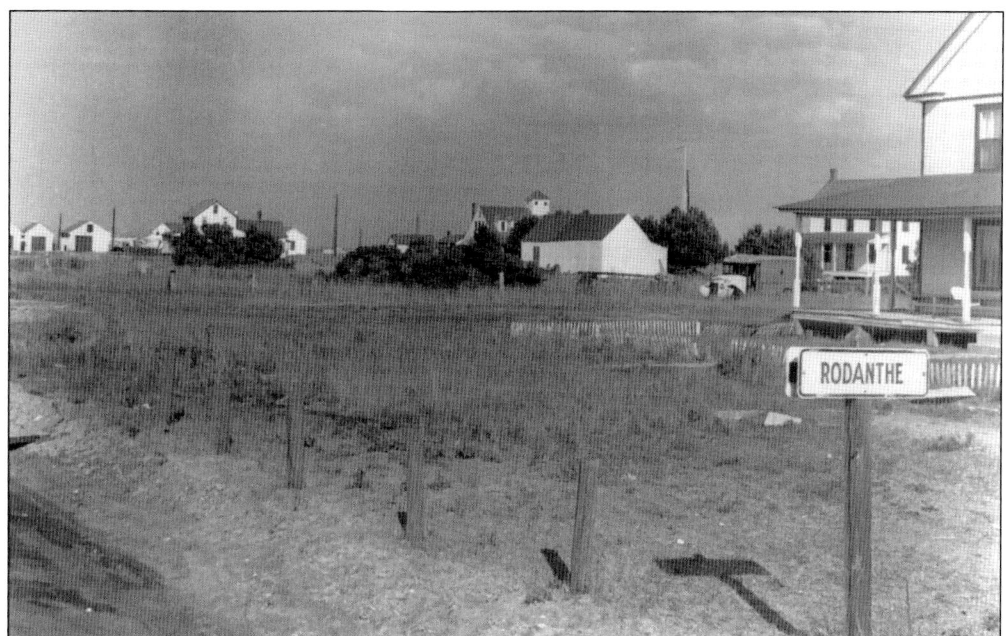

Leaving Pea Island, travelers enter the first of three villages—Rodanthe, Waves, and Salvo. Some village churches and family cemetery plots have been around since the early 18th century. Today, Rodanthe has all the modern conveniences for the many visitors who spend summer vacations in the area as well as year-round residents. (Courtesy of the Outer Banks History Center.)

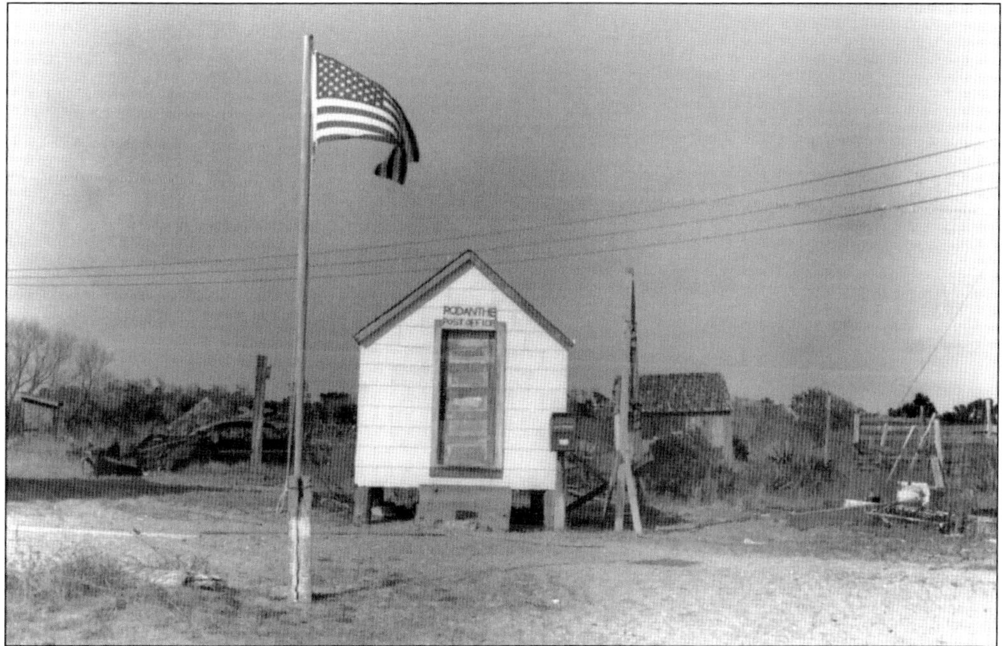

Historically, the first village was known as Chicamacomico, but in 1874 the Post Office Department began calling the village Rodanthe and the local post office was established. By the early 1900s, three distinct villages had formed, and eventually the two adjacent communities evolved into Waves and Salvo. (Courtesy of the Outer Banks History Center.)

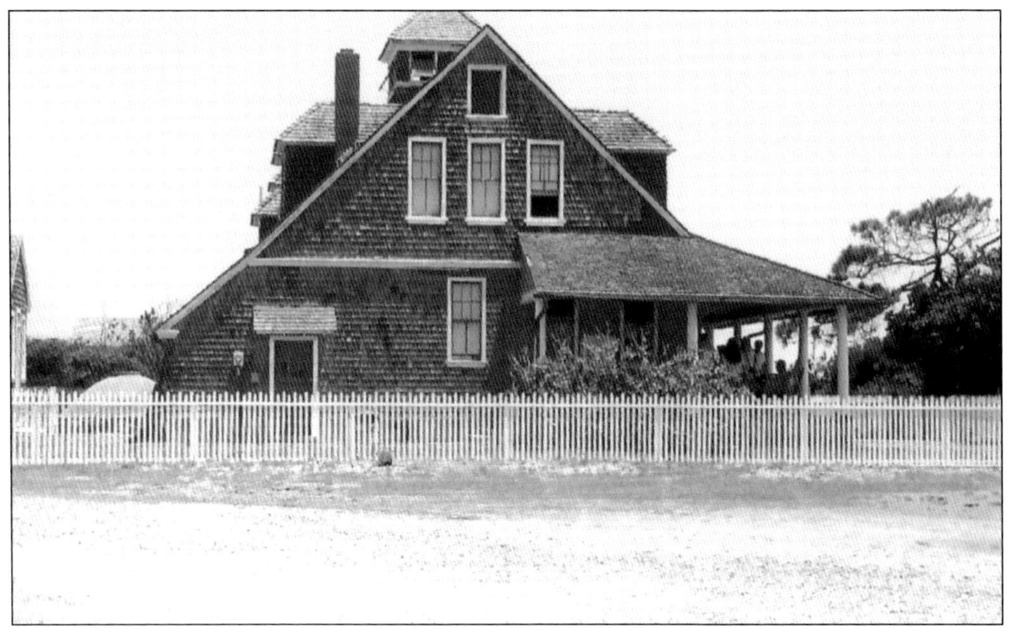

Pictured above is the old Chicamacomico Life-Saving Station, and below is a 1974 reenactment of lifesaving efforts using the beach apparatus drill, often referred to by the public as the "Breeches Buoy Reenactment." (Both, courtesy of the Cape Hatteras National Seashore.)

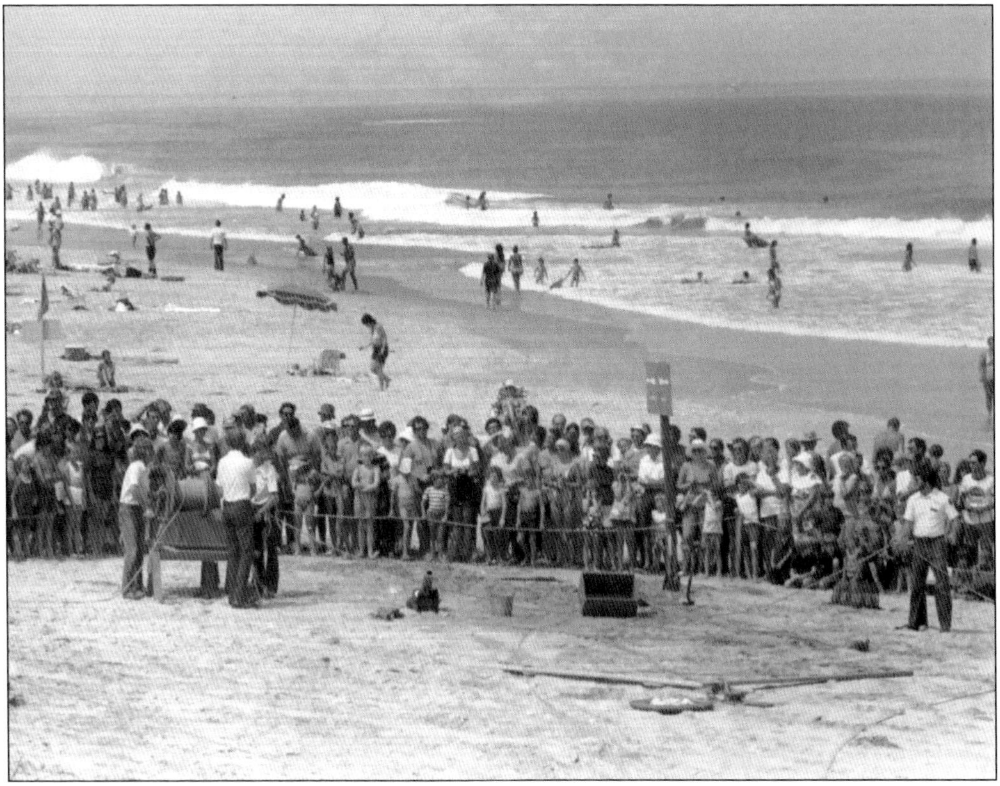

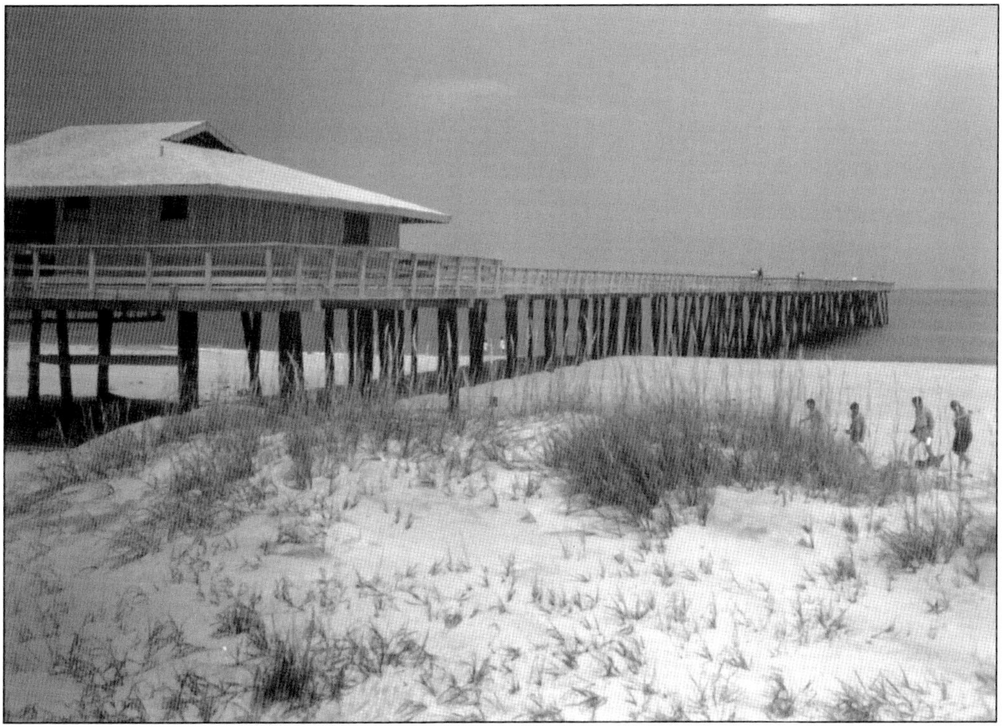

The Rodanthe Fishing Pier on Hatteras Island extends into the Atlantic Ocean. Rodanthe is considered the easternmost point of the North Carolina coast. Rodanthe is well known to water-sports enthusiasts for fishing, kayaking and paddleboarding, swimming, sailboarding, and kiteboarding. (Courtesy of the Cape Hatteras National Seashore.)

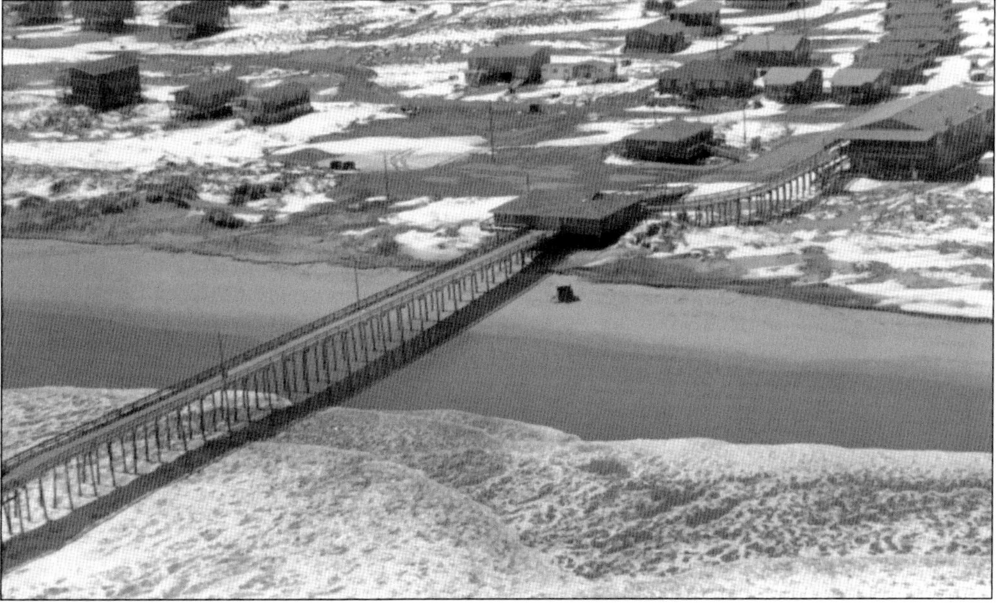

The view from the ocean is the Rodanthe Fishing Pier. In the 17th century, a prominent cape existed here known as Cape Kenrick. The cape eroded away, but remnants of it are just offshore and now known as Wimble Shoals. (Courtesy of the Cape Hatteras National Seashore.)

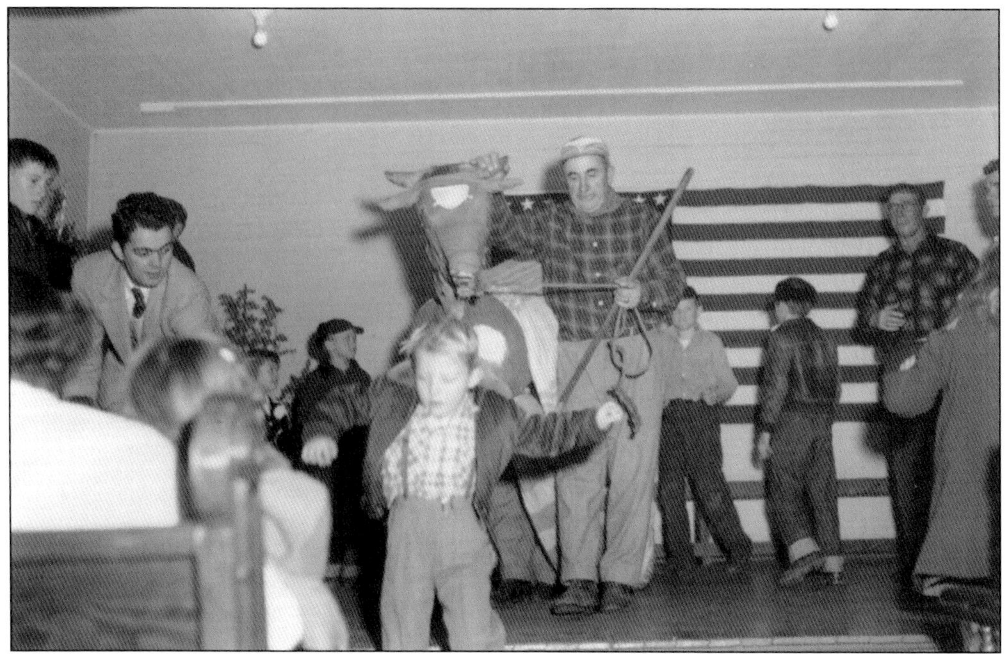

John Herbert and the Old Buck celebrate Old Christmas in Rodanthe. Some say the tradition of Old Christmas traces its origins back to 1752, when Great Britain adopted the Gregorian calendar and completely eliminated 11 dates from September that year—meaning December 25 going by the old calendar would fall on the same exact day as January 6 on the new. The story goes that folks on the Outer Banks decided to continue to recognize the January date as Old Christmas celebration. The event was never organized by a formal group, but it is celebrated by members of a handful of native Rodanthe families. (Courtesy of the Cape Hatteras National Seashore.)

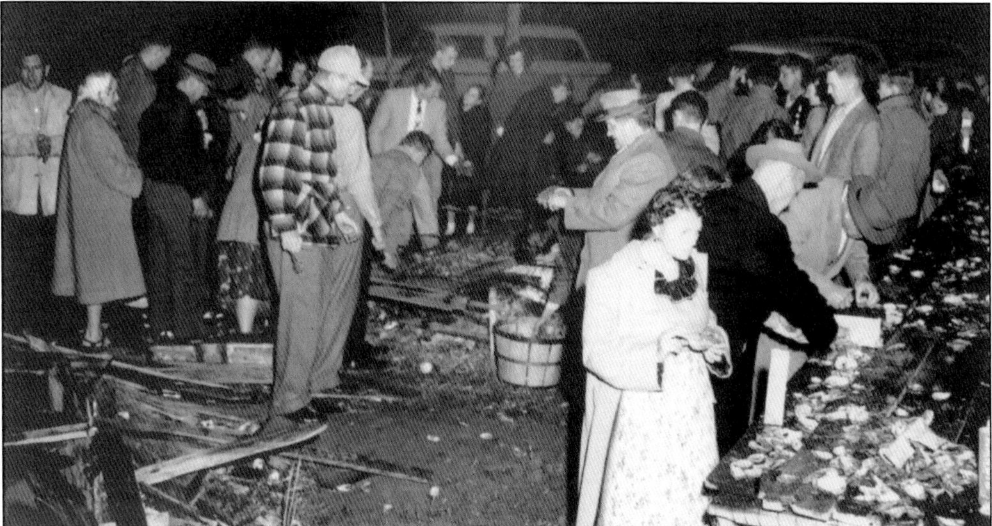

Each year, in honor of Old Christmas, drum and harmonica music plays an important role in the celebration and is one of the few remaining rituals celebrating Chicamacomico's culture. Traditional oyster roasts are hallmarks of Old Christmas, in which friends, family, and neighbors enjoy food and drink and celebrate the beginning of a new year. (Courtesy of the Cape Hatteras National Seashore.)

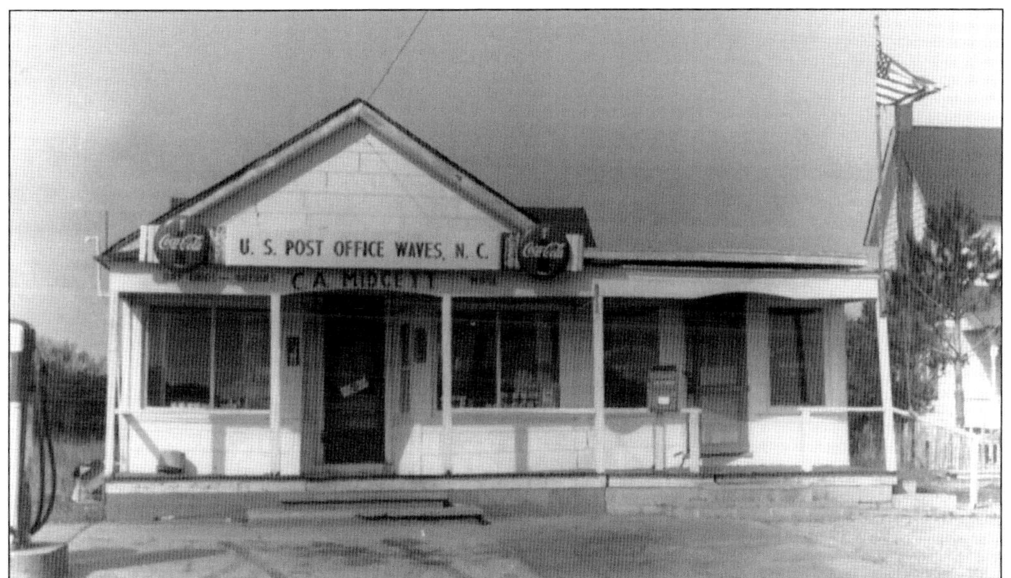

In the 1930s, the village of Waves was called South Rodanthe, until the new post office came to town and the name was changed to reflect the proximity to the rough Atlantic Ocean.

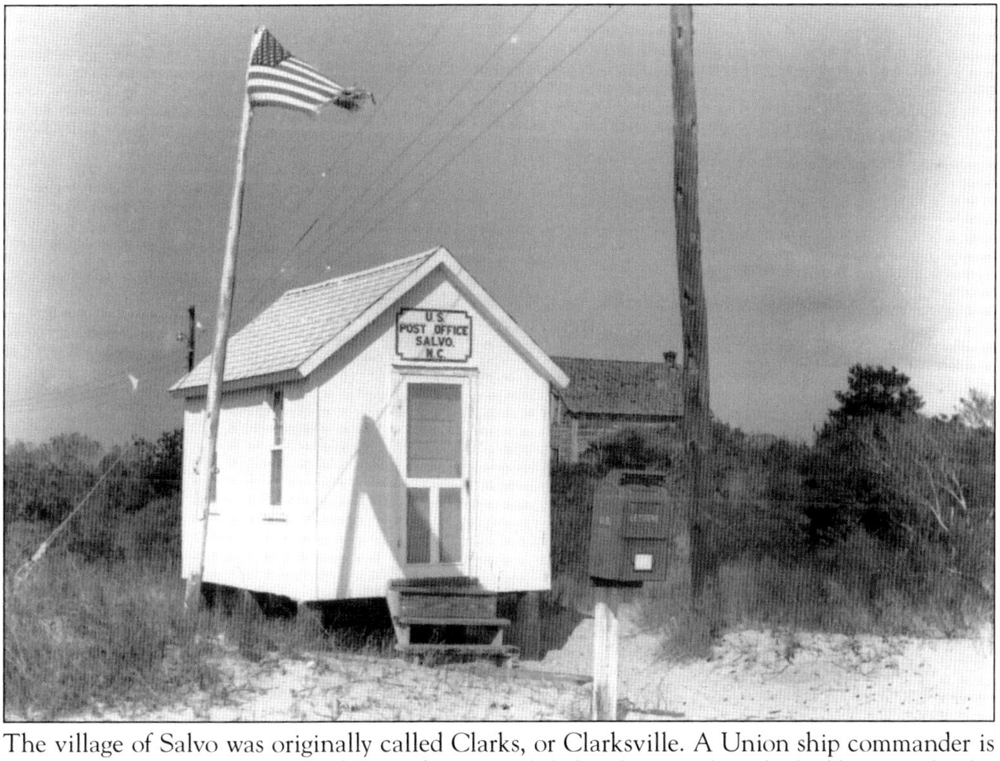

The village of Salvo was originally called Clarks, or Clarksville. A Union ship commander is reported to have spotted the settlement from sea while heading north and asked his crew for the name of the village. Checking the chart, the crew found none. The captain ordered his men to "give it a salvo anyway," which is a simultaneous firing of cannons. One of the crewmen wrote "salvo" on the chart and thus noted was the name given in 1901 when the Post Office Department established a post office here. (Courtesy of the Cape Hatteras National Seashore.)

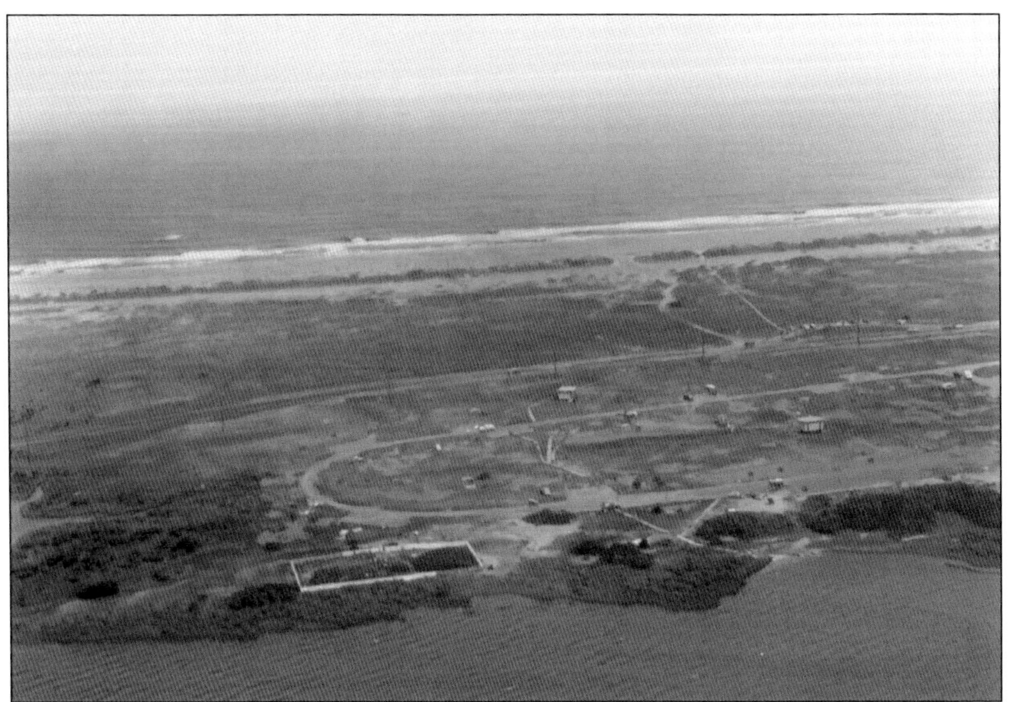

A former National Park Service campground, the Salvo day-use area now sports a new restroom facility and a small sandy sound-side beach perfect for families who prefer the calmer sound waters for swimming as well as for canoeing, kayaking, and kiteboarding. Across from the Salvo area is the beach-access Ramp No. 23 for vehicles and a parking lot. Salvo was known for its livestock and fish camps in early 1900s. (Courtesy of the Cape Hatteras National Seashore.)

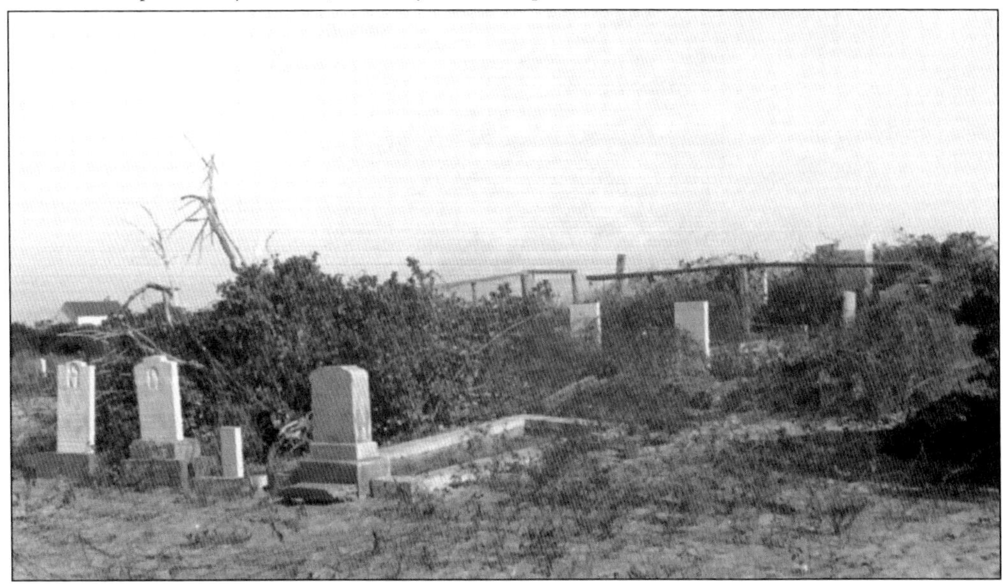

The villages have many native family cemeteries and churches dating back to the early 1800s. Salvo residents share their island with many visitors every year but remain attached to the burial sites of their loved ones and ancestors. The Salvo Cemetery is the final resting place for many natives. (Courtesy of the Cape Hatteras National Seashore.)

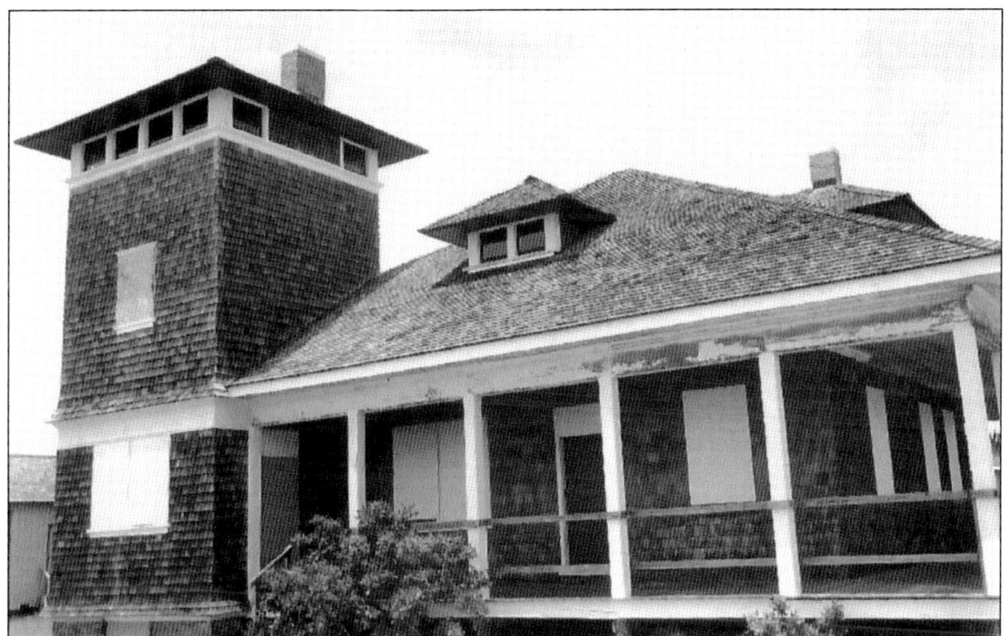

North of the community of Avon, the Little Kinnakeet Life-Saving Station is the southernmost of the original seven lifesaving stations built on the Outer Banks by the federal government. Constructed in 1874, the station was then decommissioned, and the property was transferred to the National Park Service in 1954. (Courtesy of the Cape Hatteras National Seashore.)

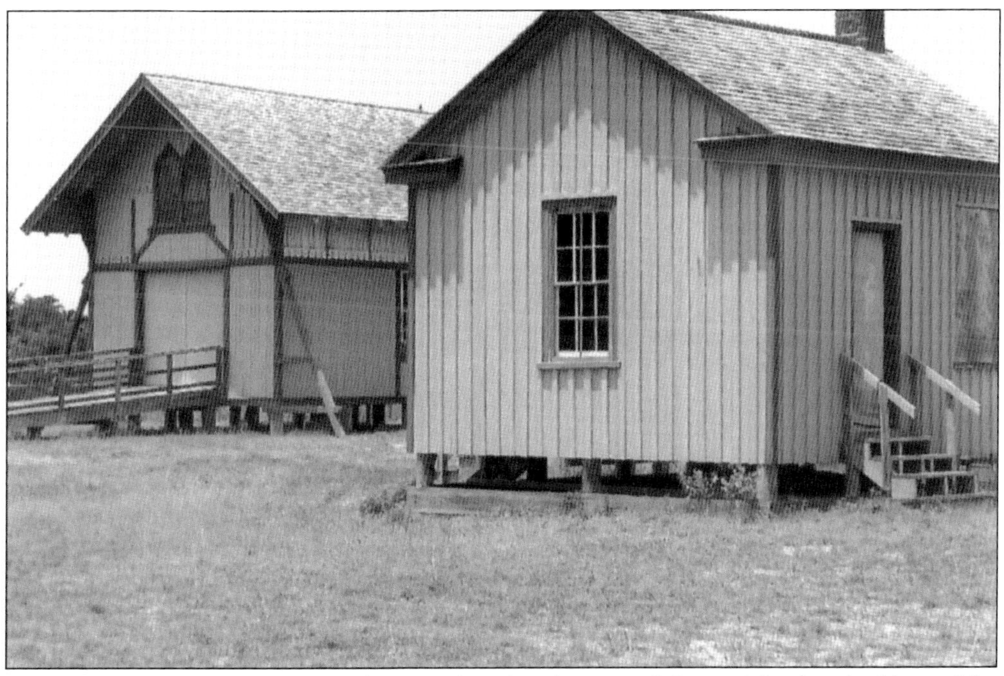

The photograph is of the 1874 Little Kinnakeet boathouse and the 1892 kitchen building of the Little Kinnakeet Life-Saving Station. (Courtesy of the Cape Hatteras National Seashore.)

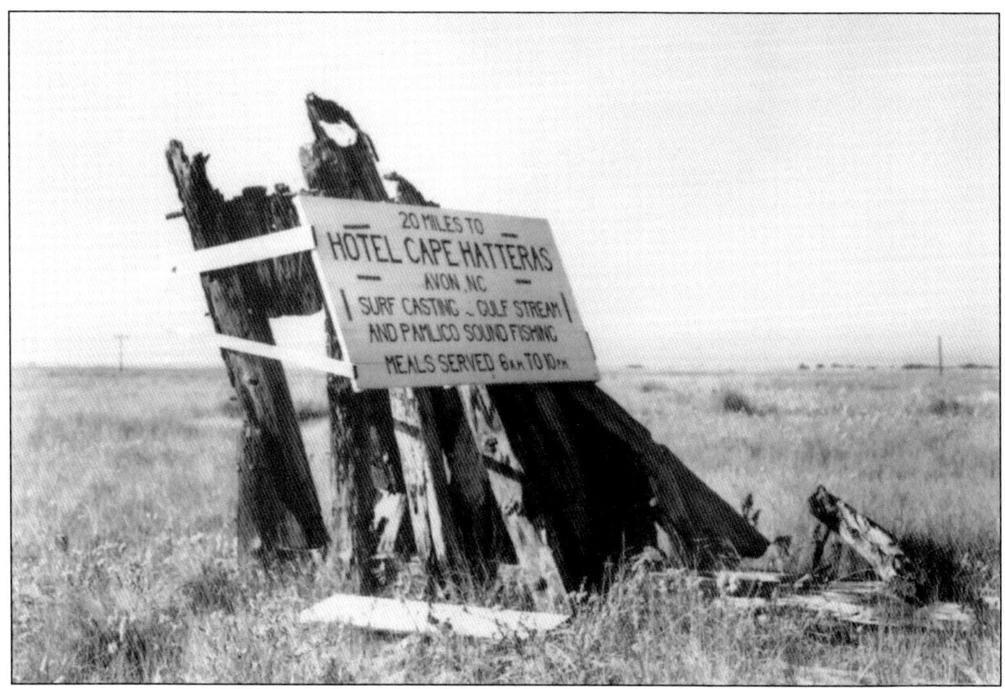

Ship wreckage was used for many purposes, including a motel sign in the early 1950s. The community of Avon was established in 1873 as "Kinnakeet," the name local Native Americans called the area. Later settlers adopted the name, but in 1883 the Post Office Department named the village Avon. (Courtesy of the Cape Hatteras National Seashore.)

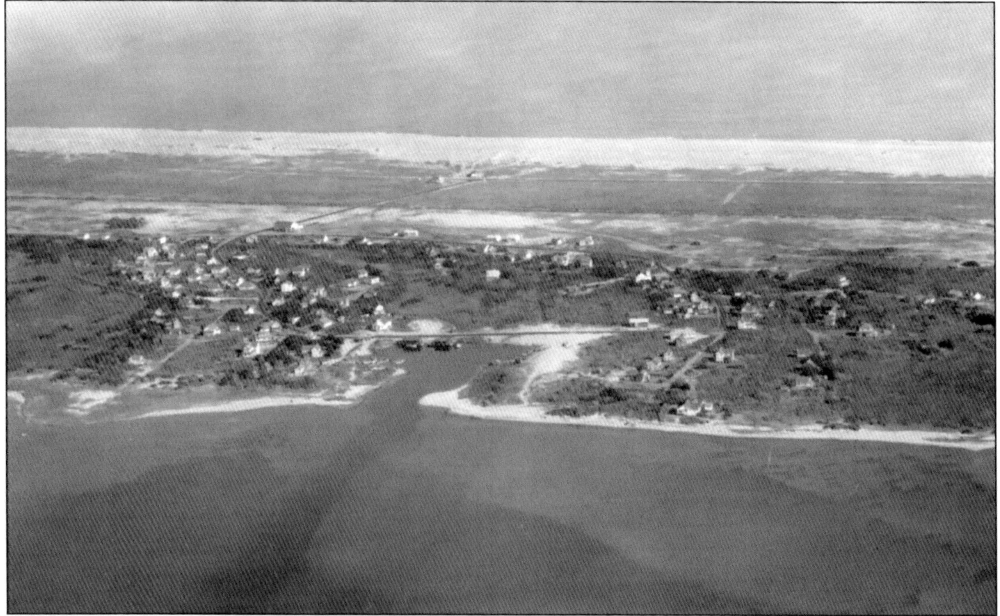

This 1960 aerial photograph is of the village of Avon. Once a small village comprised mainly of fishermen and watermen, the area today boasts beautiful beaches, vacation rental cottages, restaurants, and all the conveniences of the modern-day world. (Courtesy of the Cape Hatteras National Seashore.)

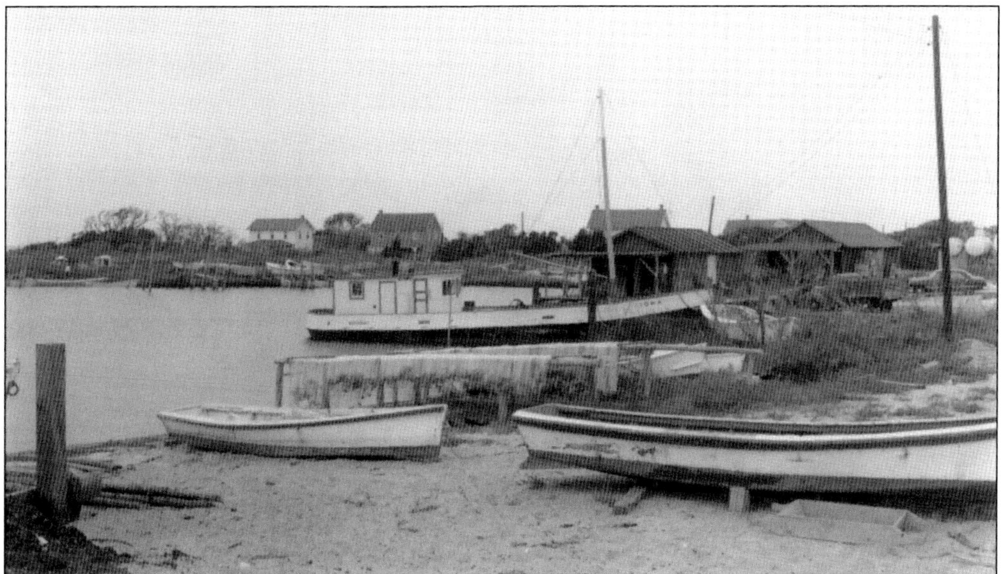

Pictured here is the historic, picturesque Avon sound-side fishing harbor where many fishing and rowboats were pulled onshore and nets were dried in the hot sun. After the Civil War, shallow-draft shad boats and sharpies were built in Avon. Today, just a few fish markets remain in the harbor. (Courtesy of the Cape Hatteras National Seashore.)

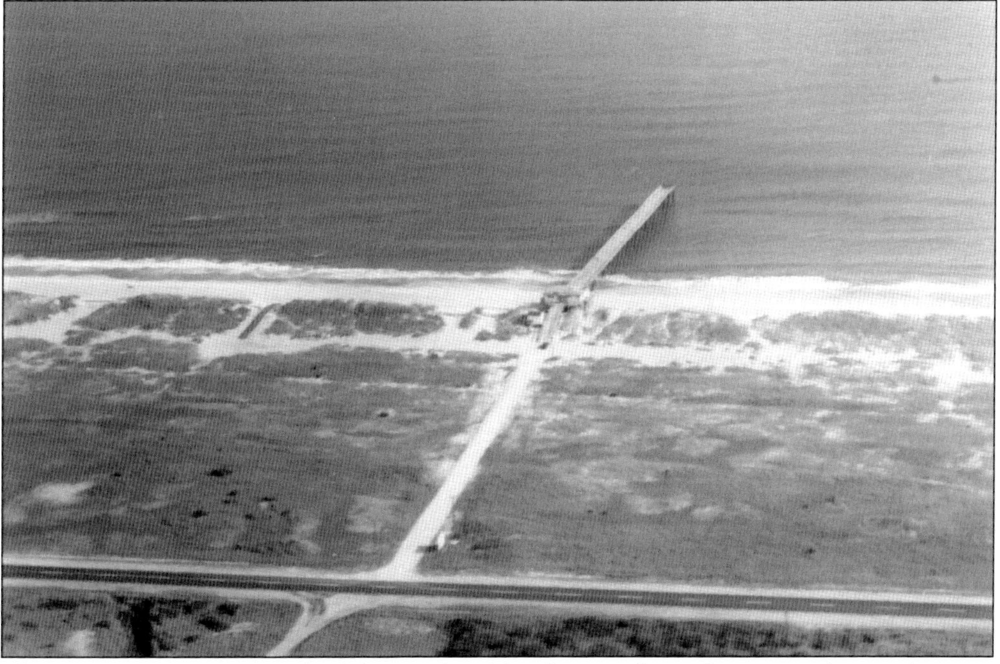

The Avon Fishing Pier was built by two local brothers in the early 1960s. The wooden pier, completed in 1963, took two years to construct and extends 665 feet into the Atlantic Ocean. The pier is world famous for the giant red drum caught offshore the barrier islands. Two miles south of Avon, in Cape Hatteras National Seashore, a sound-side parking area, formerly known as "Haulover," is today a popular spot for kiteboarding, windsurfing, kayaking, and kite or stand-up paddleboard enthusiasts. (Courtesy of the Cape Hatteras National Seashore.)

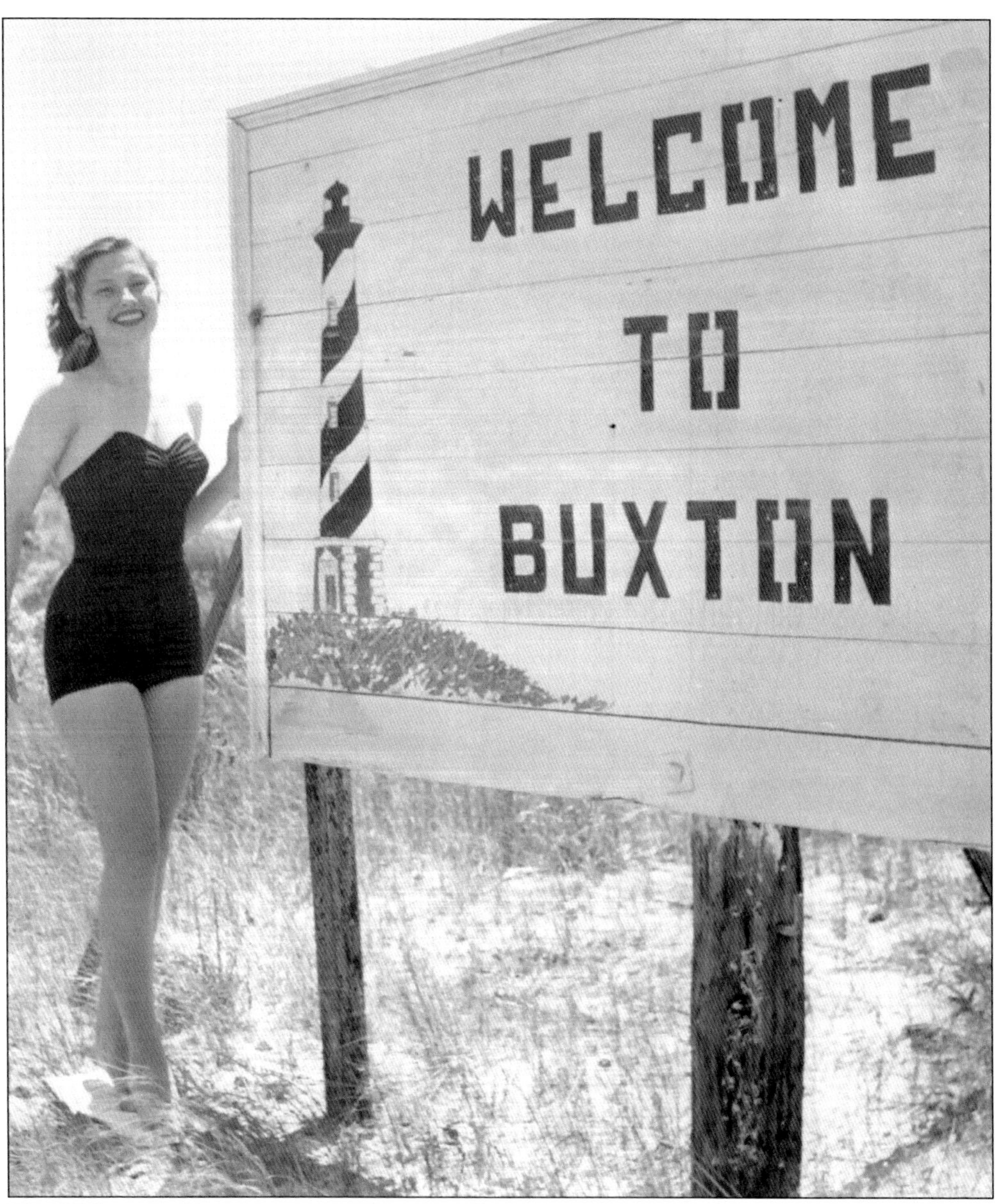

This Welcome to Buxton sign provides a prop for a Miss Dare County beauty contestant. Located six miles south of Avon, the village of Buxton is home to the famous Cape Hatteras Lighthouse, America's tallest brick lighthouse, and a famous surf-fishing spot known as Cape Point. The large shifting sandbar stretches out into the Atlantic Ocean, where the confluence of the colder Labrador Current and the warmer Gulf Steam current often clash, creating rough waters. Buxton is also known for the first wireless telegraphy experiments by Reginald Fessenden in 1902. Fessenden successfully transmitted the first musical notes received by signal from Buxton to Roanoke Island, marking the first wireless message and foreshadowing the radio. (Courtesy of the Outer Banks History Center.)

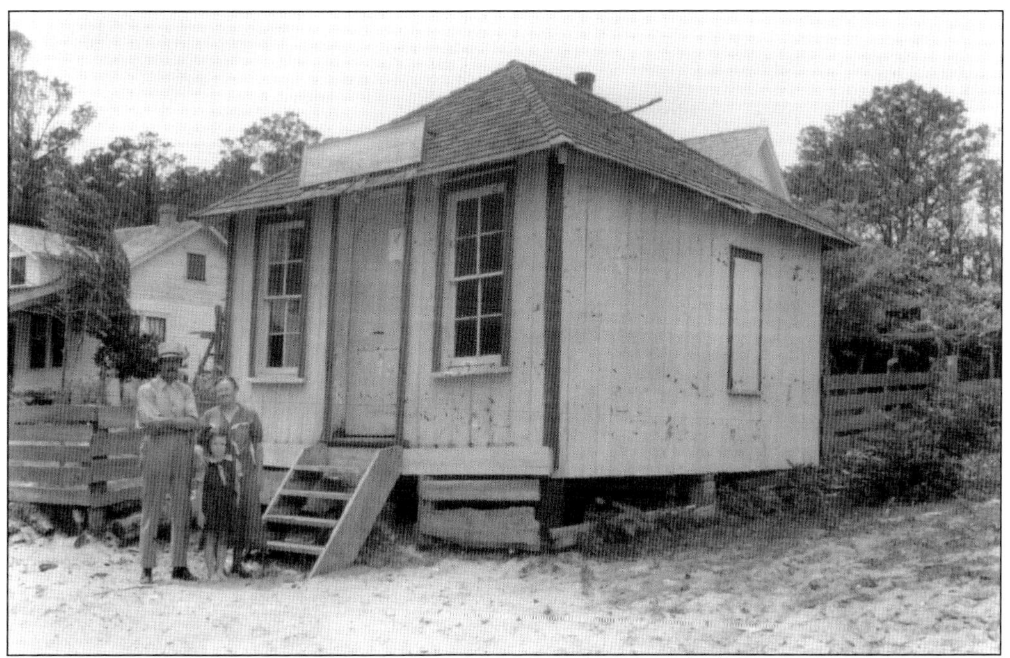

This early photograph of the Buxton Post Office with Postmaster Gray was taken in 1936. Buxton was originally known as the Cape until it was incorporated in 1882, and the village of Buxton was named after judge Ralph P. Buxton. The first post office was established in 1873. (Courtesy of the Outer Banks History Center.)

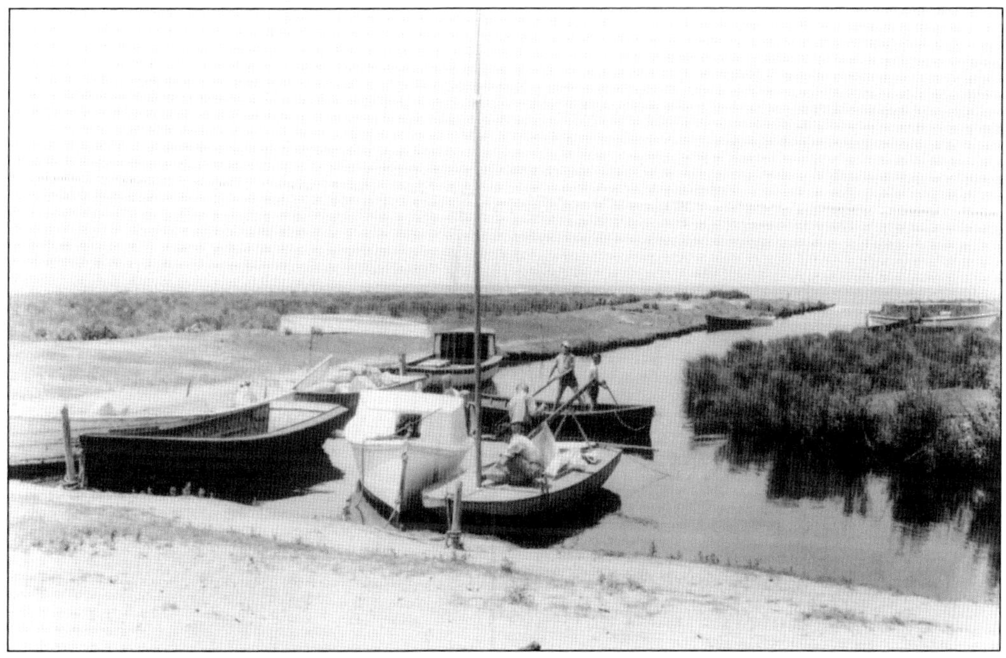

The post office was located near a cut called the Buxton Boat Landing, where a smaller skiff would be shoved out to meet the larger mail boat. The mail boat would pause or anchor offshore while mail and passengers were loaded into the smaller shove skiff for transport to dry land. (Courtesy of the Cape Hatteras National Seashore.)

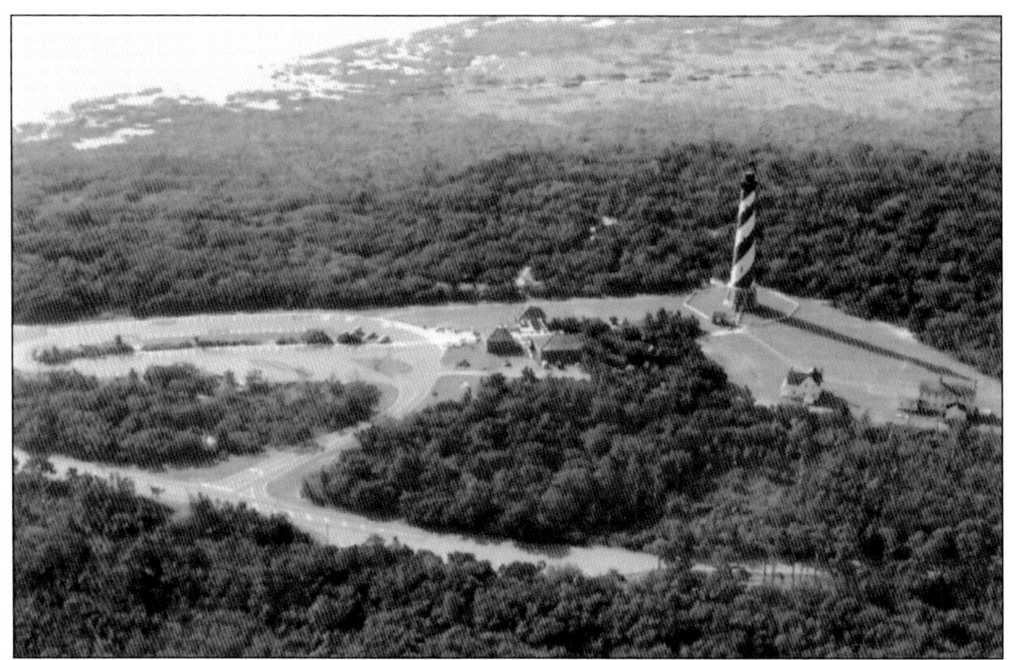

The photograph is of today's Cape Hatteras Light Station. In 1999, the lighthouse and associated buildings were successfully relocated 2,900 feet from the original site. Today, this visitors' center offers educational materials and the opportunity to climb the 248 steps of the lighthouse. The view at the top is worth every step. (Courtesy of the Cape Hatteras National Seashore.)

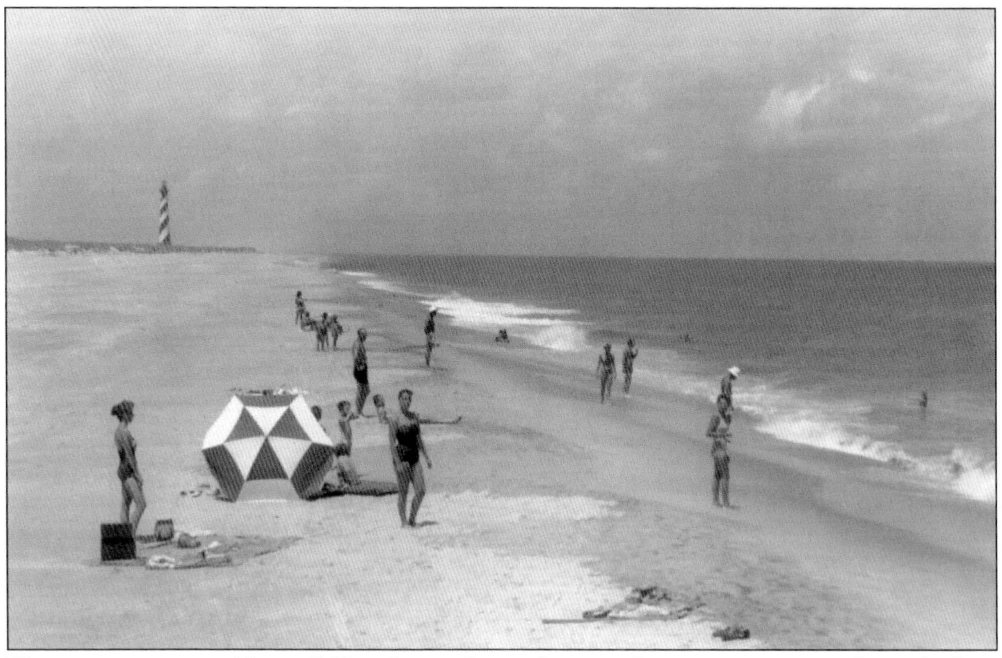

The many pristine and beautiful beaches in the seashore are favorite resting spots for sunbathers and fishermen. Buxton Beach has been named one of the top 10 beaches in the United States. Note the Cape Hatteras Lighthouse in the background. (Courtesy of the Cape Hatteras National Seashore.)

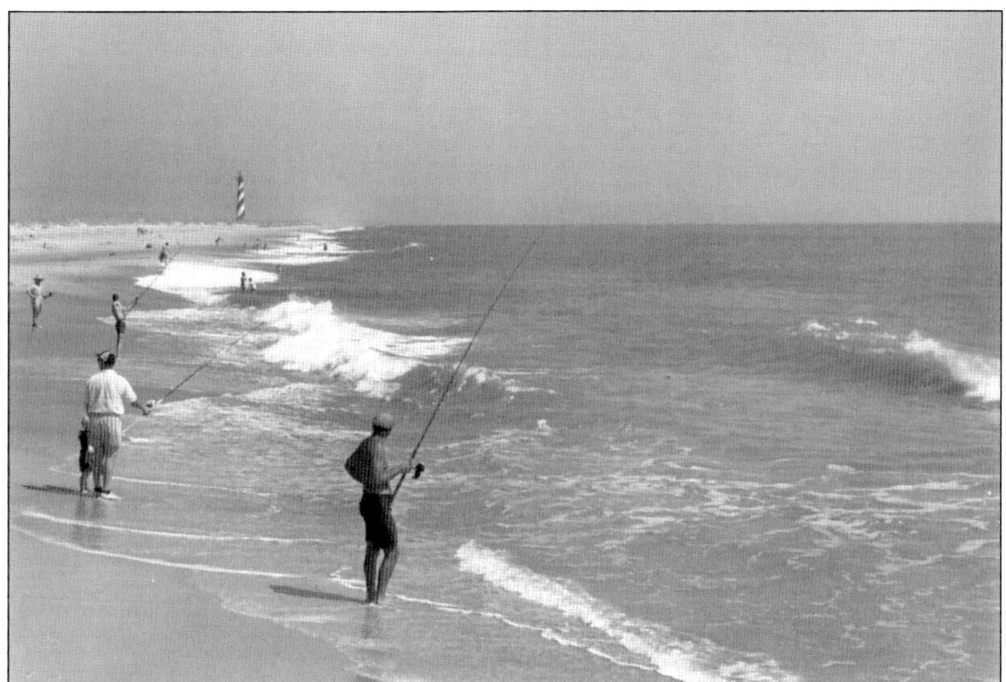

The photograph shows fishermen enjoying the beaches near Cape Hatteras Lighthouse. Nearby is the famous Cape Point, one of the best fall fishing beaches on the East Coast. (Courtesy of the Cape Hatteras National Seashore.)

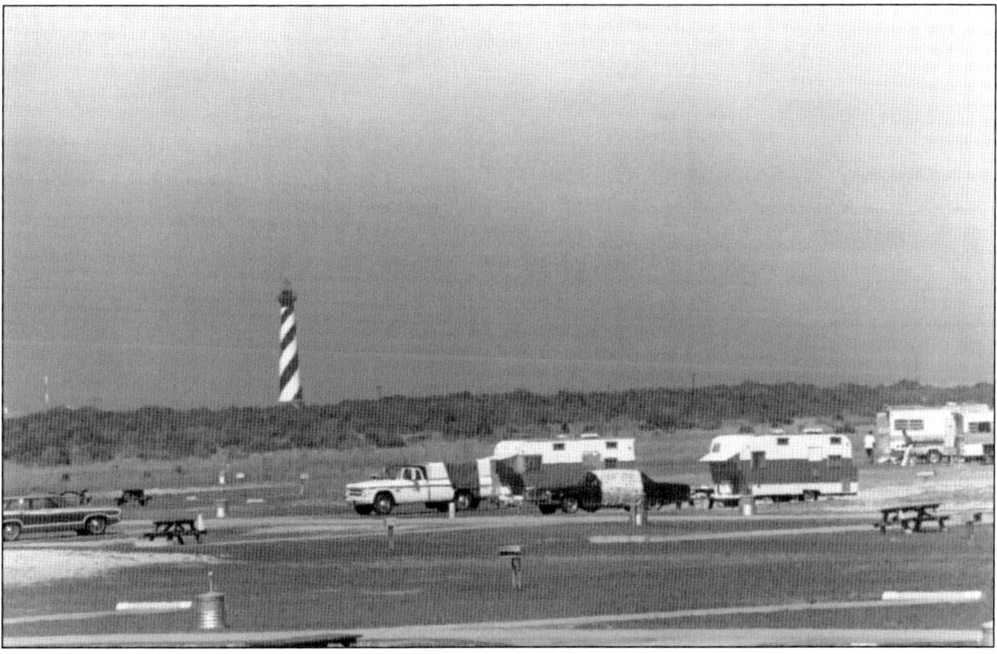

Cape Point Campground is located near the Cape Hatteras Lighthouse. Travelers can walk or drive to the beach for surfing, swimming, and surf fishing during many months of the year. The surrounding waters are known as the Graveyard of the Atlantic because of the many shipwrecks on the treacherous shoals. (Courtesy of the Cape Hatteras National Seashore.)

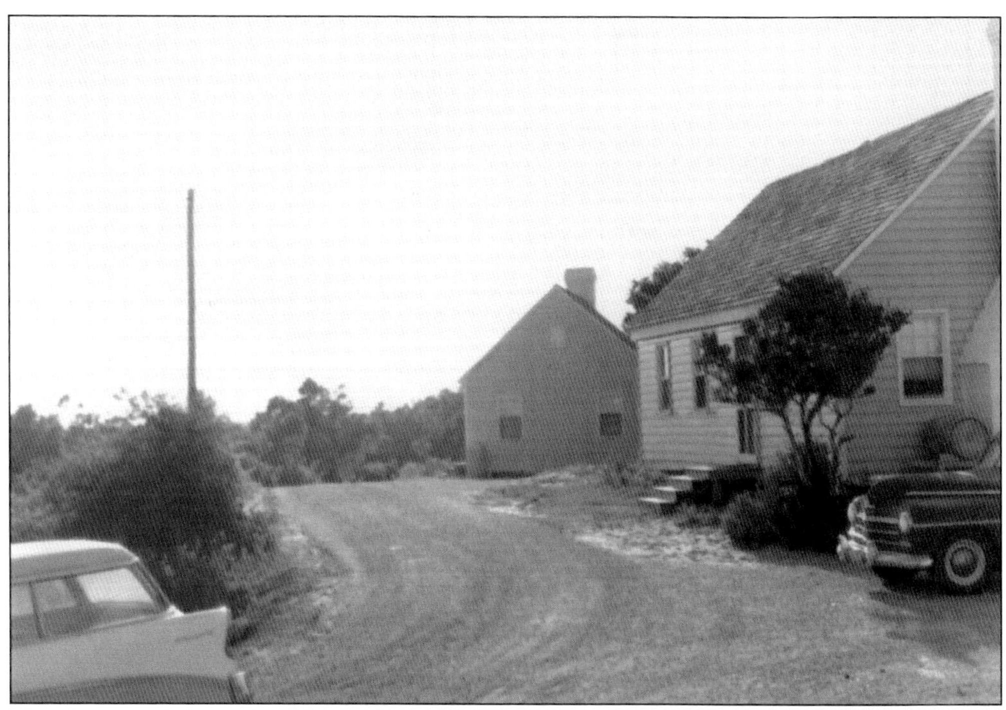

The photograph shows frame houses designed by the National Park Service and built by the CCC between 1939 and 1940. (Courtesy of the Cape Hatteras National Seashore.)

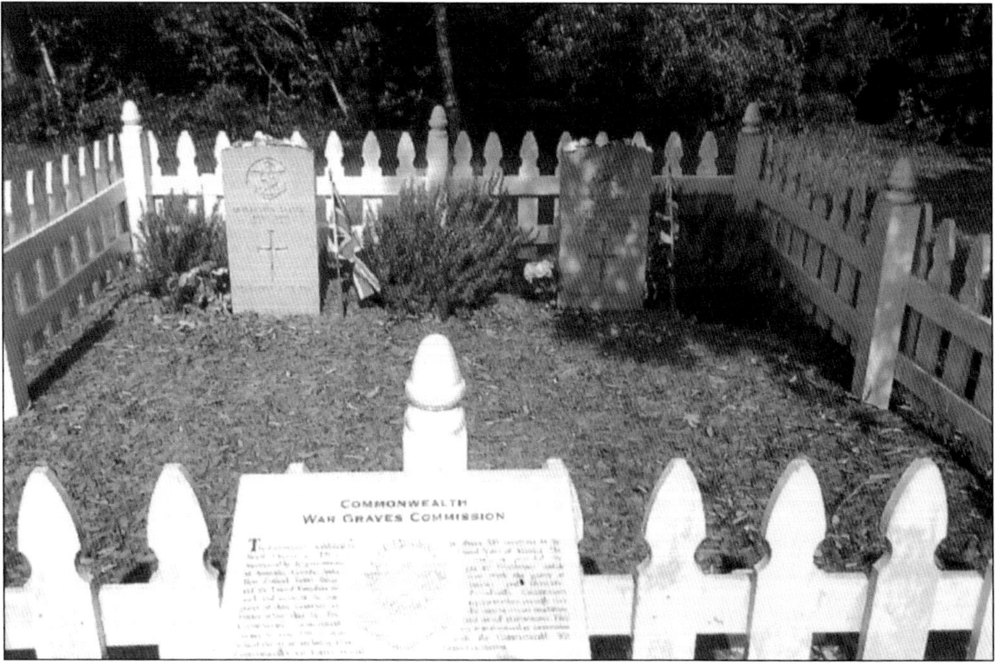

Here is a photograph of the Buxton British Cemetery. In April 1942, a British tanker carrying airplane fuel off of Cape Hatteras was hit with seven torpedoes from a lurking U-boat. Nearly half of the crew drowned, and two of them later washed up on the beach. They were buried in what is known today as the Buxton British Cemetery. (Courtesy of the Cape Hatteras National Seashore.)

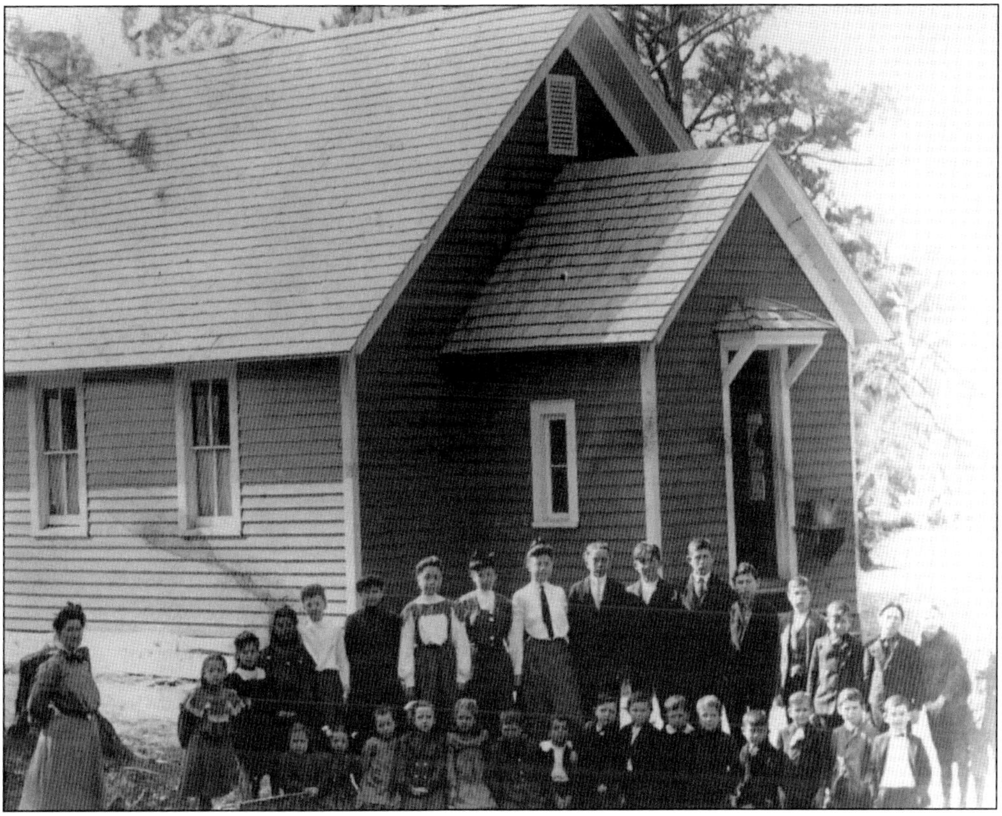

Before all village schools were consolidated in 1955, Hatteras Island had two school campuses, in Avon and Frisco. (Courtesy of the Cape Hatteras National Seashore.)

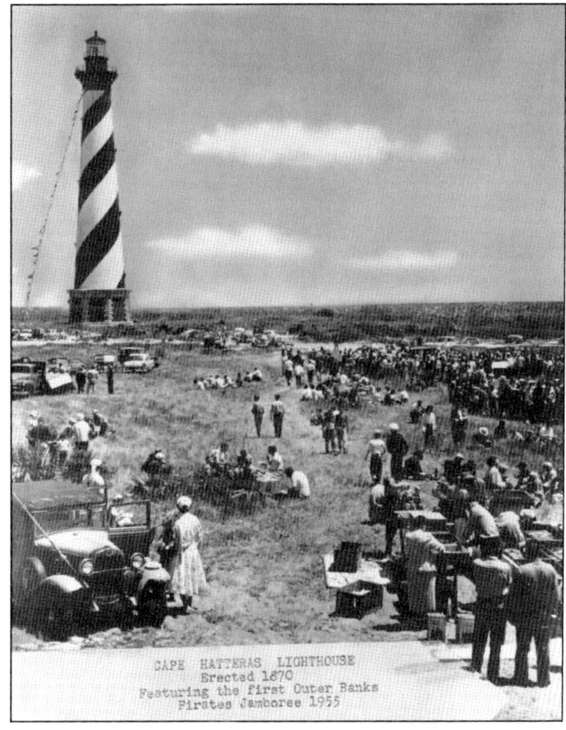

The photograph is of the Hatteras Pirates Jamboree. For many years, from the mid-1950s to 1970s, the jamboree was held every April at the Cape Hatteras Lighthouse. Today, the festival is held on Ocracoke Island. (Courtesy of the Cape Hatteras National Seashore.)

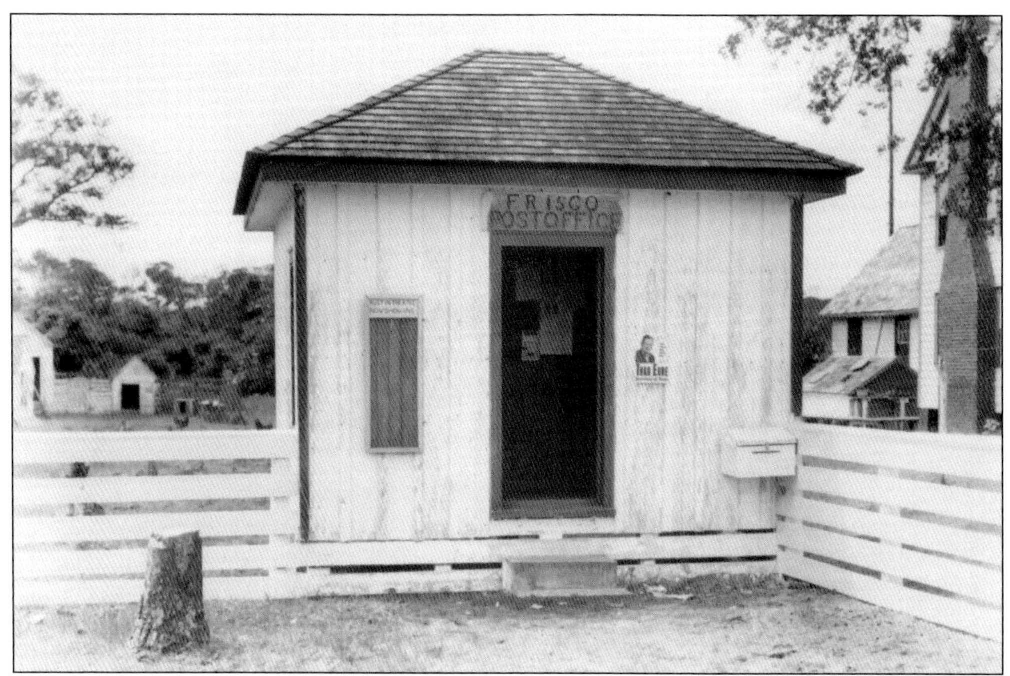

The photograph shows the Frisco Post Office in 1935. Frisco, settled in 1795, was once known as Trent. A heavily wooded maritime forest is located on the sound side. In 1898, the Post Office Department changed the village's name to Frisco. (Courtesy of the Outer Banks History Center.)

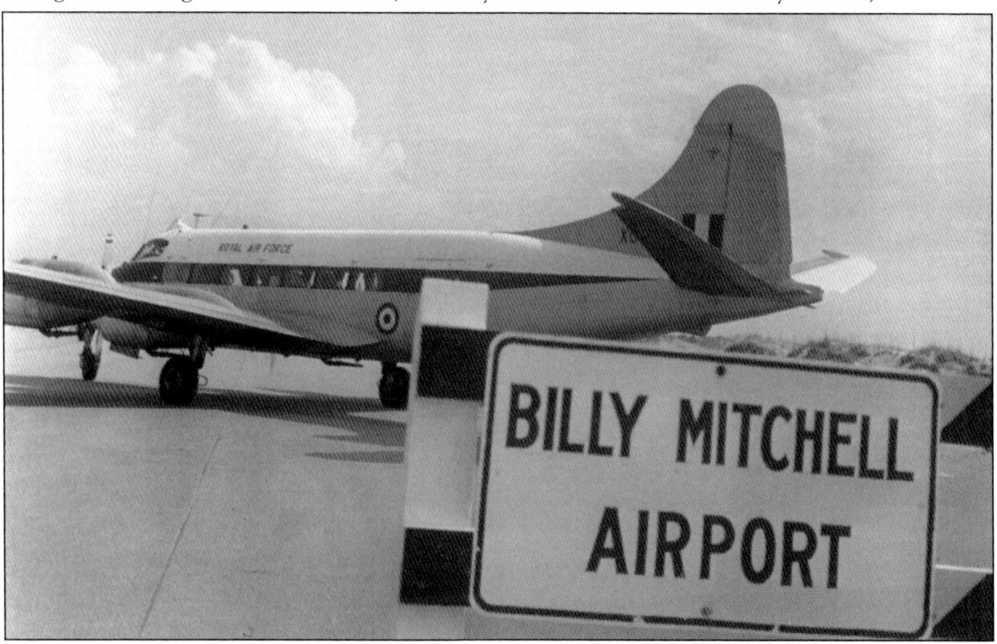

The Billy Mitchell Air Strip was constructed in the early 1960s. The photograph shows a plane carrying the British ambassador, Sir Harold Caccia, who visited the area. The airstrip is named after local legend Billy Mitchell. He was a World War I pilot and advocate for increasing development of airpower as a means of winning future wars. His efforts led to the advancement of bombing techniques that would later sink battleships. (Courtesy of the Cape Hatteras National Seashore.)

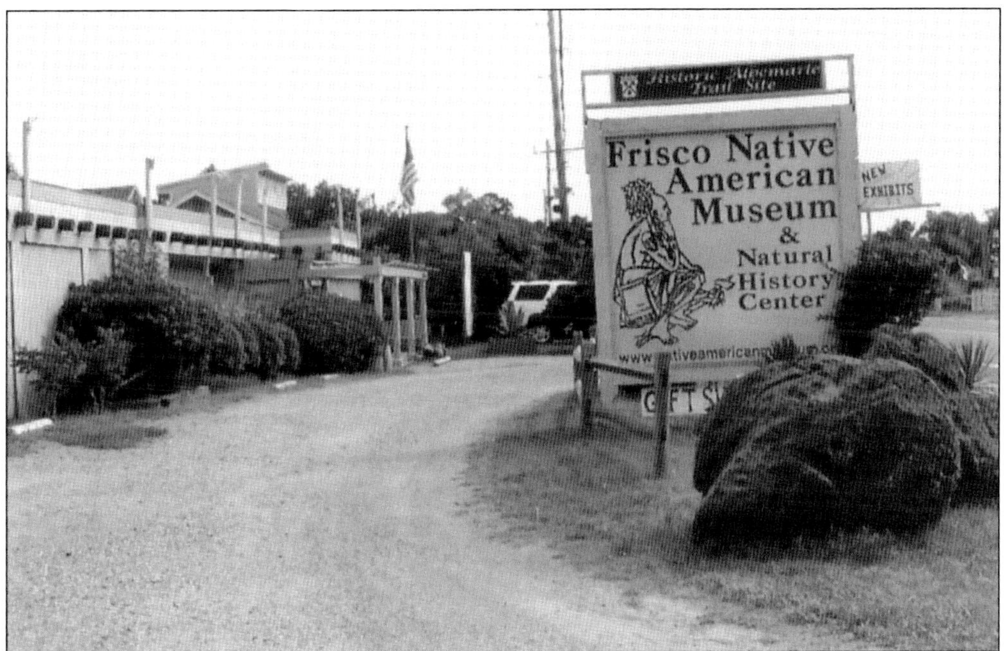

The Frisco Native American Museum is near the site of an ancient Indian village, and current excavation is being performed. The tranquil museum has authentic Indian artifacts and educational displays. The name, Indian Town, came from a population of American Indians that lived or camped near the cape. (Courtesy of the Cape Hatteras National Seashore.)

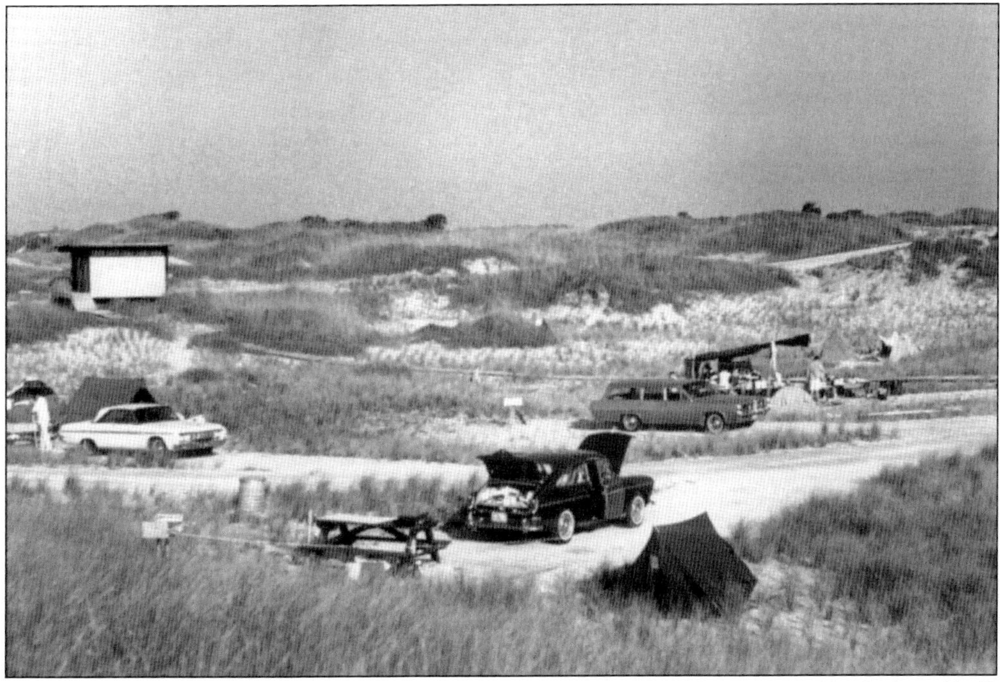

The National Park Service Frisco Campground is nestled among the trees and high dune bluffs near the village of Frisco. The campground is in proximity to the beach for great surf fishing and views of the ocean. (Courtesy of the Cape Hatteras National Seashore.)

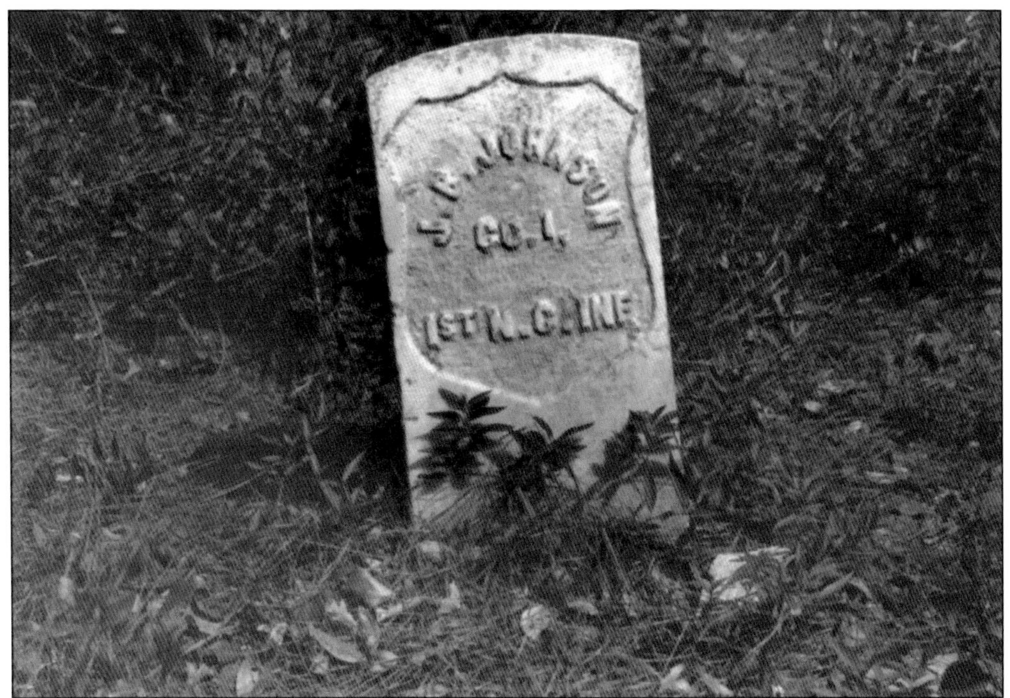

A Frisco headstone from the grave of J.B. Johnson, found in the dunes of the maritime forest, is evidence of the Civil War history on Hatteras Island. (Courtesy of the Cape Hatteras National Seashore.)

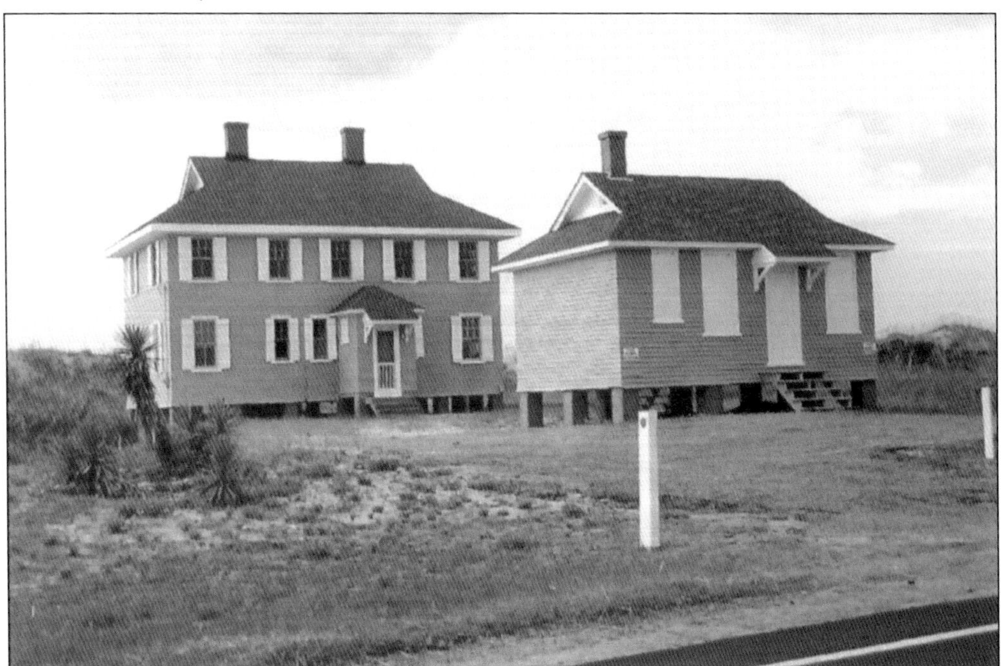

Creeds Hill Life-Saving Station (1878–1918), now a private home in the village of Frisco, is located next to Cape Hatteras National Seashore bathhouse and the Sandy Bay parking lot. (Courtesy of the Cape Hatteras National Seashore.)

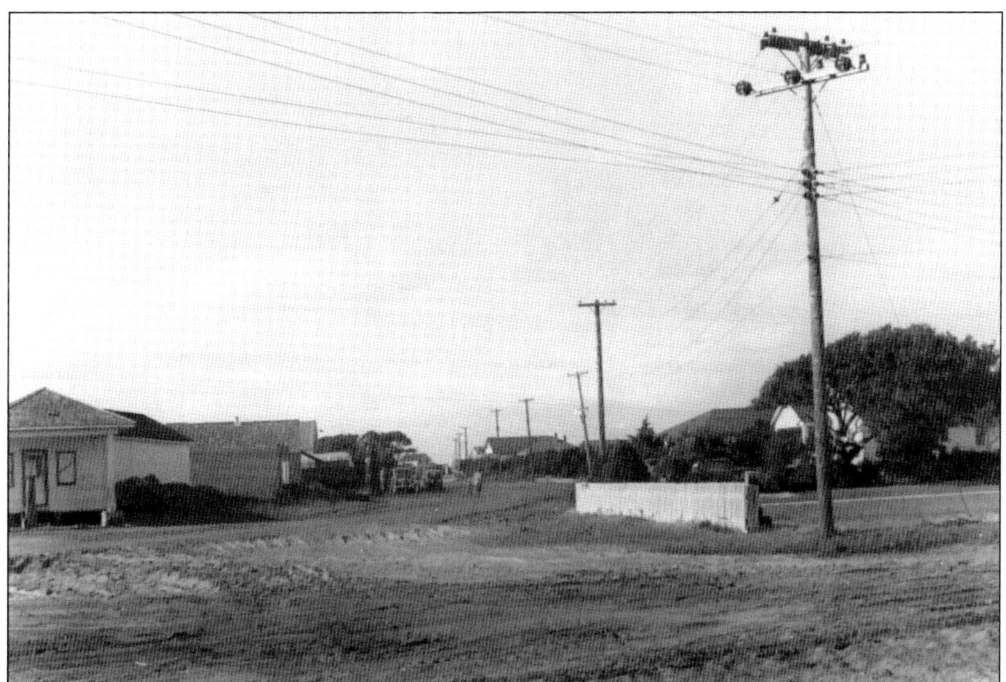

Hatteras Village is the southernmost community on Hatteras Island. The early settlers to Hatteras depended on maritime livelihoods as a way of living. The village of Hatteras retained its historical name. (Courtesy of the Cape Hatteras National Seashore.)

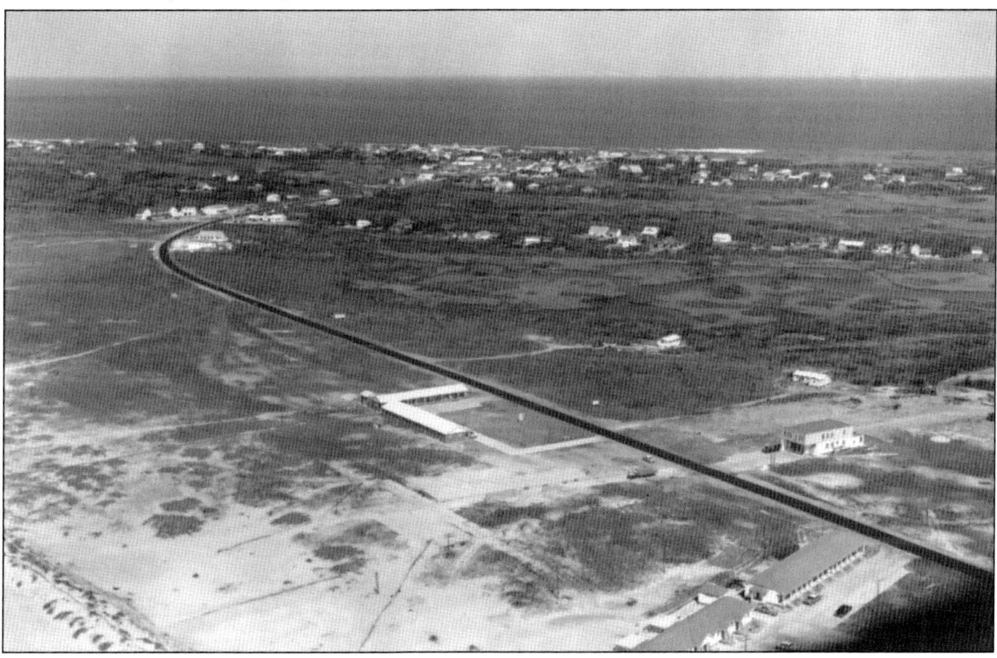

Today, Hatteras Village is home to marinas, great restaurants, large rental homes along the oceanfront, and trendy shopping areas. The village of Hatteras has retained it small-town community charm while providing summer visitors with recreational opportunities to fit anyone's vacation. (Courtesy of the Cape Hatteras National Seashore.)

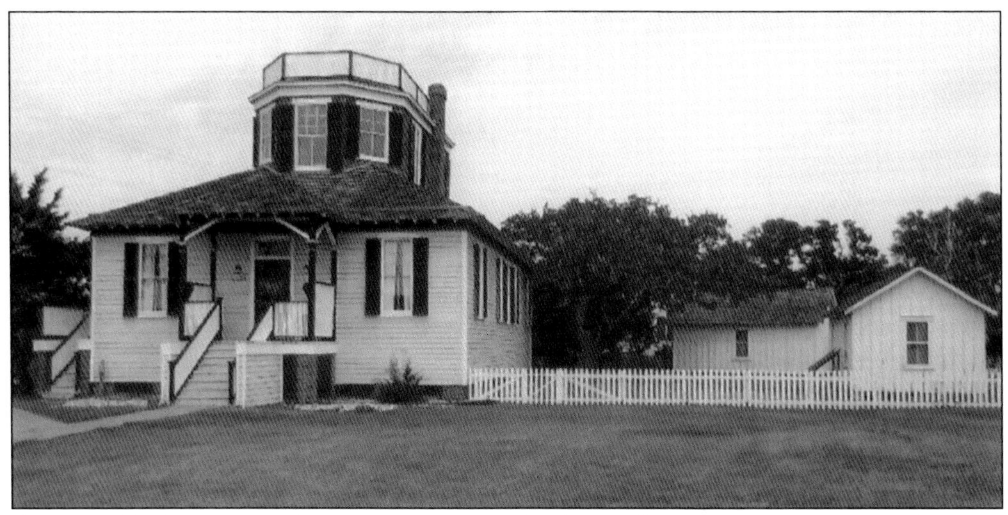

Hatteras Weather Bureau Station was built 1901. The small one-story structure is where the weather observer lived and worked to provide recorded data hourly about barometric pressure, humidity, rainfall, temperature, and wind speed. The station tower warned Hatteras villagers by displaying signal flags to caution them of approaching storms. (Courtesy of the Cape Hatteras National Seashore.)

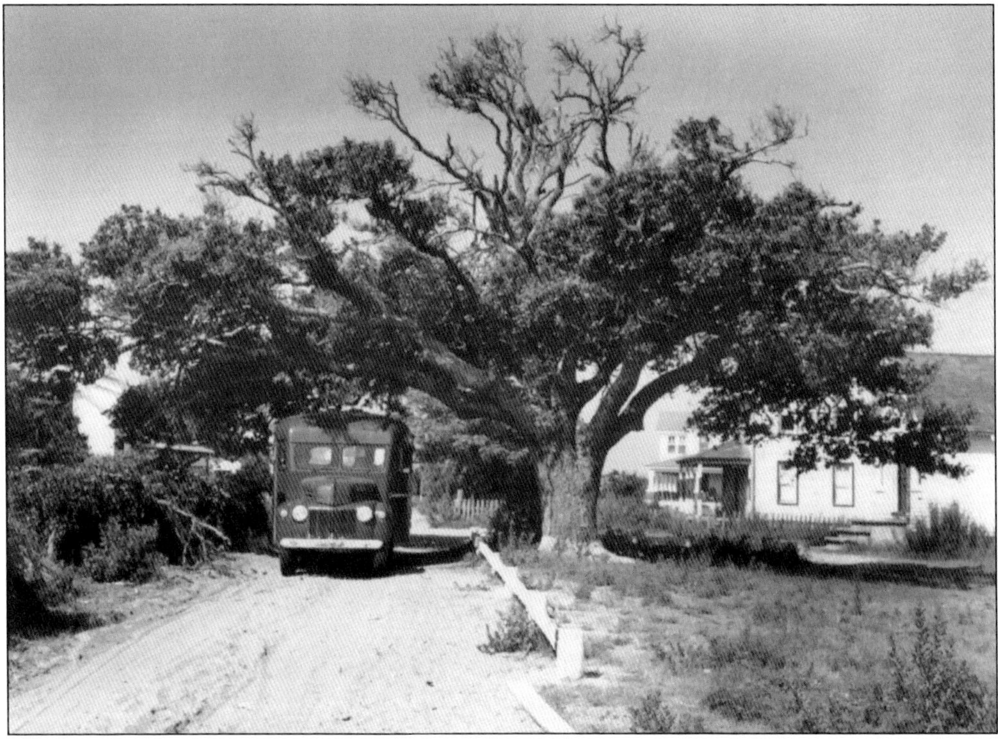

The Manteo-to-Hatteras Bus Line began in the 1930s. Prior to paved roads in the early part of the century, a bus traversed the primitive roads to deliver packages. The residents would gather up and down the sandy route to claim their deliveries. In Manteo, the local natives could catch a bus to travel to Norfolk, Virginia, if they needed medical treatment. (Courtesy of the Cape Hatteras National Seashore.)

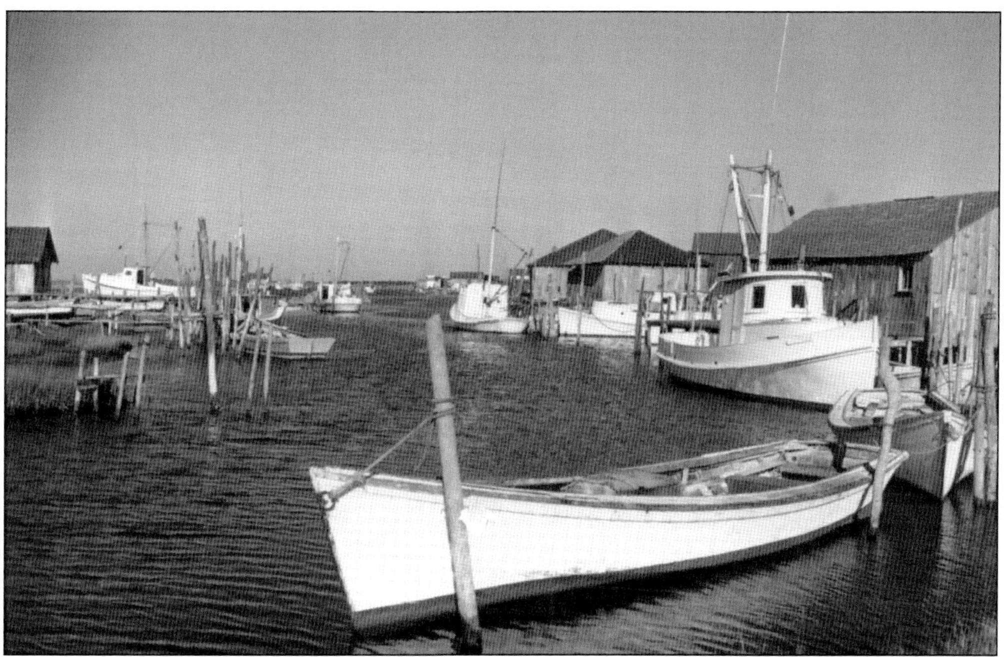

The port of Hatteras Village evolved as locals made a living from commercial fishing and other marine-related livelihoods. Today, Hatteras Village is home to a renowned charter fishing fleet, which takes many sportsmen on fishing charters to the Gulf Stream in search of blue marlin, sailfish, and other large game fish off the coast. (Courtesy of the Cape Hatteras National Seashore.)

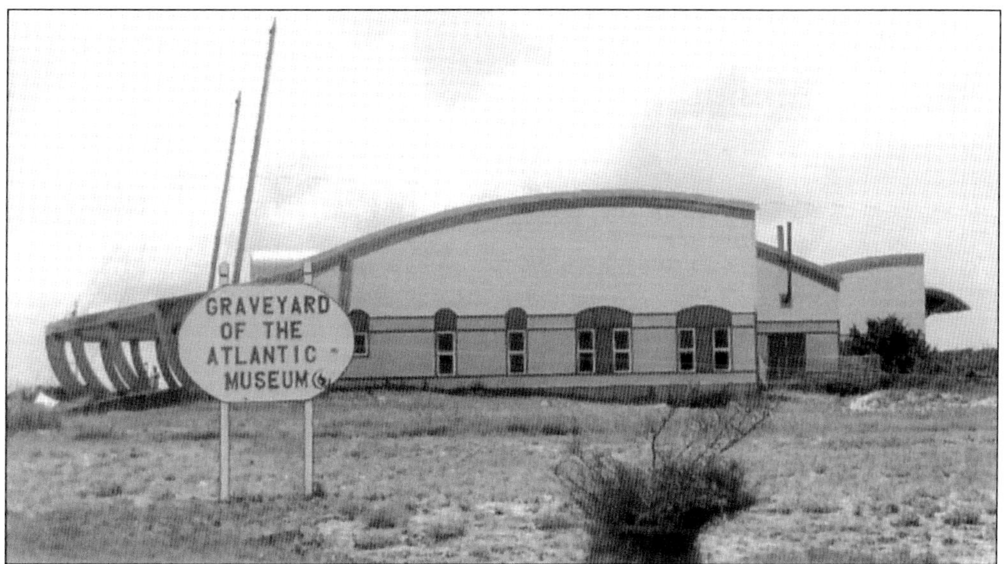

The Graveyard of the Atlantic Museum displays the remaining pieces of the original Fresnel lens and rotating pedestal of Cape Hatteras Lighthouse along with the USS *Monitor* artifacts. The Hatteras Island Ocean Center, located nearby, provides a wide variety of environmental-education programs. Just south of the museum is the former site of Fort Clark and Fort Hatteras, where a chapter of the Civil War played out. The byway begins a unique leg of the trip as it continues by state-owned ferries and crosses Hatteras Inlet to Ocracoke Island. (Courtesy of the Cape Hatteras National Seashore.)

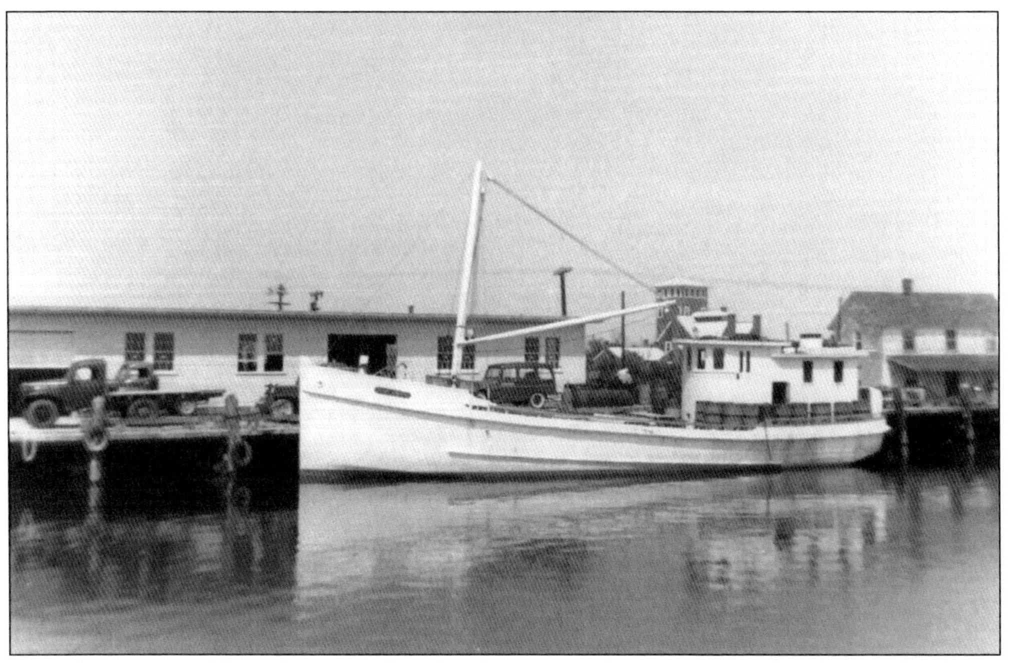

The *Aleta* was a mail boat that carried mail and passengers between Ocracoke Island and Atlantic in Carteret County during the 1940s and 1950s. Ocracoke first appeared on European maps in 1585 following John White's explorations along the North Carolina shoreline. (Courtesy of the Cape Hatteras National Seashore.)

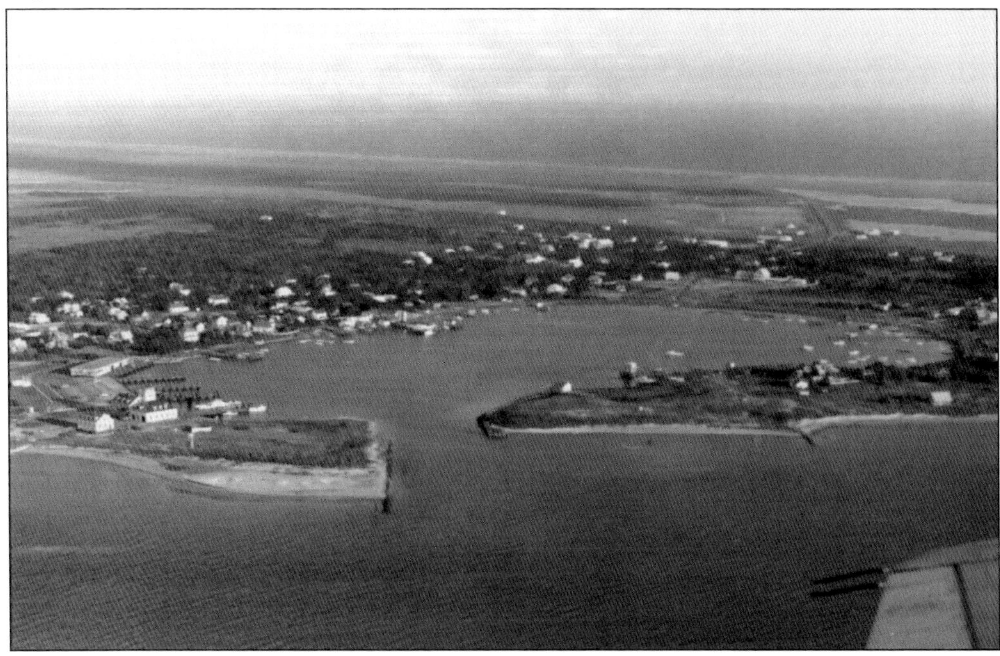

This is an aerial view of Ocracoke Harbor. Ocracoke has a unique history that revolves around pirates, shipwrecks, and the Civil War, World War I, and World War II. The island was home to a small Confederate fort abandoned in 1861 when the Union troops captured Hatteras Island. (Courtesy of the Cape Hatteras National Seashore.)

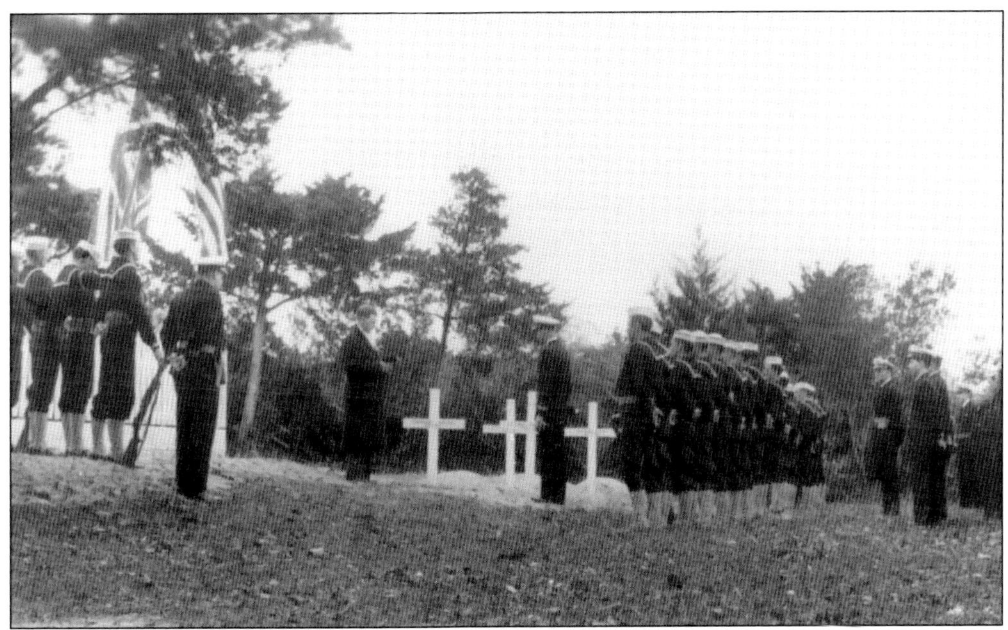

The Ocracoke British Cemetery is the final resting place of four British sailors who drowned at sea and washed ashore after their trawler, the HMS *Bedfordshire*, was torpedoed by a German submarine on May 11, 1942. The cemetery, identified by a small white picket fence and a British flag that flies overhead, holds a commemorative service annually in May to recognize the connection between the United States and Britain. (Courtesy of the Cape Hatteras National Seashore.)

In the 1940s, the Silver Lake waterfront was home to the Ocracoke Naval Base operation (1942–1944) and then used as an amphibious training station (1944–1945.) Loop Shack Hill is the site of a top secret "loop shack," which received pulses from a magnetic cable that ran from Ocracoke to Buxton and detected when underwater vessels, such as the German submarines, were navigating in the waters surrounding Ocracoke. Additionally, in 1943, the US Navy trained servicemen as beach jumpers—predecessors to today's Navy Seals—on Ocracoke Island. (Courtesy of the Cape Hatteras National Seashore.)

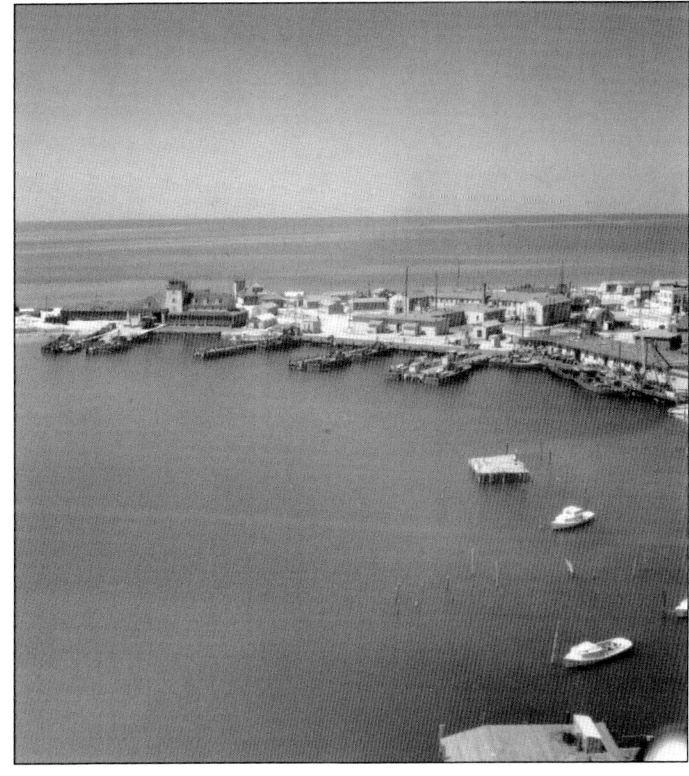

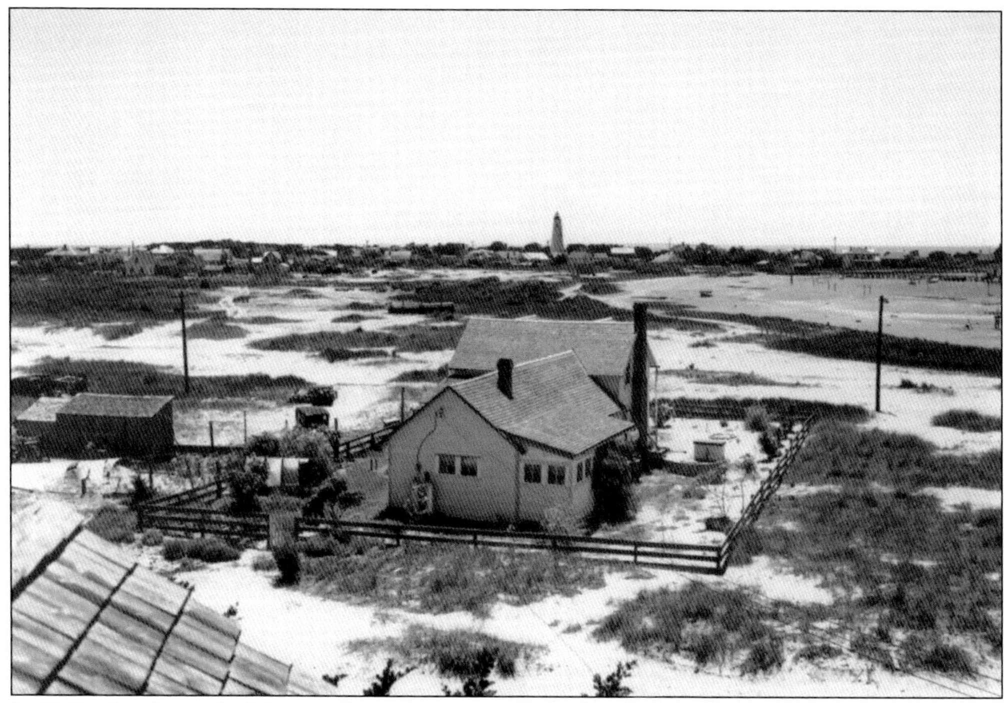

In 1990, the Ocracoke Historic District was established with more than 200 structures that are still visible today. The Ocracoke Island Lighthouse, shown in the background, was built in 1823. The National Park Service owns most of the island except for the village. Ocracoke has some of the finest beaches in the United States and has been recognized one of the top 10 beaches several times. (Courtesy of the Cape Hatteras National Seashore.)

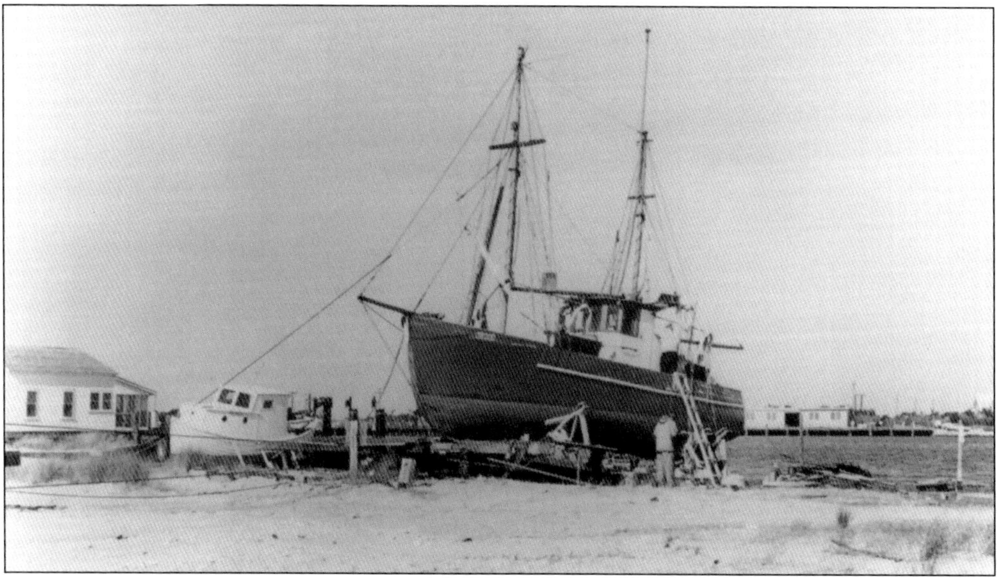

The photograph shows the Ocracoke boat railway on the south shore of Silver Lake Harbor used for hauling boats out of the water to work on their hulls. The traditional wooden sailing vessels, schooners, and skipjacks were part of the early boatbuilding efforts. (Courtesy of the Cape Hatteras National Seashore.)

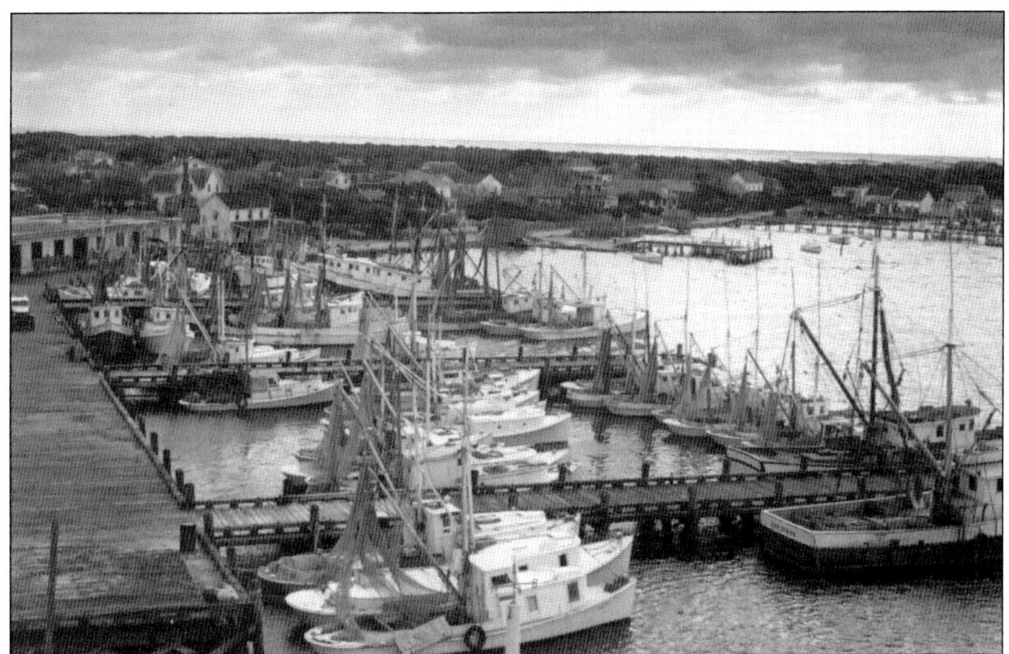

Ocracoke fishing boats often took shelter on Silver Lake. Today, Ocracoke is home to Cape Hatteras National Seashore's visitors' center, the Ocracoke Preservation Museum, and the former US Coast Guard Station, which was converted into a campus of North Carolina Center for the Advancement of Teaching (NCCAT). (Courtesy of the Cape Hatteras National Seashore.)

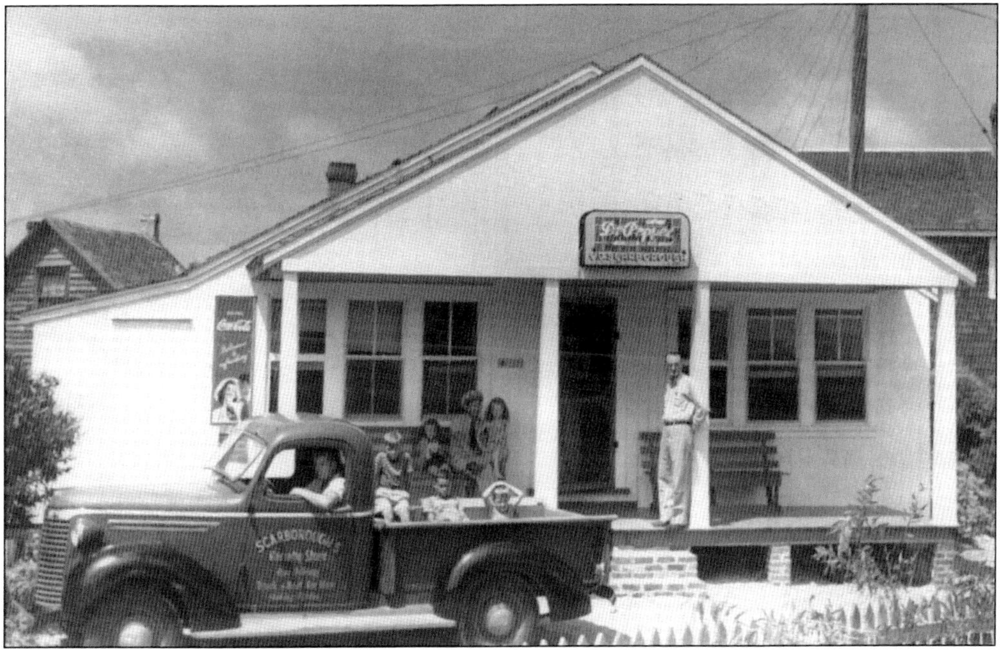

Ocracoke is a quaint little village filled with interesting hometown community and variety stores, gift shops, and art galleries. Many of Ocracoke's restaurants, motels, and places of business have been family-owned for many generations. One will find no modern-day chain establishments on Ocracoke Island. (Courtesy of the Outer Banks History Center.)

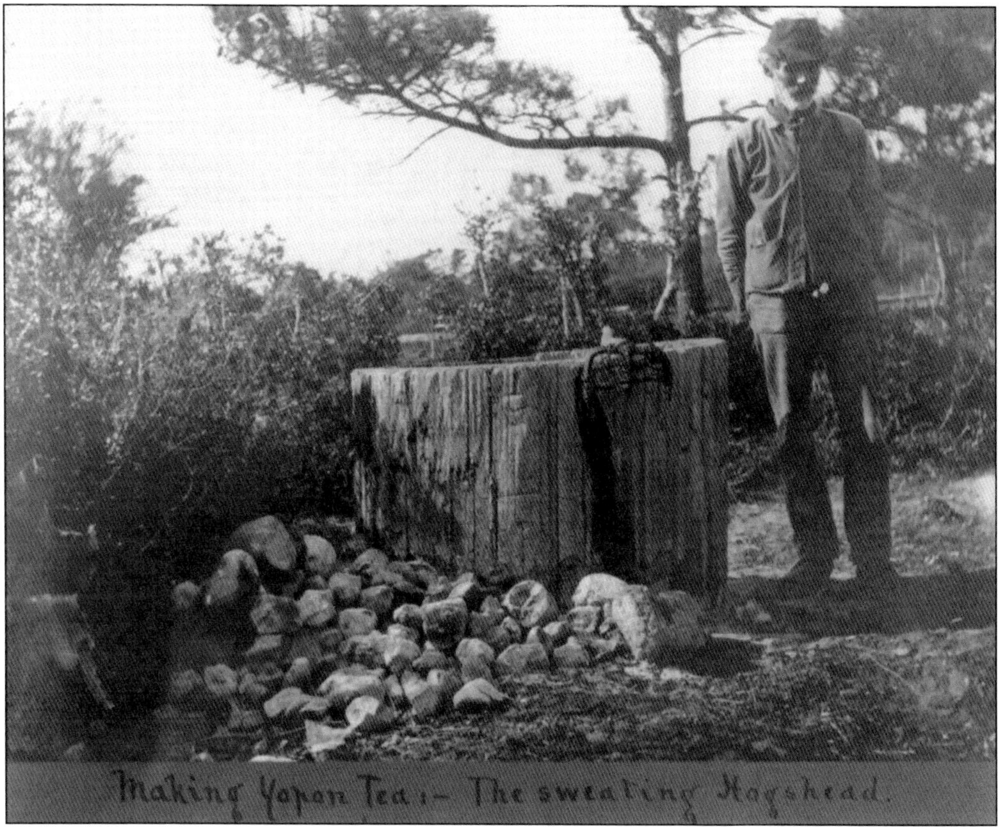

Making Yapon Tea:- The sweating Hogshead.

Yaupon tea, or "black drink," was made from the dried leaves of the indigenous yaupon, a native holly. The drink was used ceremonially by Native Americans in the area. (Courtesy of the Outer Banks History Center.)

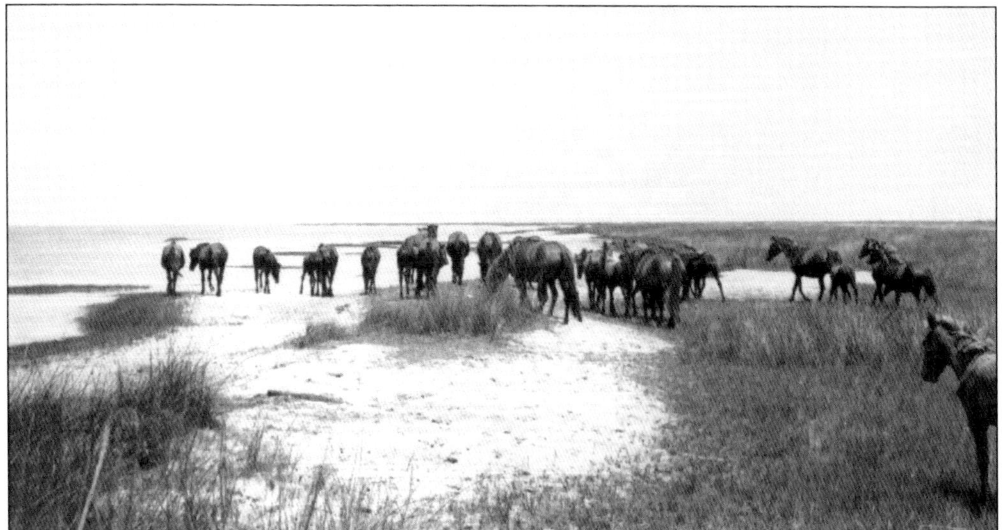

Ocracoke Pony Pens are located just a few miles south of the Hatteras Ferry Docks and are home to the famed Banker ponies, thought to be the descendants of horses from Spanish shipwrecks from the 1500s and 1600s. (Courtesy of the Cape Hatteras National Seashore.)

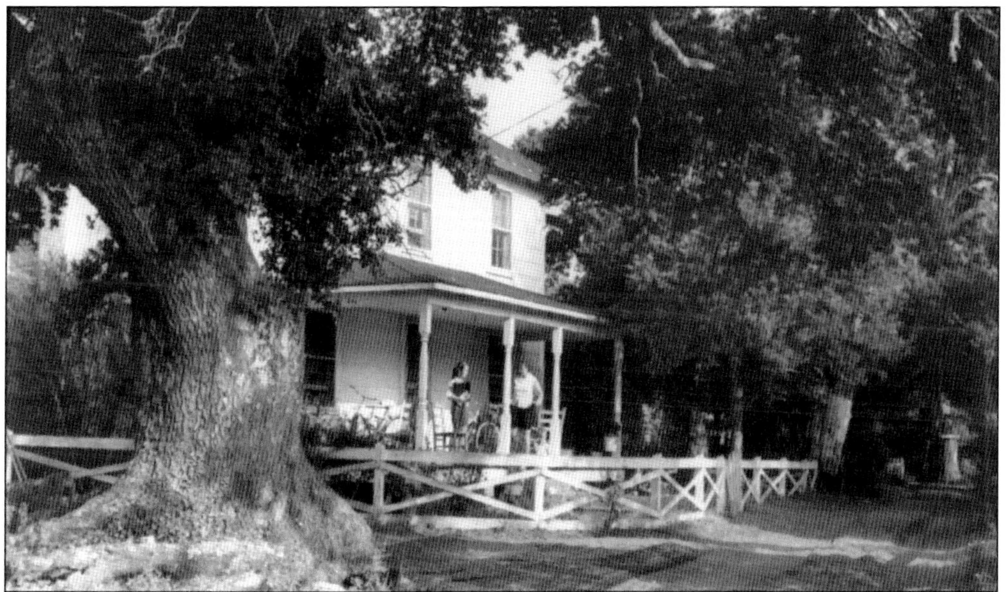

Ocracoke's Howard Street is the last one-lane unpaved street on the island. Visitors can capture a glimpse of the past by walking or biking down this sandy tree-lined road and also visit the local merchants along the way for a pleasant morning stroll. The North Carolina Coastal Springer's Point Preserve offers great bird-watching, hiking, and views from the beach overlooking the Pamlico Sound. This site, historically referred to as Teach's Plantation, is the reputed favorite haunt of the legendary pirate Blackbeard. (Courtesy of the Cape Hatteras National Seashore.)

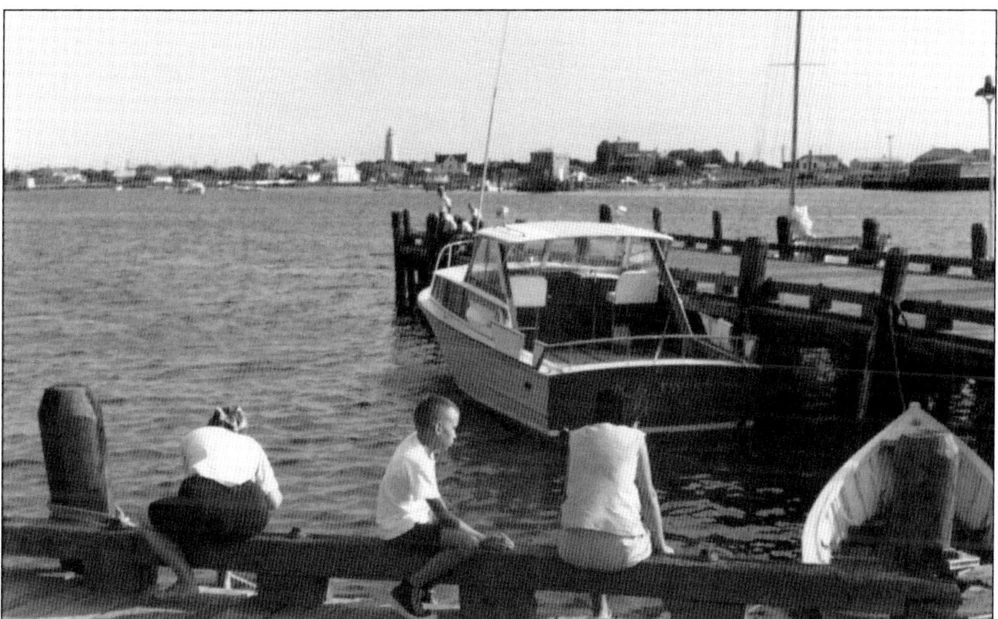

Silver Lake, Ocracoke, is a destination vacation where families and friends can find great fishing, pirate lore, fascinating history, and a quaint little white lighthouse; it is a beachcomber's and sun worshipper's paradise, artists in residence abound, and a variety of local festivals celebrate everything from traditional Fourth of July parades to the annual fig festival and great opportunities for some of the clearest night skies on the East Coast. (Courtesy of the Cape Hatteras National Seashore.)

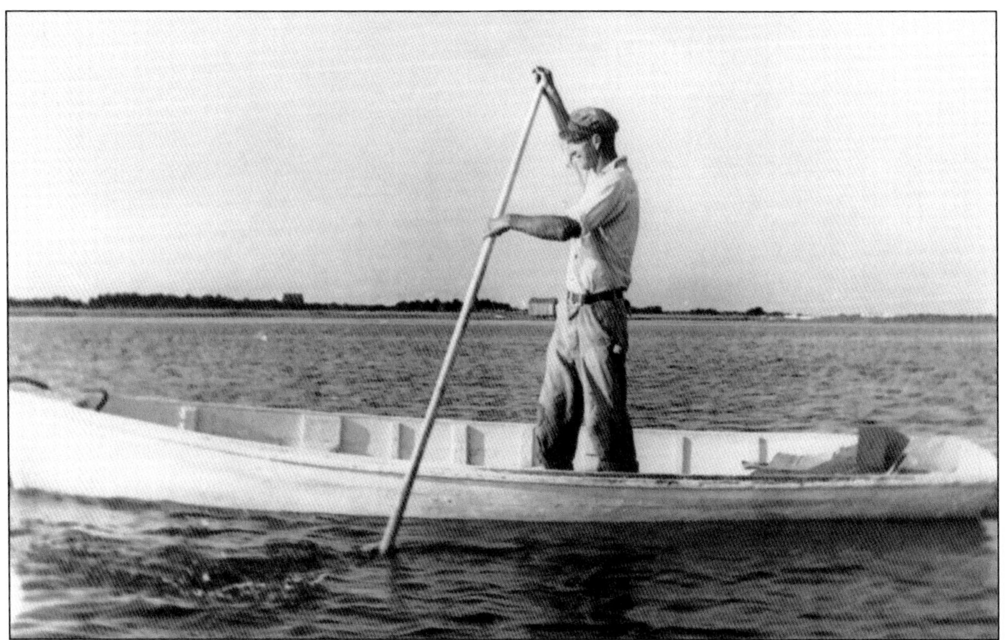

Carl Dixon poles out to meet the mail boat from Portsmouth Island. Today, only a handful of Outer Banks visitors even make the long and arduous trek to the island. It is only accessible by a small boat from Ocracoke or privately operated ferry in Atlantic, North Carolina. Portsmouth Island is a tidal island connected, under low-water conditions, to the north end of the North Core Banks. The tiny community in Carteret County was officially established in 1752, and by 1770, it was the largest European settlement on the Outer Banks, boasting approximately 700 residents at that time. Due to storms and the isolation of this area, the village was abandoned in 1970. Cape Lookout National Seashore maintains the few remaining structures as part of a historic district. (Courtesy of the Ocracoke Preservation Society.)

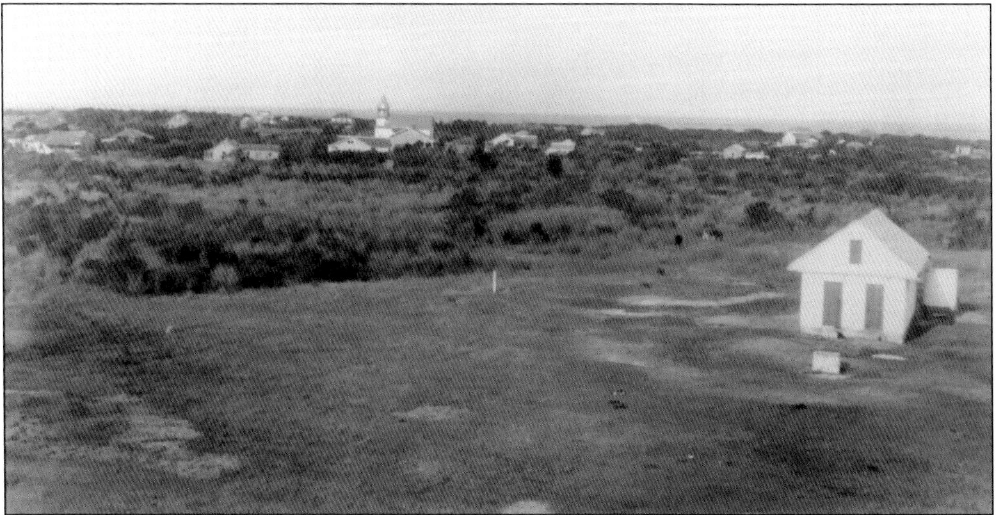

The Portsmouth Island Post Office is one of the few remaining structures from this once-bustling coastal maritime village. This isolated island has no vacation homes or modern conveniences but offers a glimpse into the past of an early 19th-century barrier-island village. (Courtesy of the Ocracoke Preservation Society.)

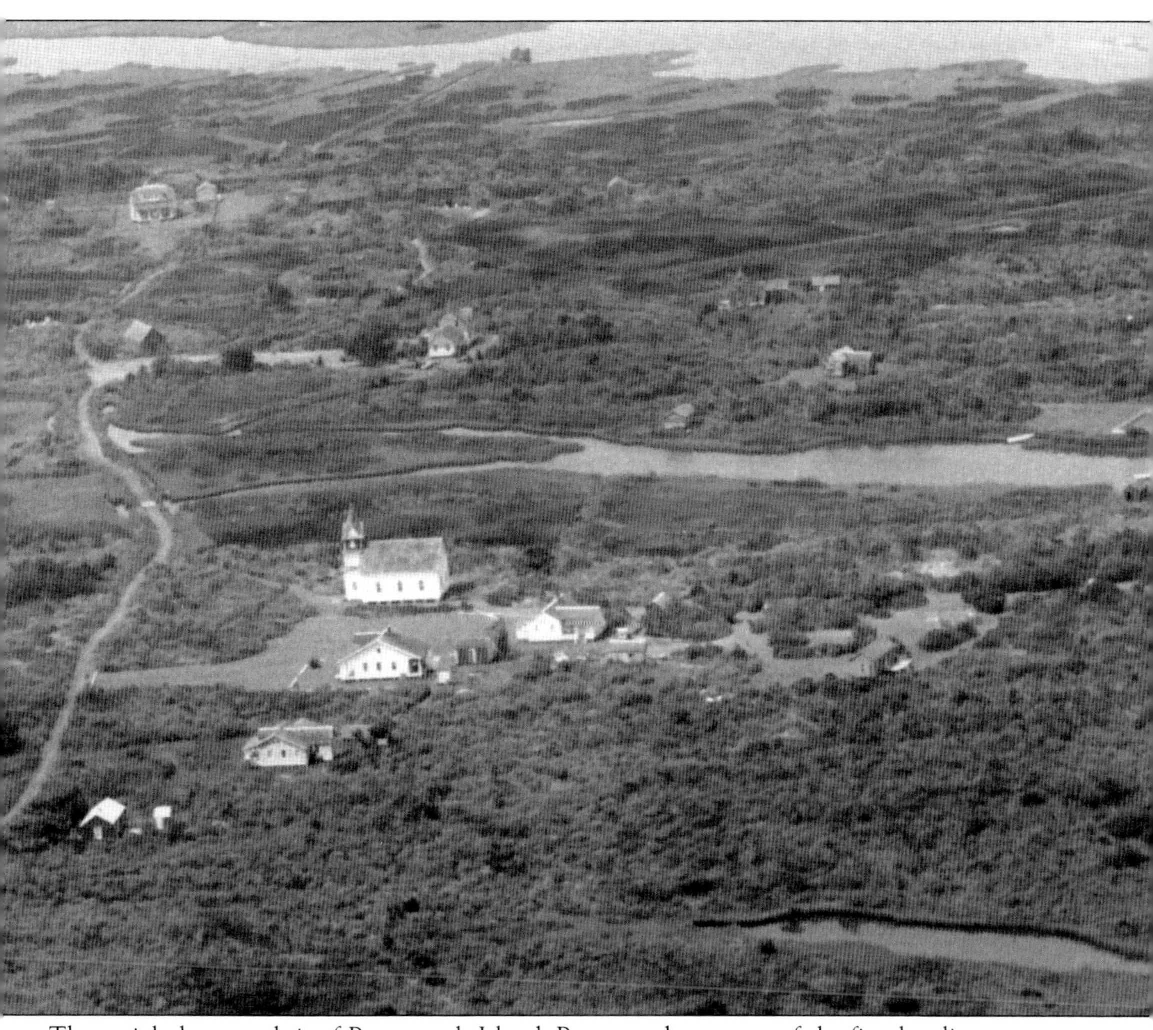

The aerial photograph is of Portsmouth Island. Portsmouth was one of the first bustling ports following European colonization. The community provided settlers, sailors, and businessmen with easy trade and shipping routes through the narrow inlets along the coast. The isolated Portsmouth Island area remains one of the last wild and open landscapes on the Outer Banks. The lack of modern amenities attracts some vacationers who prefer to rough it and provides a glimpse of the past. (Courtesy of the Ocracoke Preservation Society.)

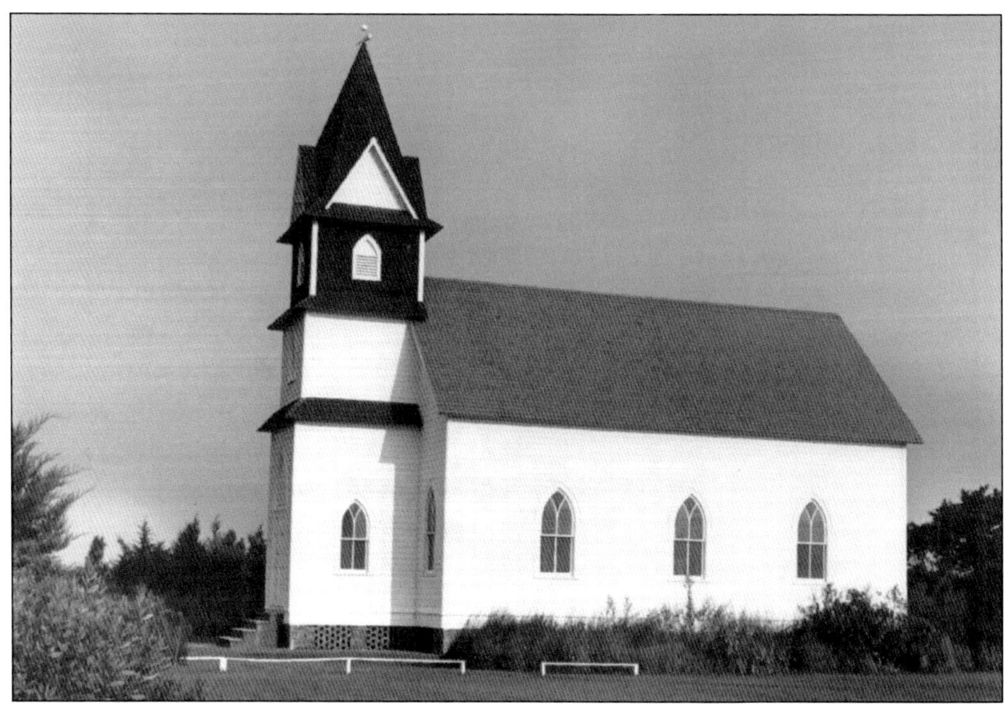

The Methodist Church of Portsmouth Island remains today. Once, it was part of a thriving community with homes, churches, a general store, and a post office. (Courtesy of the Cape Lookout National Seashore.)

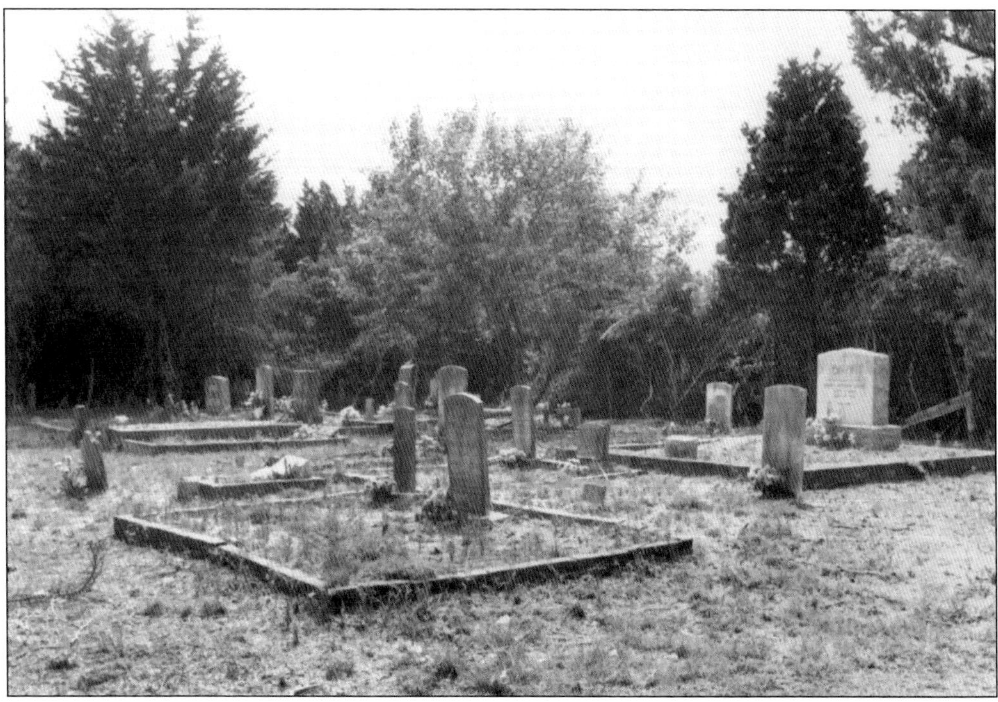

Pictured here are Portsmouth Island Cemetery and the tombstone of John Wallace, governor of Shell Castle, who died in Portsmouth in 1810. (Courtesy of the Cape Lookout National Seashore.)

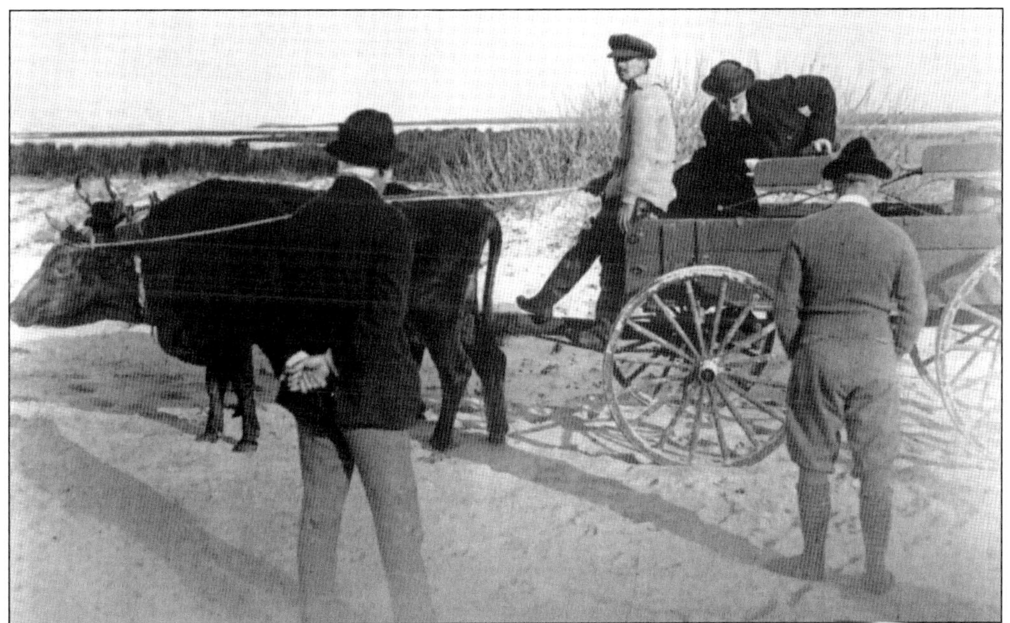

Pictured here in 1915 are early visitors to Portsmouth Island. The Pilontary Gun Club catered to all sorts of visitors. The ox wagon, driven by Alvin Mason, carried wildlife artist Arthur Duane (standing left), then–assistant secretary of the Navy Franklin D. Roosevelt (sitting in the cart), and owner of the club J.L. Mott (standing right) around the island to a boat, which took them to the railroad station in Beaufort. (Courtesy of the Cape Lookout National Seashore/FDR Library.)

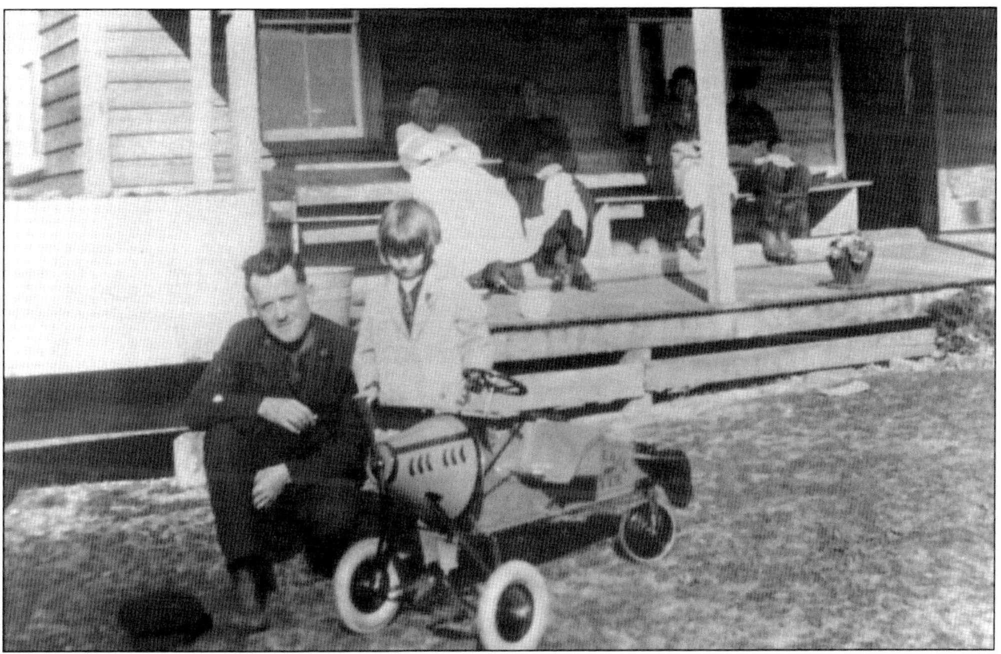

The photograph is of the Walker Styron family. Four-year-old Dorothy Styron lived with her father, who worked at the Portsmouth Life-Saving Station. The toy airplane was a Christmas gift. (Courtesy of the Cape Lookout National Seashore.)

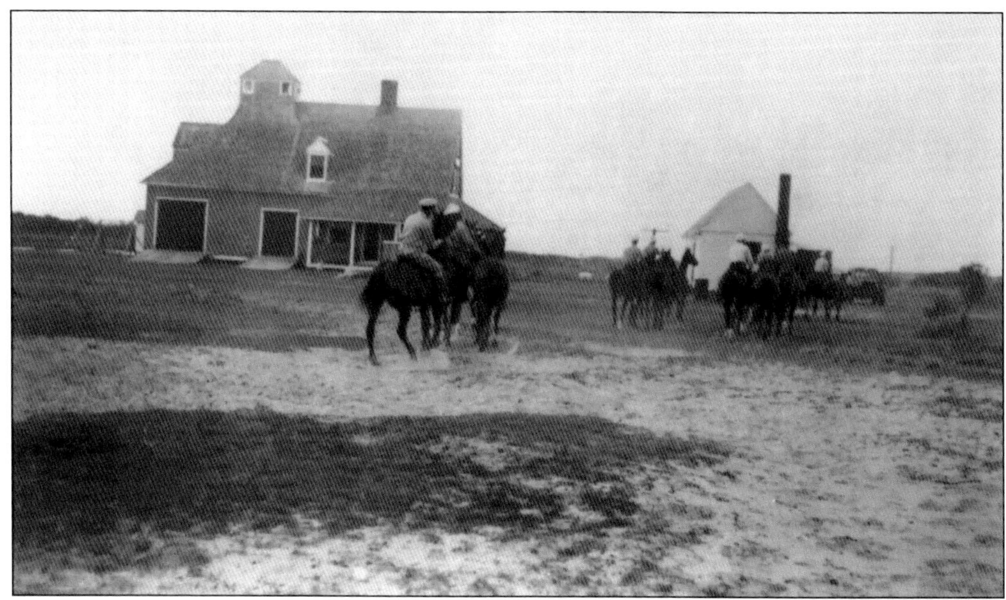

Pictured here in 1930 is the US Coast Guard station that was reactivated during World War II. Men from several branches of the armed forces, including the Navy, Army, and Marines, shared the station with the Coast Guardsmen. The men were equipped with a truck and a dozen horses for patrols. (Courtesy of the Cape Lookout National Seashore.)

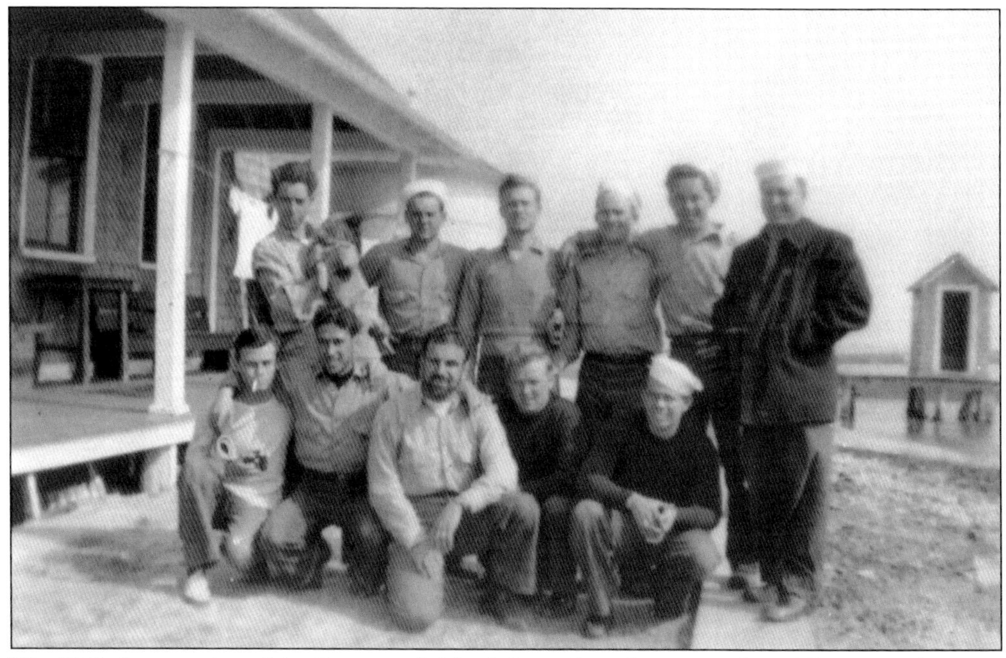

The 1942 photograph is of the Portsmouth Island Coast Guard crew members. The remote location of this station forced the men to deal with primitive conditions, including the outhouse at the end of the pier over the creek. (Courtesy of the Cape Lookout National Seashore.)

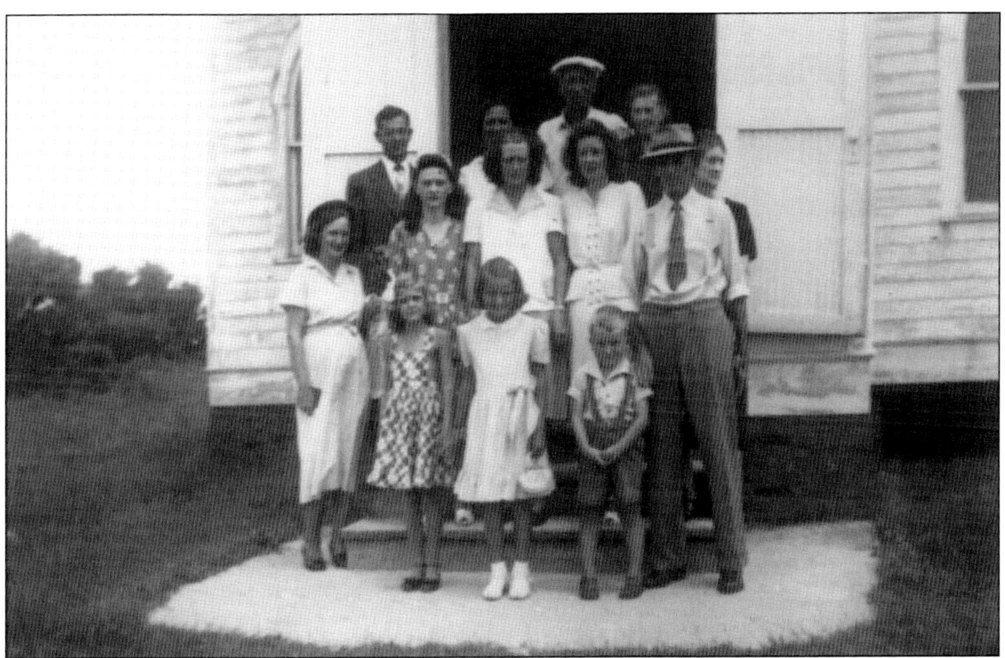

Pictured here is a Portsmouth Island family attending the only church on the island, the Methodist church. Portsmouth lacked even the most basic comforts even in the 1950s. (Courtesy of the Cape Lookout National Seashore.)

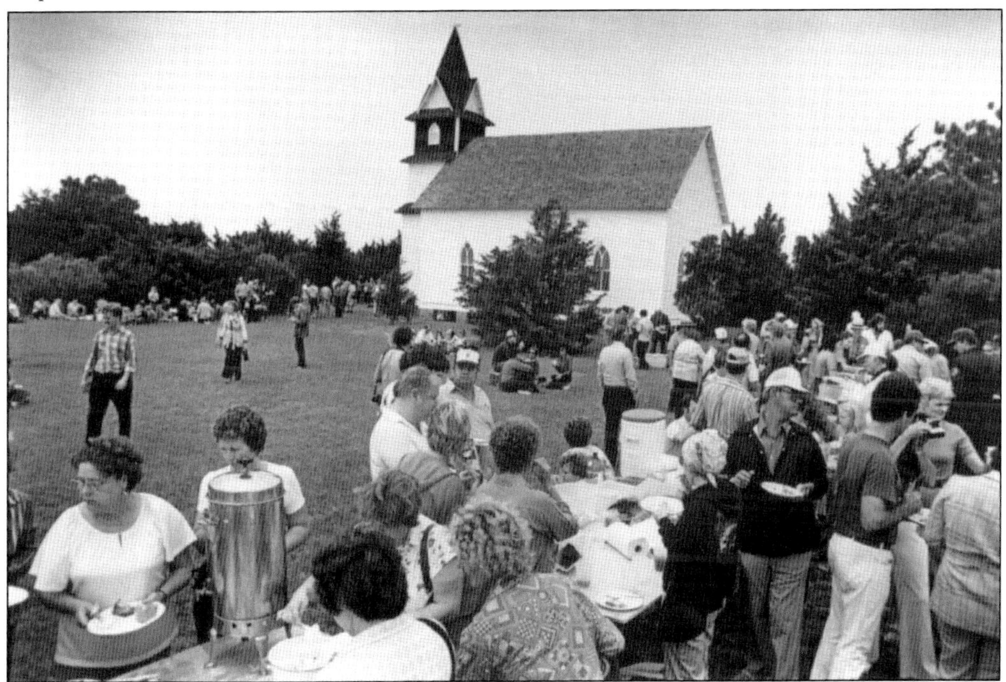

This photograph shows a typical Portsmouth Island homecoming. The last two Portsmouth Island residents were elderly ladies and longtime residents who left in 1970. The first homecoming event was held on April 25, 1992, and these continue today. (Courtesy of the Cape Lookout National Seashore.)

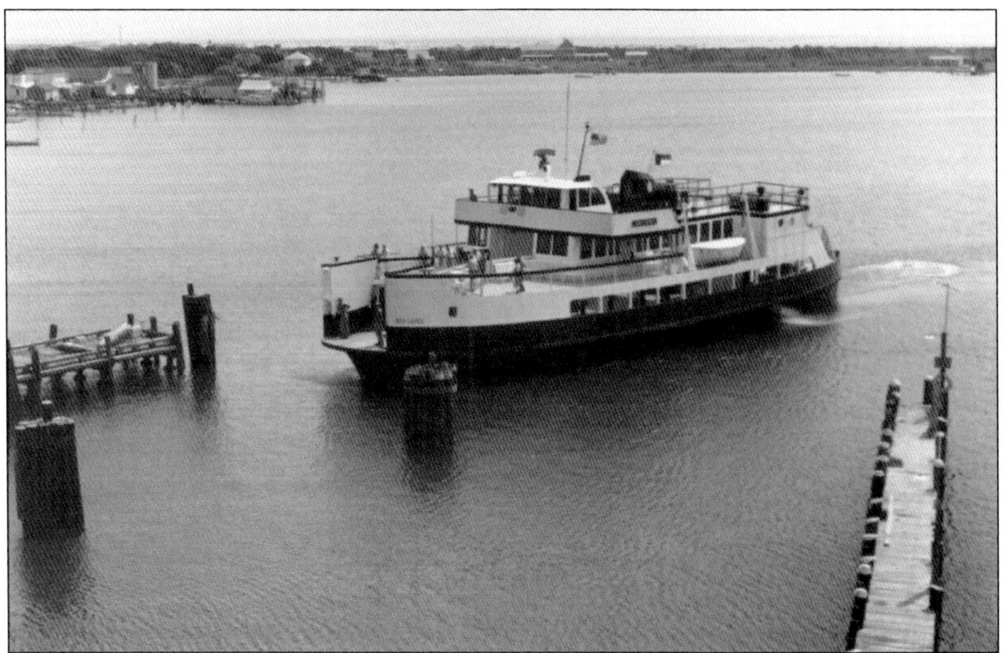

Ferries leave from Ocracoke and deliver passengers and cars to Cedar Island. When one visits the Down East area, there is opportunity to explore the 13 unincorporated byway communities of Atlantic, Bettie, Cedar Island, Davis, Gloucester, Harkers Island, Marshallberg, Otway, Sea Level, Smyrna, Stacy, Straits, and Williston. (Courtesy of the Cape Lookout National Seashore.)

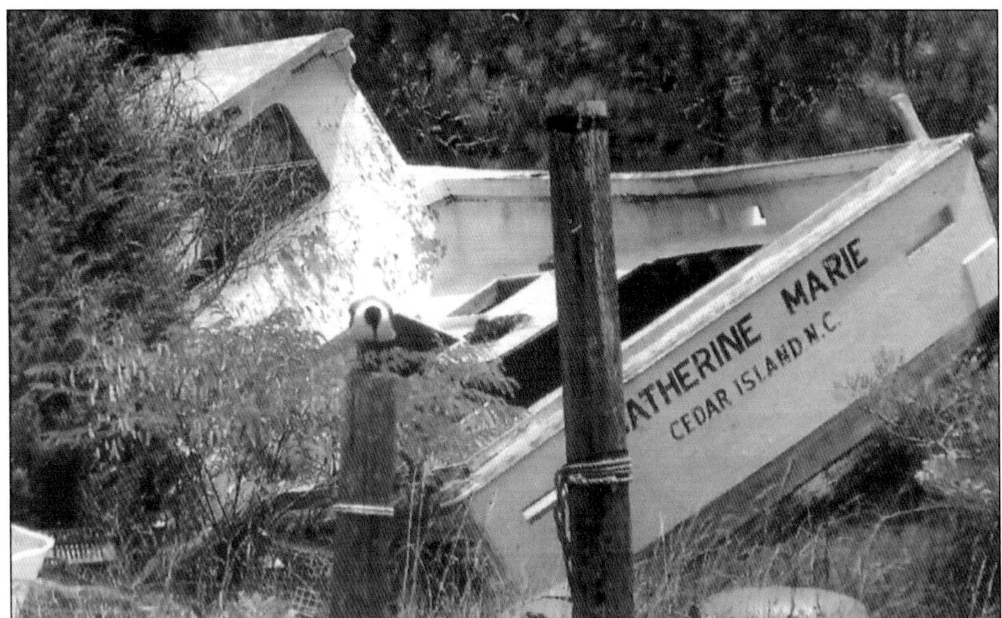

In this section of the byway, the traveler glimpses a slower pace of life in the coastal villages. Many of the communities still have hunting clubs, small-town grocery and hardware stores, wholesale-retail fish houses, stables, several rental vacation cottages, and a church and a post office. The main village of Cedar Island, formerly known as "Roe," is located along the north central portion of the island. (Courtesy of the Core Sound Waterfowl Museum & Heritage Center.)

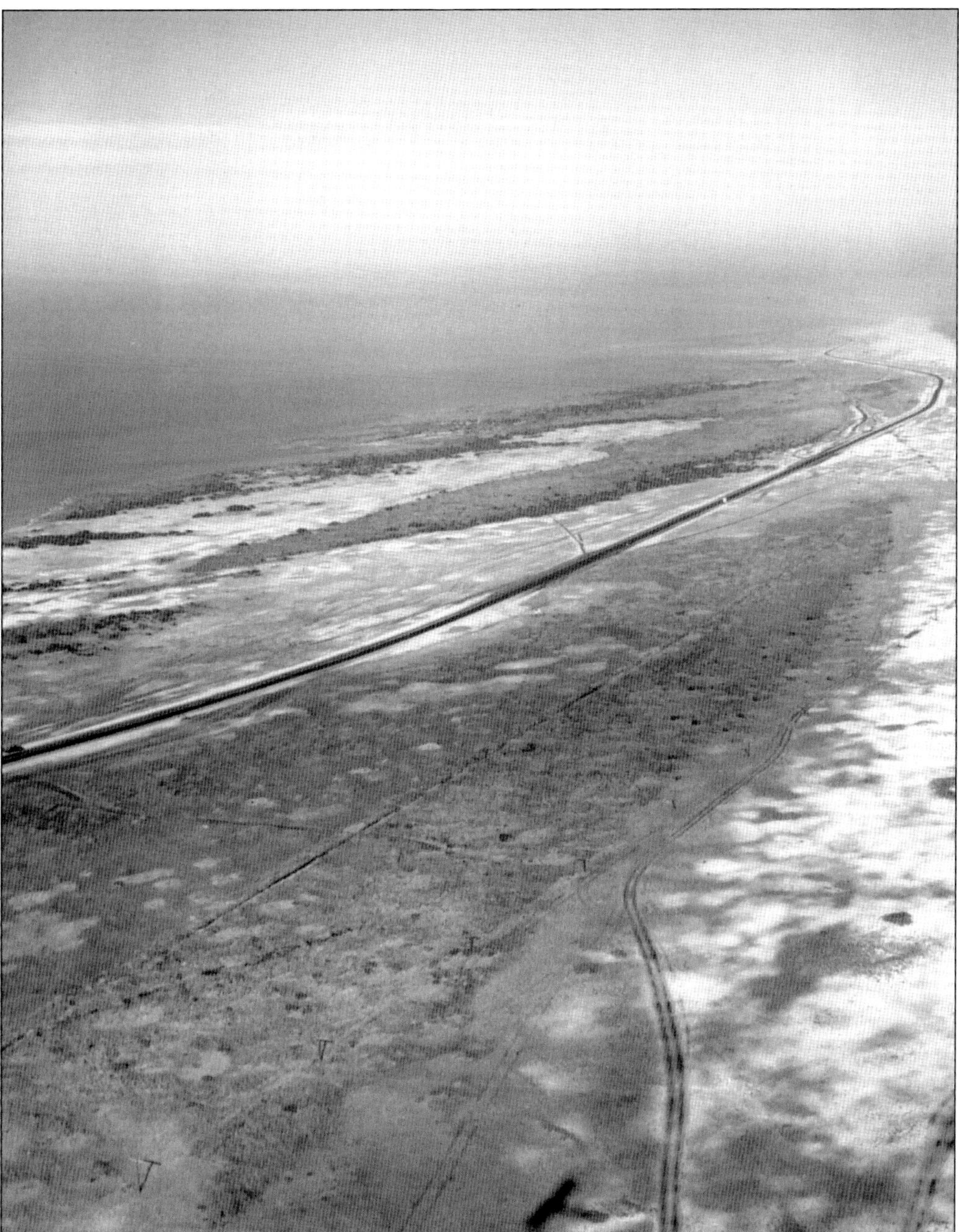

This aerial photograph of Cedar Island National Wildlife Refuge reveals the remoteness of this region. Cedar Island National Wildlife Refuge, established in 1964, consists of 11,000 acres of irregularly-flooded, brackish marsh and pocosin, woodland habitat. Brackish and salt marshes are some of the most productive acreage found in the food chain on earth. Many local residents are fishermen. The body of water to the left is the Core Sound, named for the Coree Indians, who once lived in this area. (Courtesy of the Core Sound Waterfowl Museum & Heritage Center.)

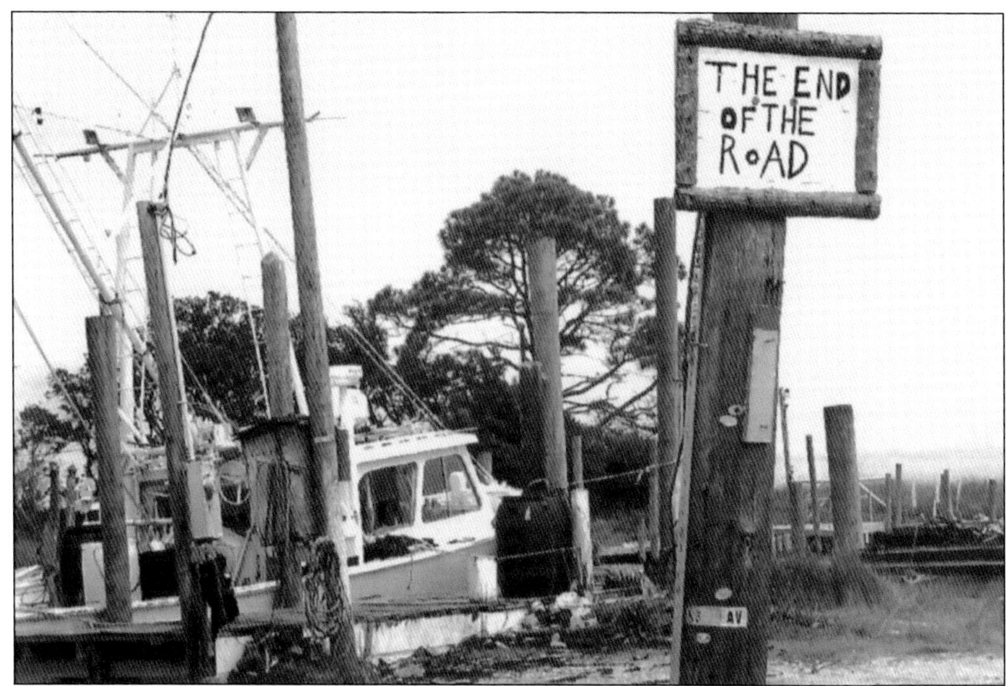

One end of US 70 is in Atlantic, North Carolina. This east-west highway extends for 2,385 miles from Atlantic, North Carolina, to east-central Arizona. (Courtesy of the Core Sound Waterfowl Museum & Heritage Center.)

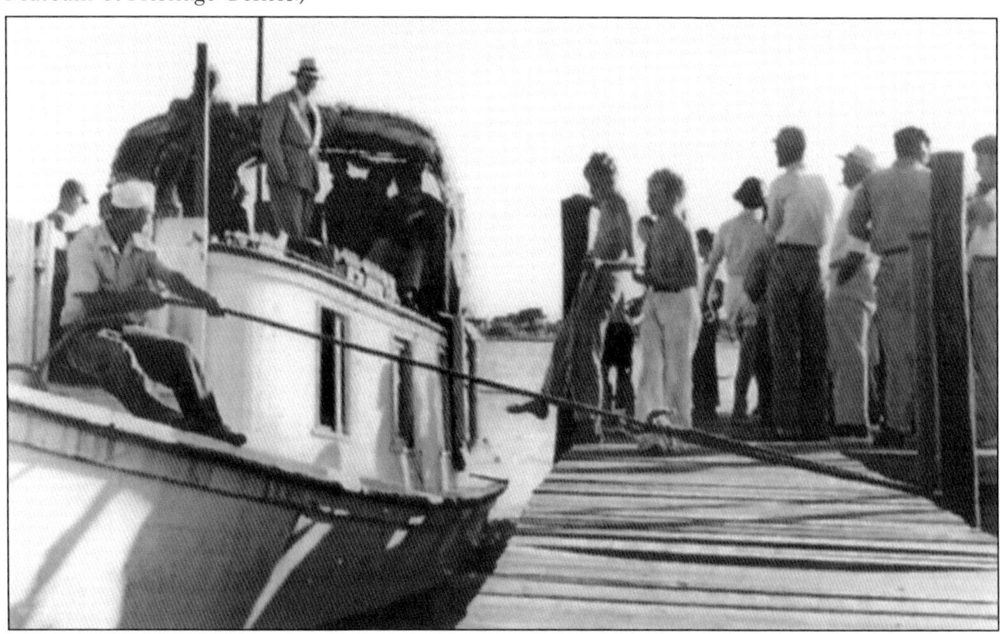
The *Aleta* mail boat, operating between Atlantic and Ocracoke, arrives to a crowded dock in Atlantic. Before bridges were built, this isolated community was only accessible by water. In the early 1900s, daily passenger and mail services began. The community of Atlantic was originally called Hunting Quarters, named by the Tuscarora Indians and the Coree. In 1890, the name was changed to Atlantic. (Courtesy of the North Carolina Maritime Museum.)

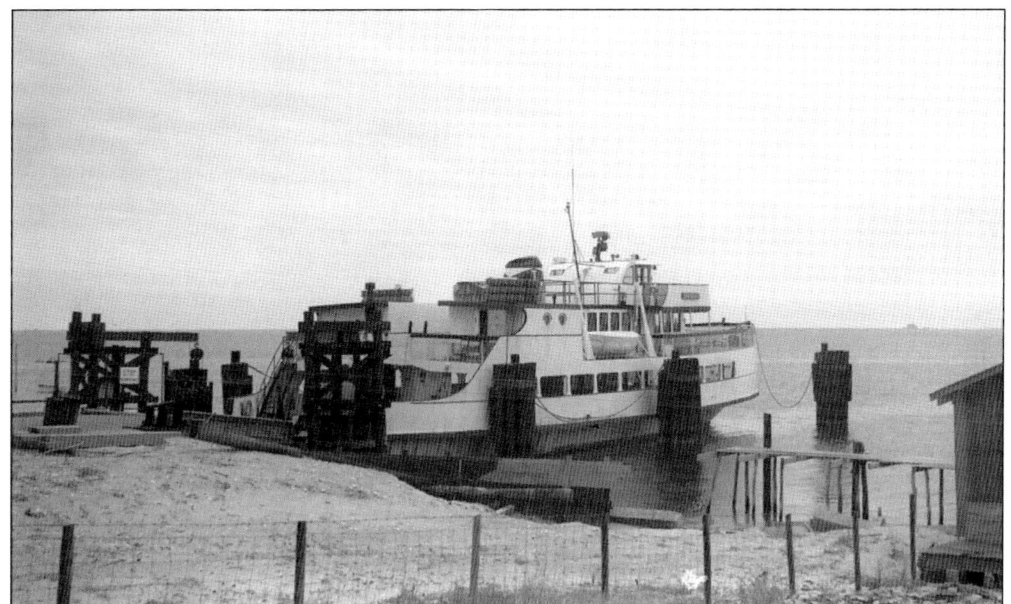

A former state-operated ferry route from Atlantic to Ocracoke was discontinued, and service now runs from Cedar Island to Ocracoke. Today, the Morris Marina Ferry serves as a private vehicle ferry to North Core Banks and Portsmouth Island. (Courtesy of the North Carolina Maritime Museum.)

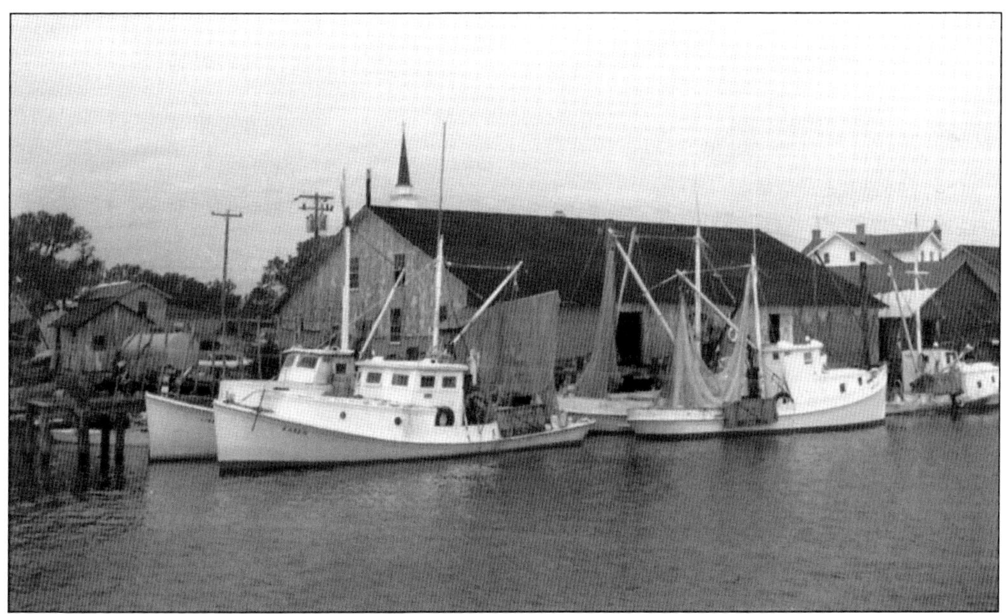

The byway along US 70 meanders past old workboats at rest along the waterfront of Atlantic Harbor, a community of rich commercial-fishing heritage. Today, the community is a pleasant mixture of traditional churches, family gathering places, and cemeteries, and the commercial waterfront is filled with fishing boats. Atlantic was once known for its many fish houses, fish factories, a fish meal plant, an oyster factory, and boatbuilding. (Courtesy of the North Carolina Maritime Museum.)

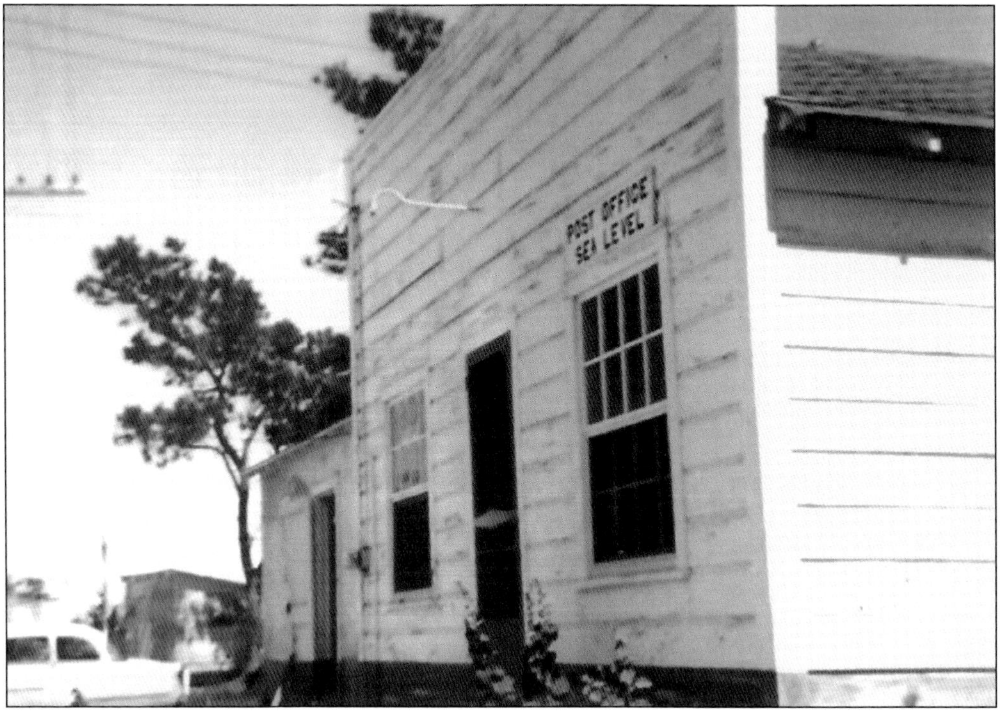

Sea Level is another maritime village found along this stretch of the byway, and it is appropriately named. Because Sea Level has one of the lowest elevations in North Carolina, it is estimated that approximately 75 percent of the community floods when hurricanes pass through. (Courtesy of the Core Sound Waterfowl Museum & Heritage Center.)

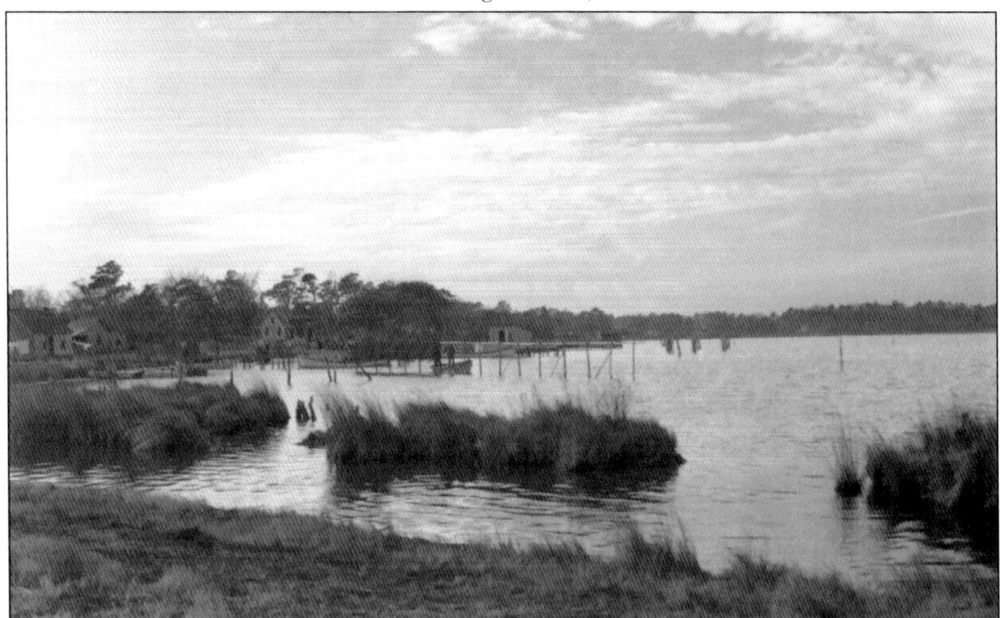

Sea Level was once known for its hunting and fishing camps. Drum Inlet is an outlet to the Core Sound waters, and commercial fishing has long been the primary means of earning a living in this community. (Courtesy of the Core Sound Waterfowl Museum & Heritage Center.)

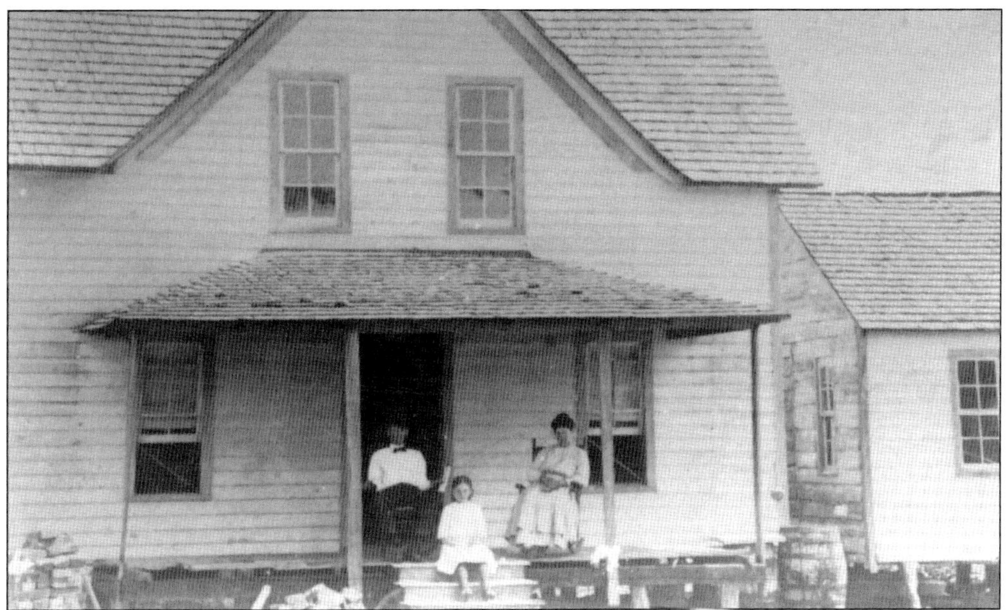

The village of Stacy was known as Piney Point until 1888. Today, a post office and a country store are the hub of the community. In 1888, Dr. William Paul brought the post office to the village and changed the name from Piney Point to Stacy. The area was once home to many of the area's best-known waterfowl carvers. (Courtesy of the Core Sound Waterfowl Museum & Heritage Center.)

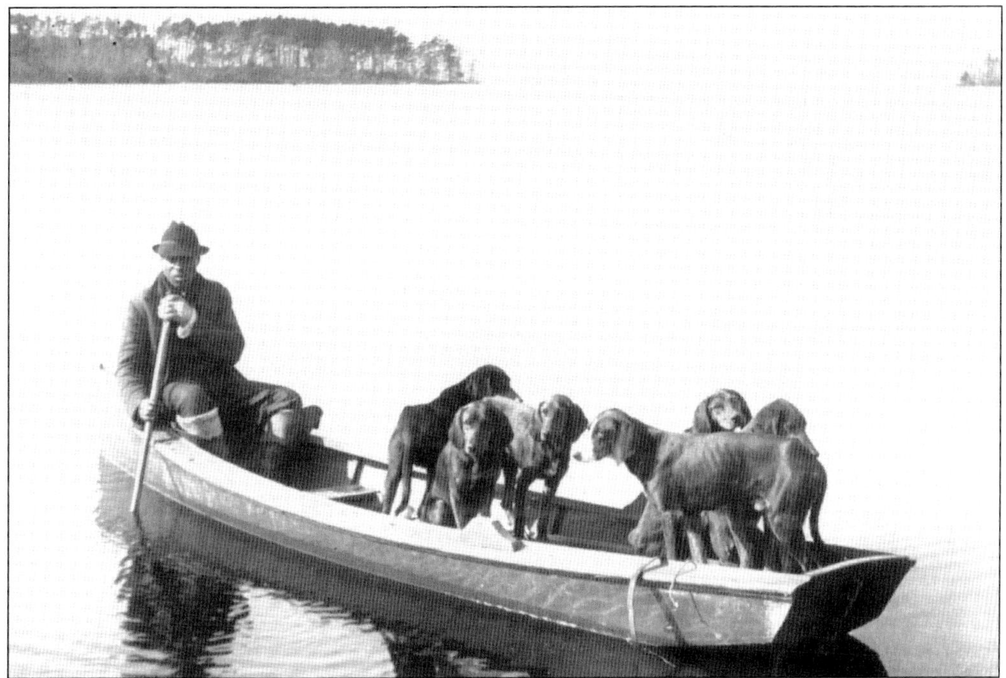

The 1918 photograph is of a Davis resident with his hunting dogs. Davis was known to many for its local waterfowl hunting and fishing guides. The Carteret Gun and Rod Club House was built in 1902; it burned down on May 25, 1970. (Courtesy of the North Carolina Maritime Museum.)

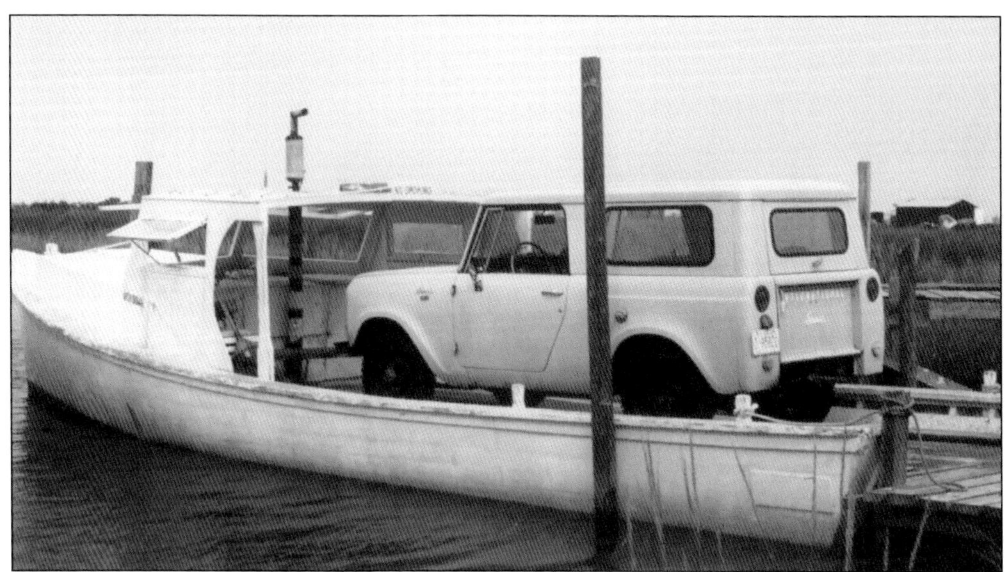

The Davis Ferry Company, located in both Davis and Atlantic, uses makeshift ferries to carry vehicles to Long Point Cabin Camp, which is located on North Core Banks. The historic camp, a favorite of fisherman and beachgoers, can only be reached by boat. (Courtesy of the Cape Lookout National Seashore.)

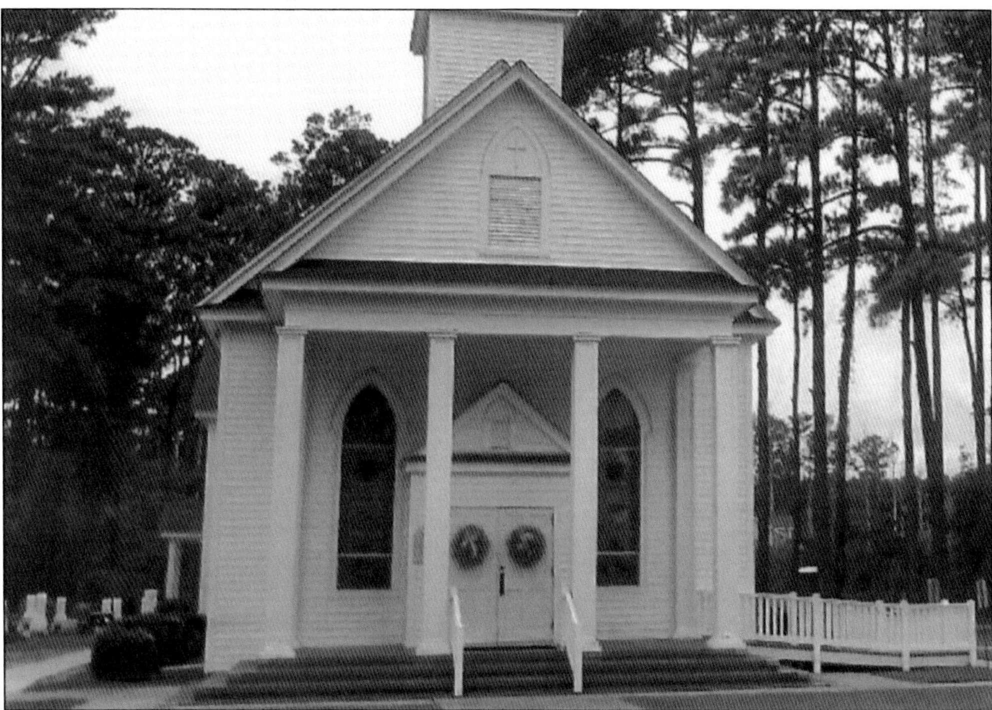

Williston, a small coastal community along the Core Sound, has a rich history of commercial fishing. Although little industry remains today, the small waterfront community was once home to several fish houses, boatbuilding operations, and even its own schoolhouse. Today, the community's picturesque setting includes historic churches and ancient, gnarled live oaks that grace the well-kept homes and streets. (Courtesy of the Core Sound Waterfowl Museum & Heritage Center.)

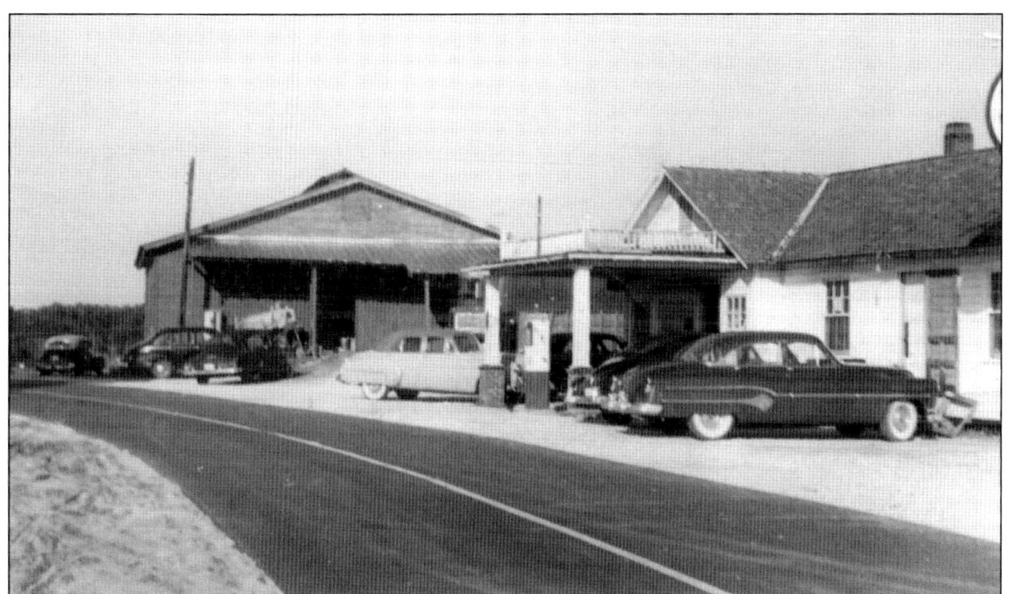

The Williston Village Store sold all household needs, as well as oysters, clams, finfish, and fowl that residents either hunted or raised domestically. The byway continues and turns left into the town of Smyrna. (Courtesy of the Core Sound Waterfowl Museum & Heritage Center.)

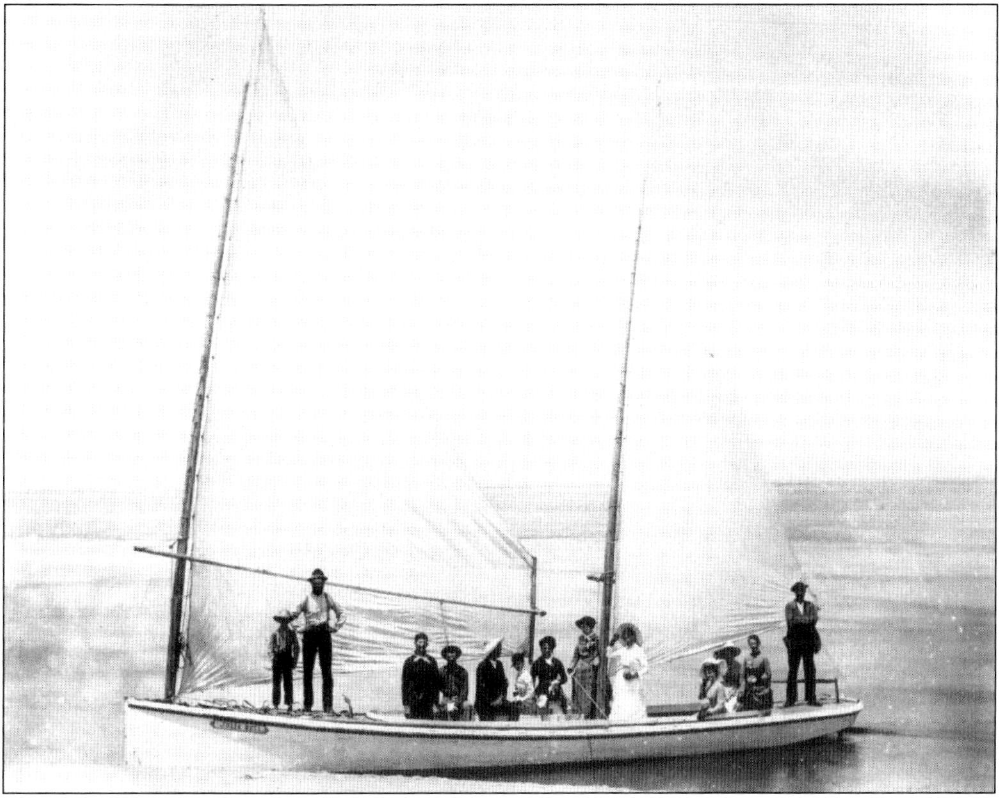

This seven-ton, 45-foot sharpie was built at Smyrna, North Carolina. It is a good example of what was called a Core Sound sharpie. (Courtesy of the North Carolina Maritime Museum.)

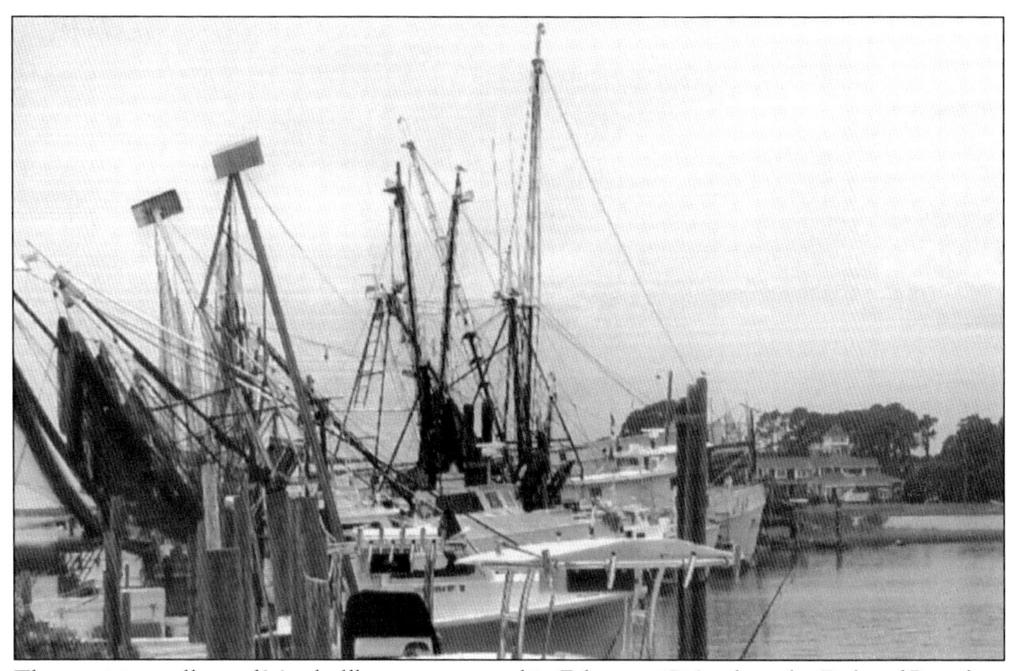

The maritime village of Marshallberg was created in February 1713, when the Duke of Beaufort, one of the Lords Proprietors, issued a land patent to George Bell for 287 acres of land. The post office named the community Marshallberg in honor of Matt Marshall, who ran the mail boat that served the community. Marshallberg Harbor was home to three seafood dealers buying and selling soft crabs, hard crabs, shrimp, clams, and oysters. (Courtesy of the Core Sound Waterfowl Museum & Heritage Center.)

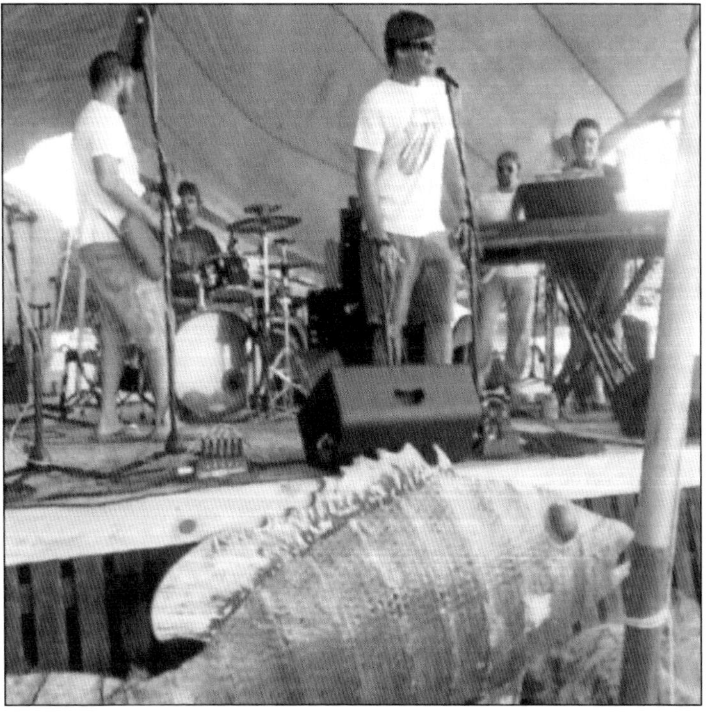

The Wild Caught Festival is an annual event that brings the communities together to celebrate root music, local seafood, summer produce, and heritage. Capt. Joe Pigott, who had visited and admired Gloucester, Massachusetts, requested that the post office name the town Gloucester. Today, it is a community of farmers who grow tobacco, potatoes, beans, tomatoes, and broccoli as their principal crops. (Courtesy of the Core Sound Waterfowl Museum & Heritage Center.)

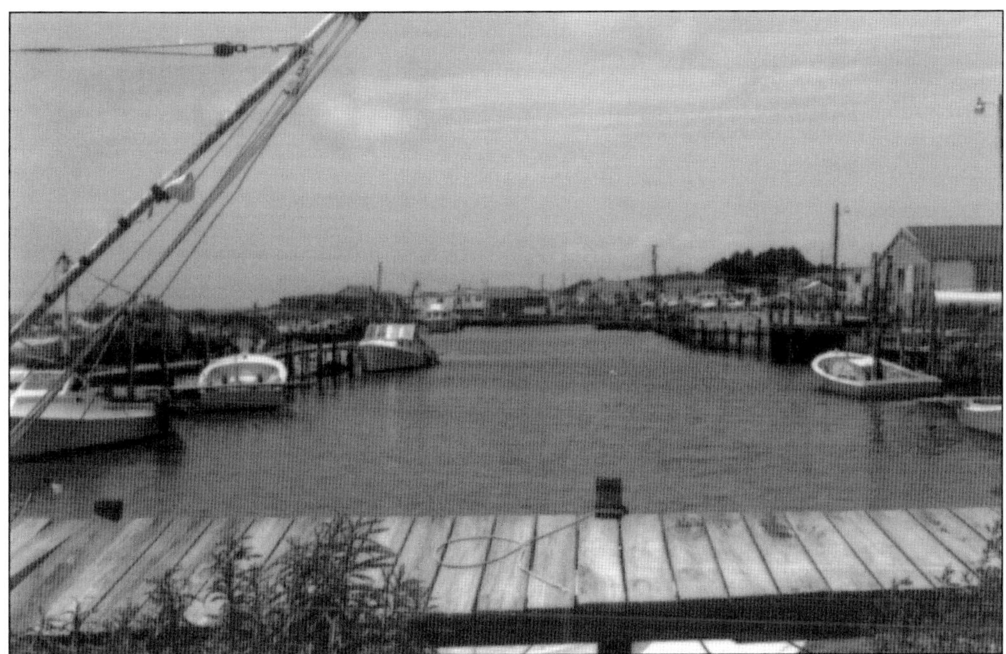

With the construction of the permanent bridge in 1941, Harkers Island was linked to the mainland forever. Today, Harkers Island Bridge causeway is a prime wildlife-viewing spot and a favorite bird-watching area complemented by a fishing pier, public access, and a boat launch for the sportsman. (Courtesy of the Core Sound Waterfowl Museum & Heritage Center)

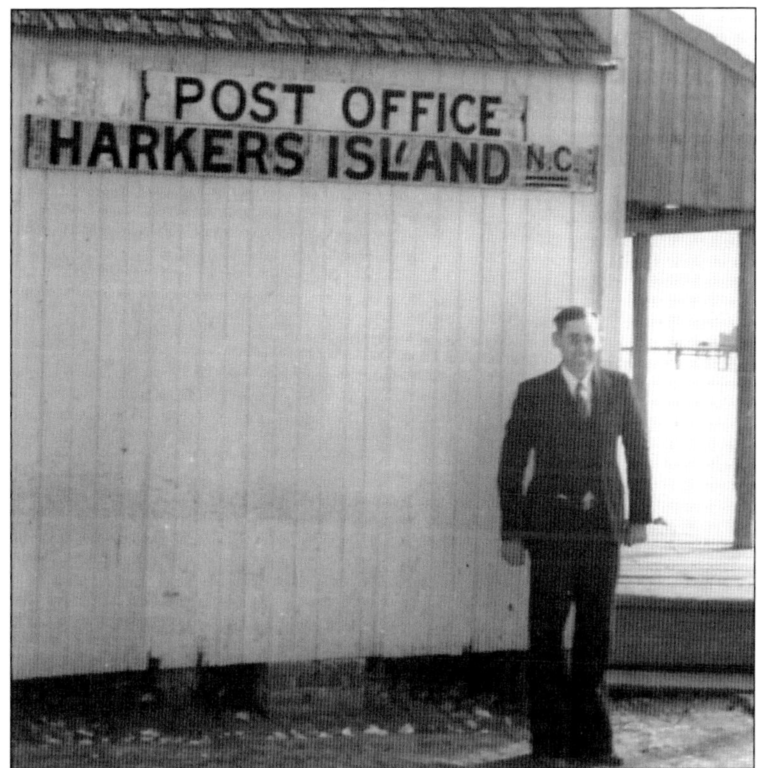

In 1730, Ebenezer Harker purchased the island, where he then settled with his family and built a plantation and boatyard. The island became known as Harkers Island soon after his death. (Courtesy of the Core Sound Waterfowl Museum & Heritage Center)

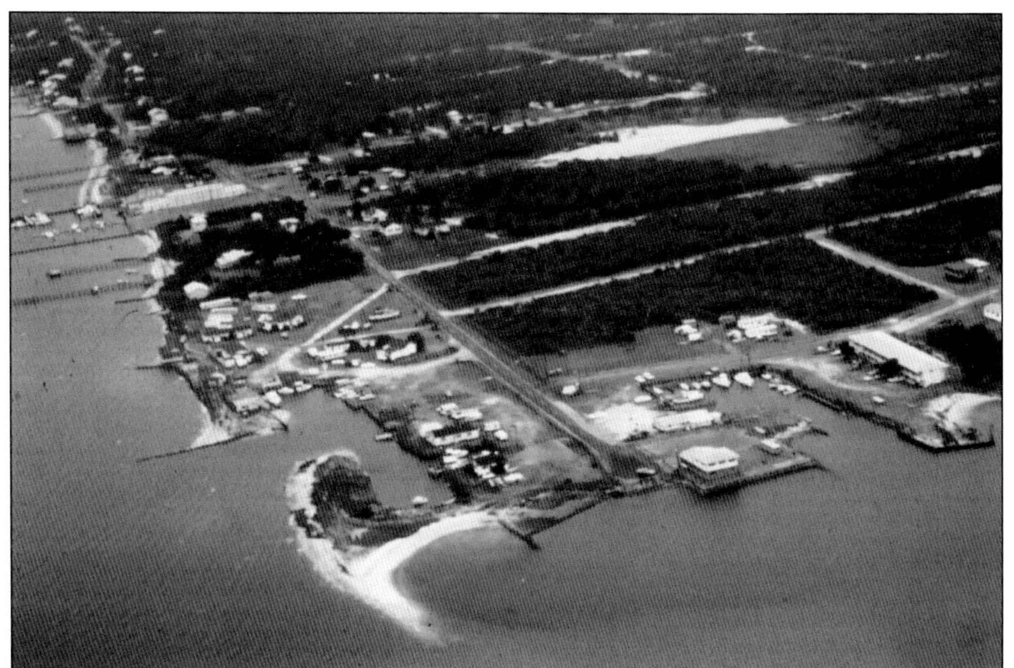
Today, the Harkers Island community consists of side roads to private island homes and small businesses dedicated to decoy carving, model boat construction, harvesting fresh seafood, and the island's famed boatbuilding industry. (Courtesy of the Core Sound Waterfowl Museum & Heritage Center.)

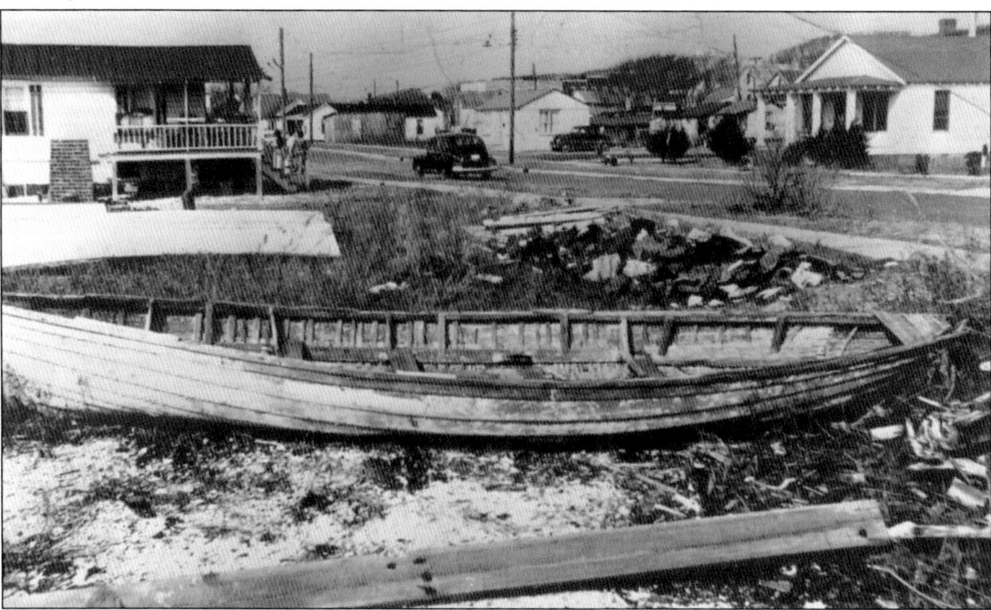
Diamond City was a settlement on the eastern end of Shackleford Banks in Carteret County. Due to impacts from the August 1899 hurricane that made landfall in the area, approximately 500 residents of the settlement decided to move farther inland. The last of the residents left by 1902 and many even relocated their homes to nearby places such as Harkers Island (pictured) and Morehead City. (Courtesy of the North Carolina Maritime Museum.)

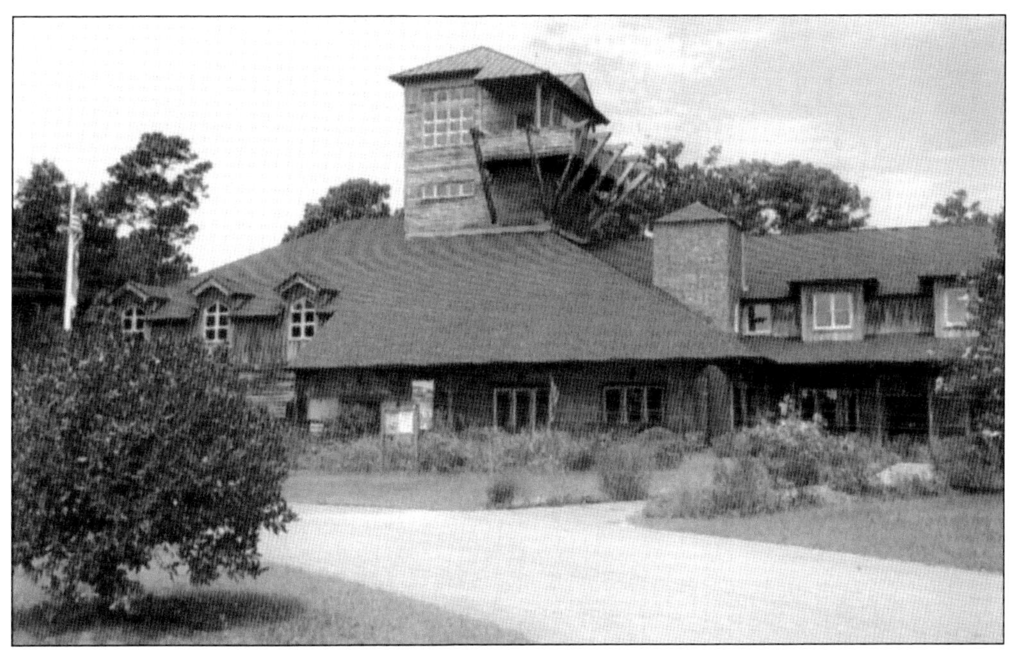

Core Sound Waterfowl Museum & Heritage Center on Harkers Island has a large collection and displays local traditions of this region. Displays of traditional boatbuilding, decoy carving, duck calls, folklore, and community artifacts can be found in the museum. (Both, courtesy of the Core Sound Waterfowl Museum & Heritage Center.)

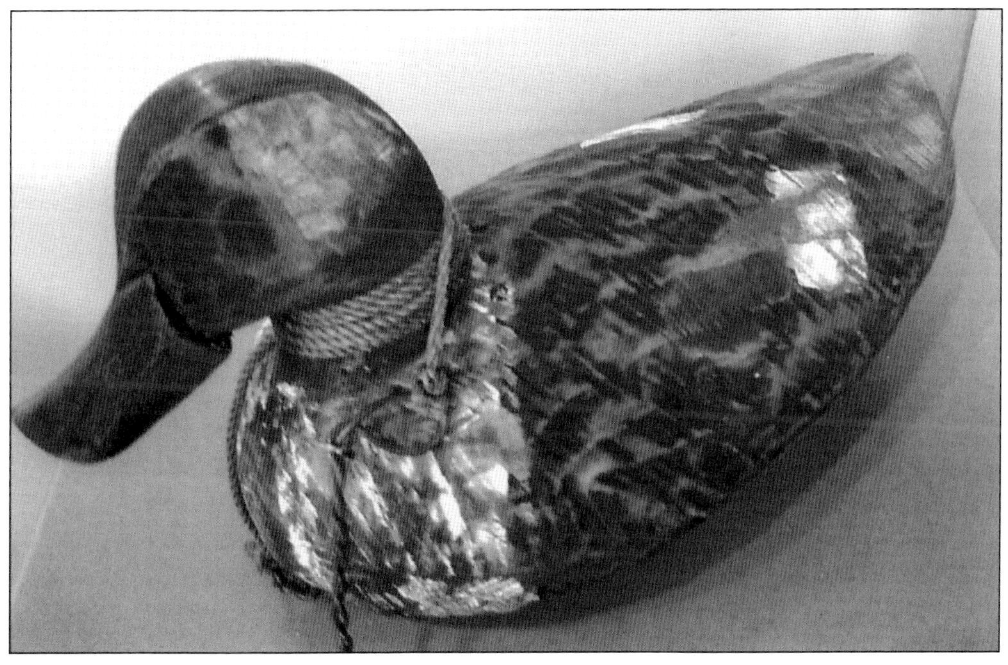

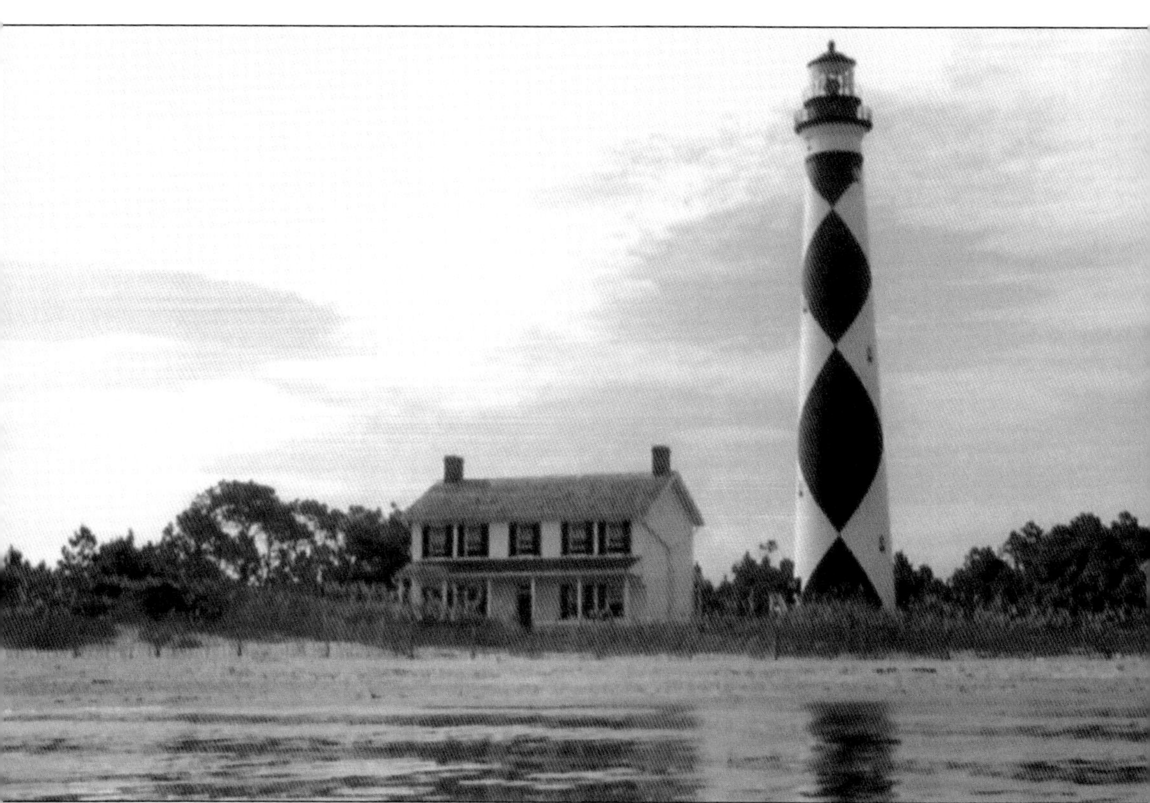

Just past the museum, the Cape Lookout National Seashore Visitor Center is located at the end of the road. This low narrow ribbon of barrier island sand extends from Ocracoke Inlet on the northern end to Beaufort Inlet on the southwest end. This seashore, authorized by the federal government in 1966, extends for approximately 56 miles and consists mainly of pristine white sand beaches with low dunes covered by grasses and bordered by expansive salt marsh along the sound waters. The Cape Lookout Lighthouse is accessible by ferry from Harkers Island. (Courtesy of the Cape Lookout National Seashore.)

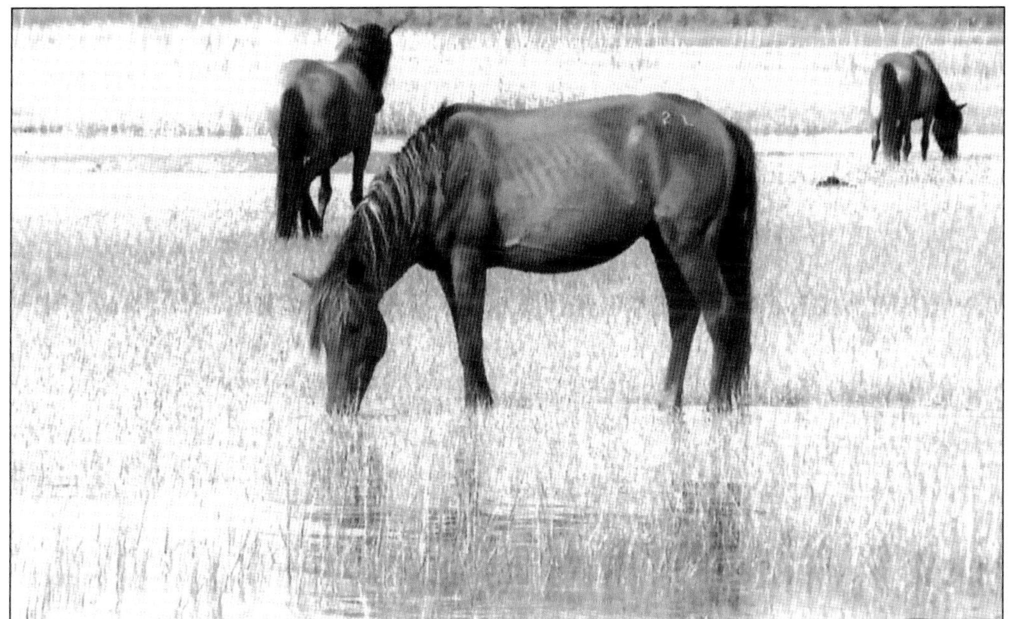

Shackleford Banks, the southernmost barrier island in Cape Lookout National Seashore, is home to more than 100 wild horses. Visitors can enjoy the rare privilege of watching these island residents. The Shackleford Banks is accessible by ferry from Harkers Island and Beaufort. (Courtesy of the Cape Lookout National Seashore.)

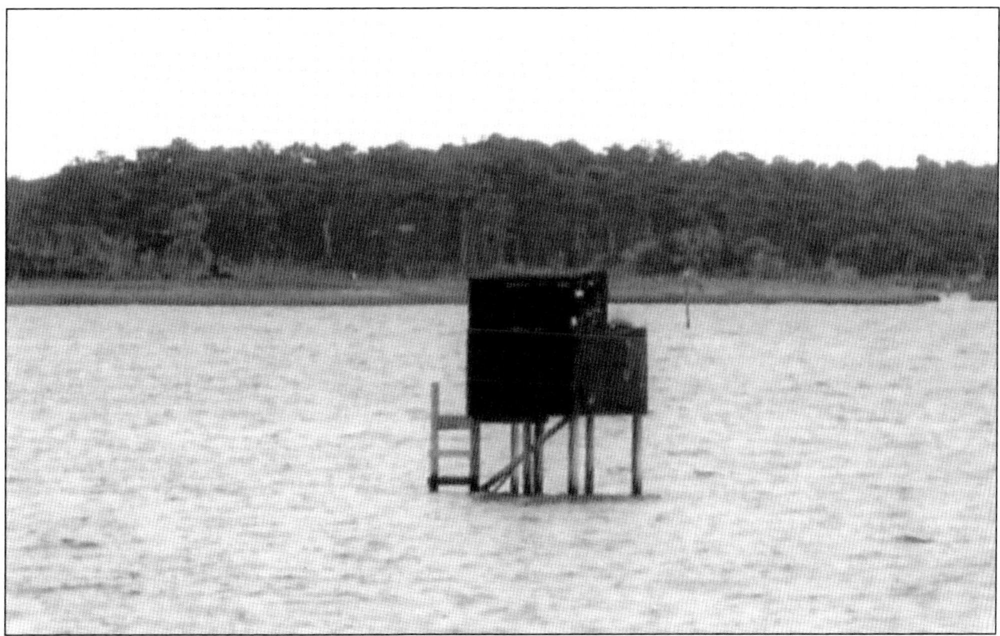

From the road to the village of Otway, the traveler gets a closer glimpse of traditional duck blinds, which blend into the landscape and waterways of the area. Otway was named in honor of Otway Burns, who was in command of a boat sailing from New Bern, North Carolina, to Portland, Maine. (Courtesy of the Core Sound Waterfowl Museum & Heritage Center.)

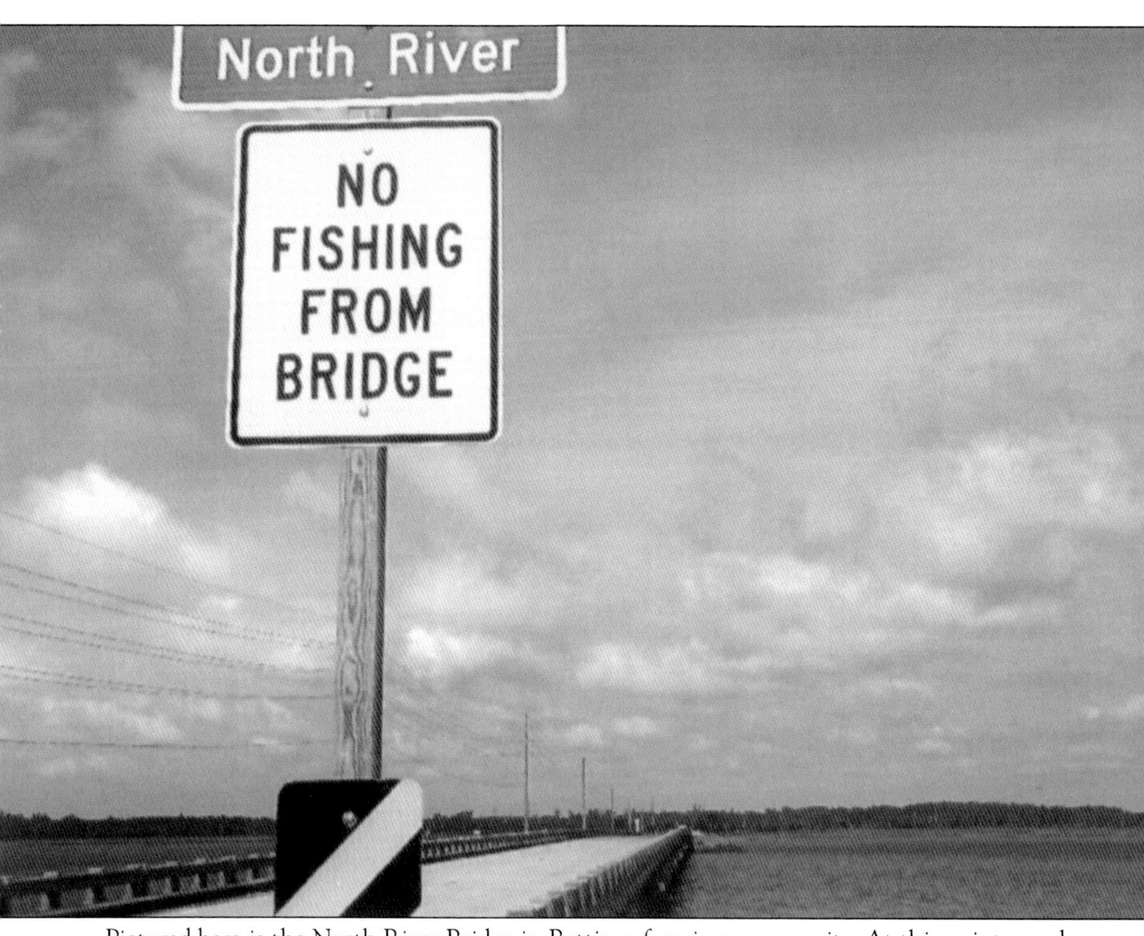

Pictured here is the North River Bridge in Bettie, a farming community. At this point, one has arrived at the National Scenic Byway's southern entrance. A state-designated byway continues for six miles to the town of Beaufort. A walk along the waterfront provides a great place to stretch one's legs and enjoy the storied coastal community with a diverse history. (Courtesy of the Core Sound Waterfowl Museum & Heritage Center.)

Five

A Water Highway, Forever Changing

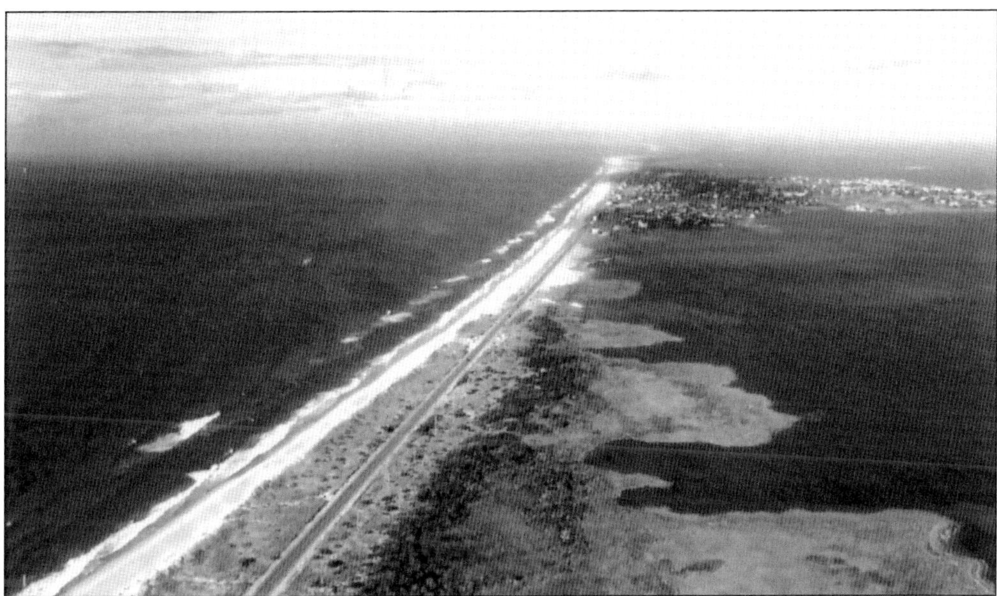

The Outer Banks National Scenic Byway is a two-lane highway on a coastal chain of barrier islands that constantly shift and are exposed to ocean overwash during storms. It passes through 21 coastal villages. Tourism is the main activity in the area and the economic driver in this transportation corridor. Impacts from hurricanes and nor'easters, severed roadways, beach erosion, storm damage, and anticipated sea level rise as a result of climate change can all have effects on the scenic byway. Man is constantly seeking long-term solutions to ensure access to these treasured villages and landscapes. A new Herbert C. Bonner Bridge replacement is currently planned, new alternative passenger ferries are being discussed, and the dredging operations will continue. (Courtesy of the Cape Hatteras National Seashore.)

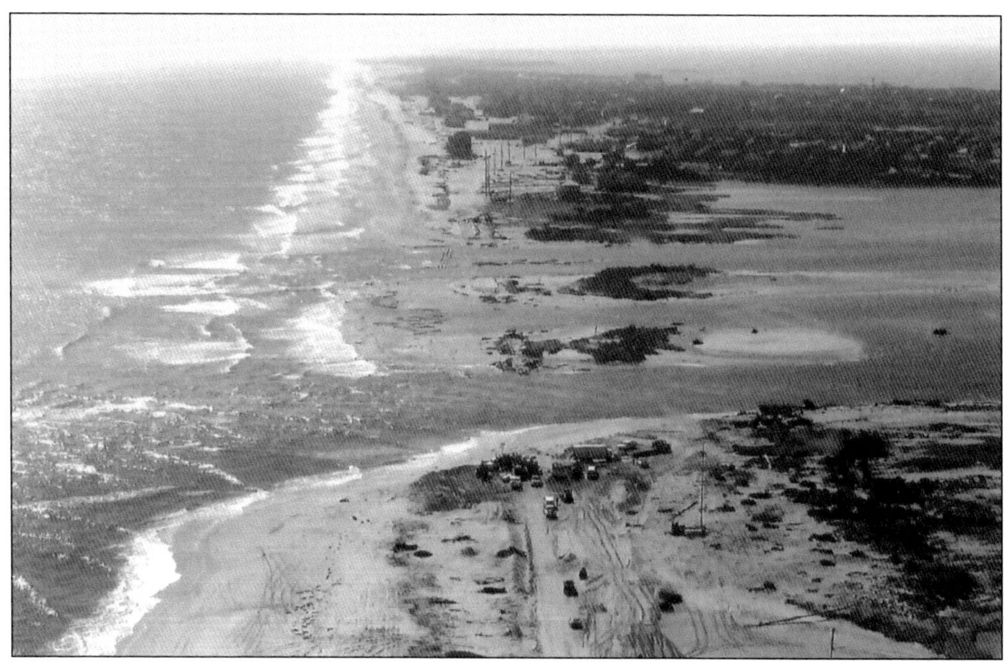

In the aftermath of Hurricane Isabel in September 2003, the devastating effects of a strong storm surge produced a 2,000-foot-wide new inlet between Frisco and Hatteras Village that temporarily disconnected NC Route 12, thereby isolating Hatteras Village for two months. (Courtesy of the Cape Hatteras National Seashore.)

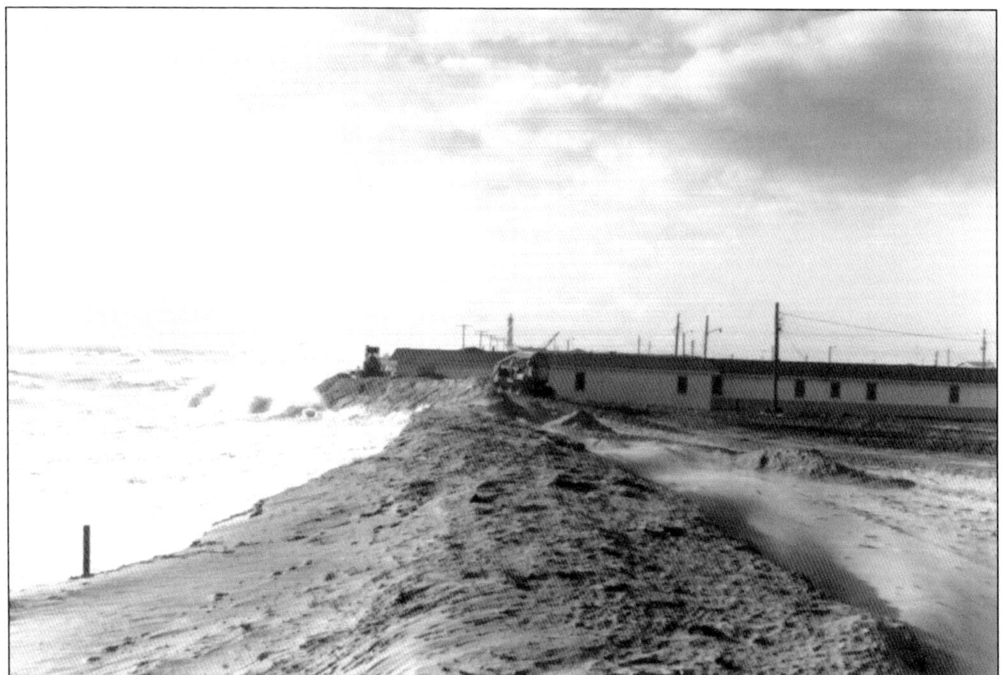

This 1971 photograph shows damage to the dune line near the village of Buxton after a storm, and attempts are being made to save a hotel on the oceanfront. The Cape Hatteras Lighthouse can be seen in the background. (Courtesy of the Cape Hatteras National Seashore.)

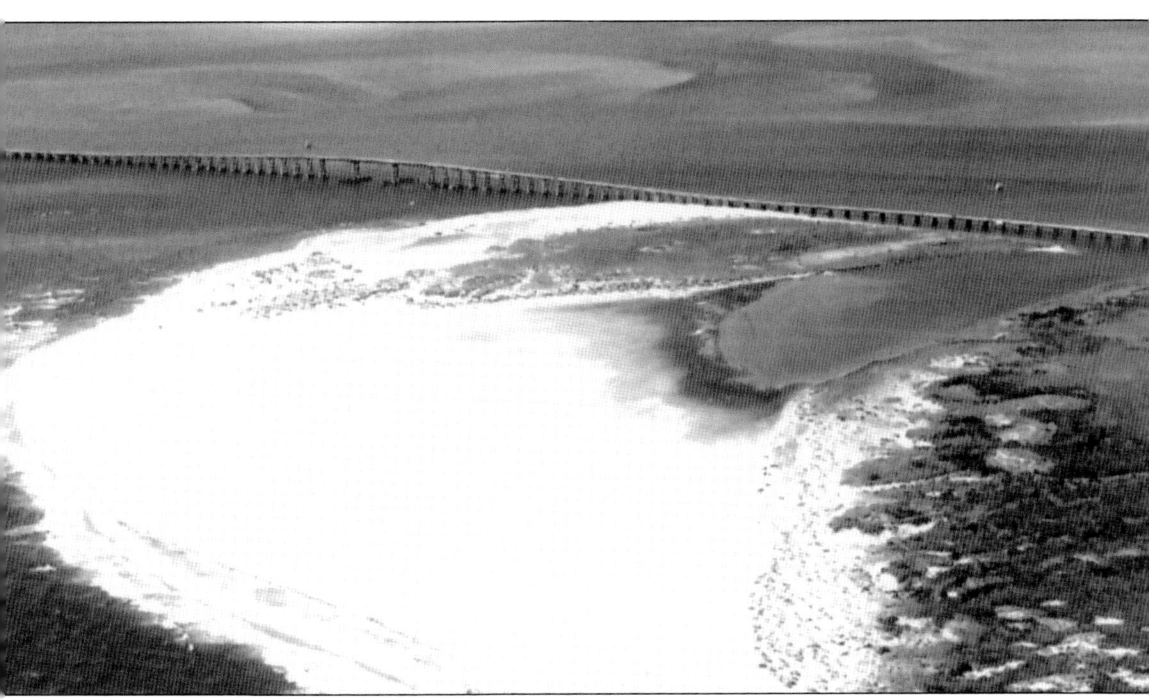

The Herbert C. Bonner Bridge spans Oregon Inlet and is the longest bridge on the byway and the only one that connects to Hatteras Island. (Courtesy of the Cape Hatteras National Seashore.)

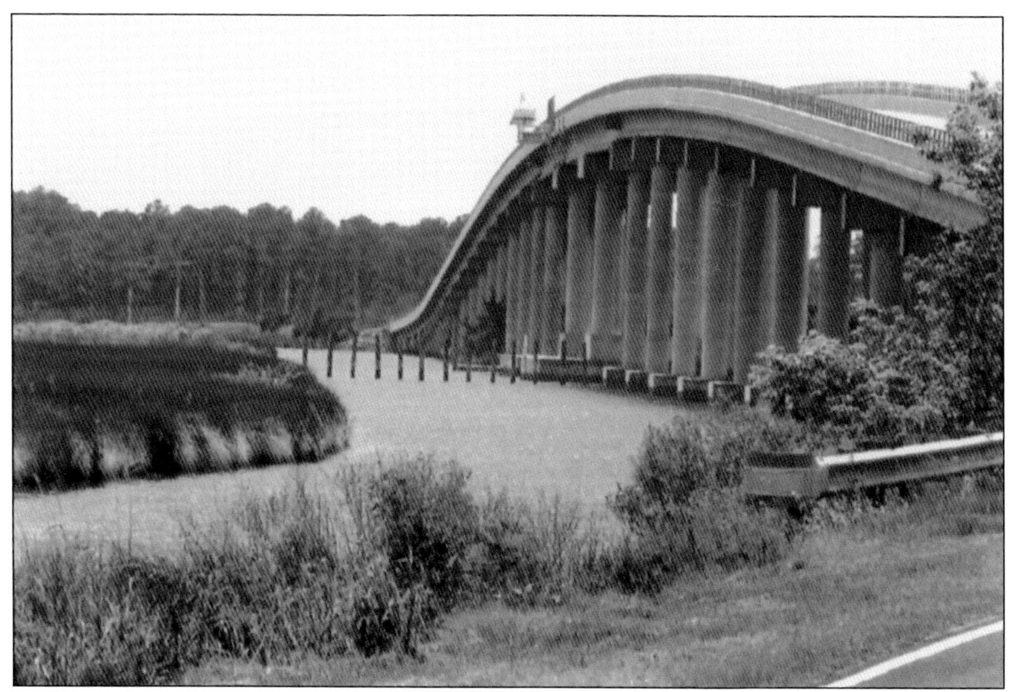

Bridge replacements are being constructed with higher elevations and stronger spans along all sections of the byway. (Courtesy of the Core Sound Waterfowl Museum & Heritage Center.)

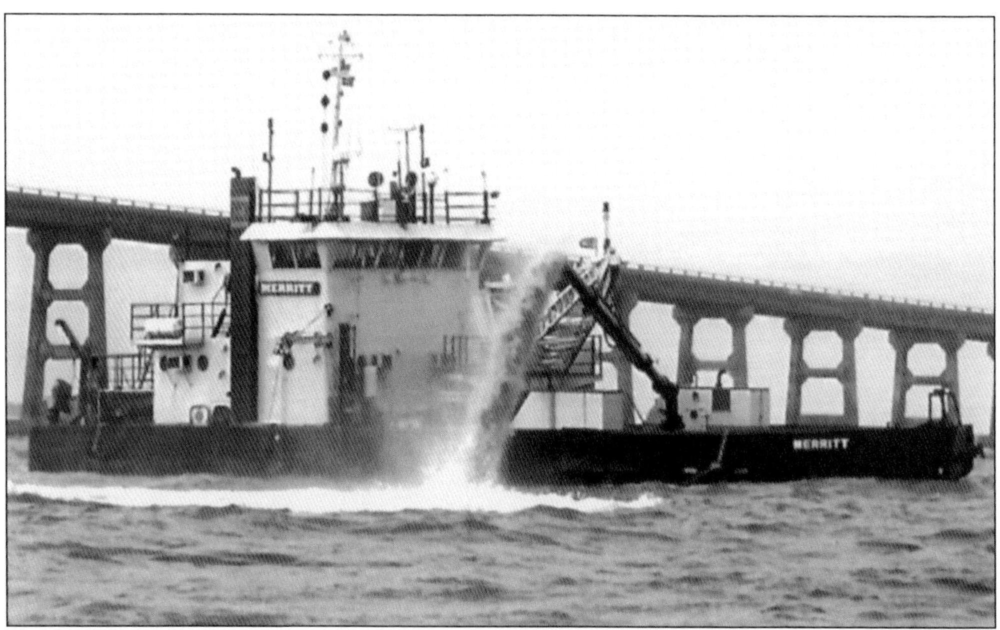

Pictured here is a dredge in Oregon Inlet. Modern-day dredging is needed to enlarge and maintain waterway channels along the Outer Banks and Cape Lookout areas. Maintenance of the channels requires dredging to keep inlets open for use by the US Coast Guard, private vessels, ferry vessels, commercial fishing, and charter fishing boats. (Courtesy of the Cape Hatteras National Seashore.)

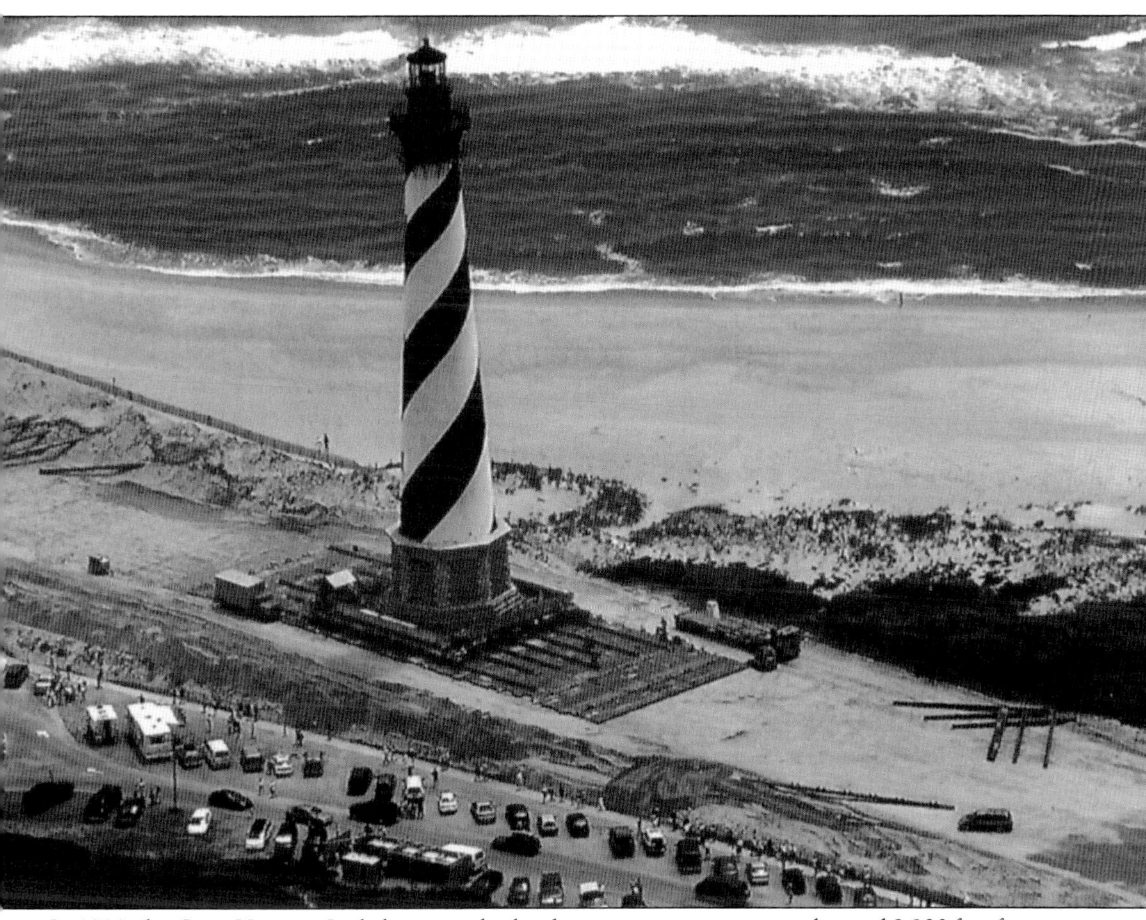

In 1999, the Cape Hatteras Lighthouse and other historic structures were relocated 2,900 feet from the ocean. The lighthouse was precariously located only 120 feet from the ocean's edge and faced almost certain destruction prior to this move. This is a classic example of man's attempt to rescue historic structures from coastal erosion. (Courtesy of the Cape Hatteras National Seashore.)

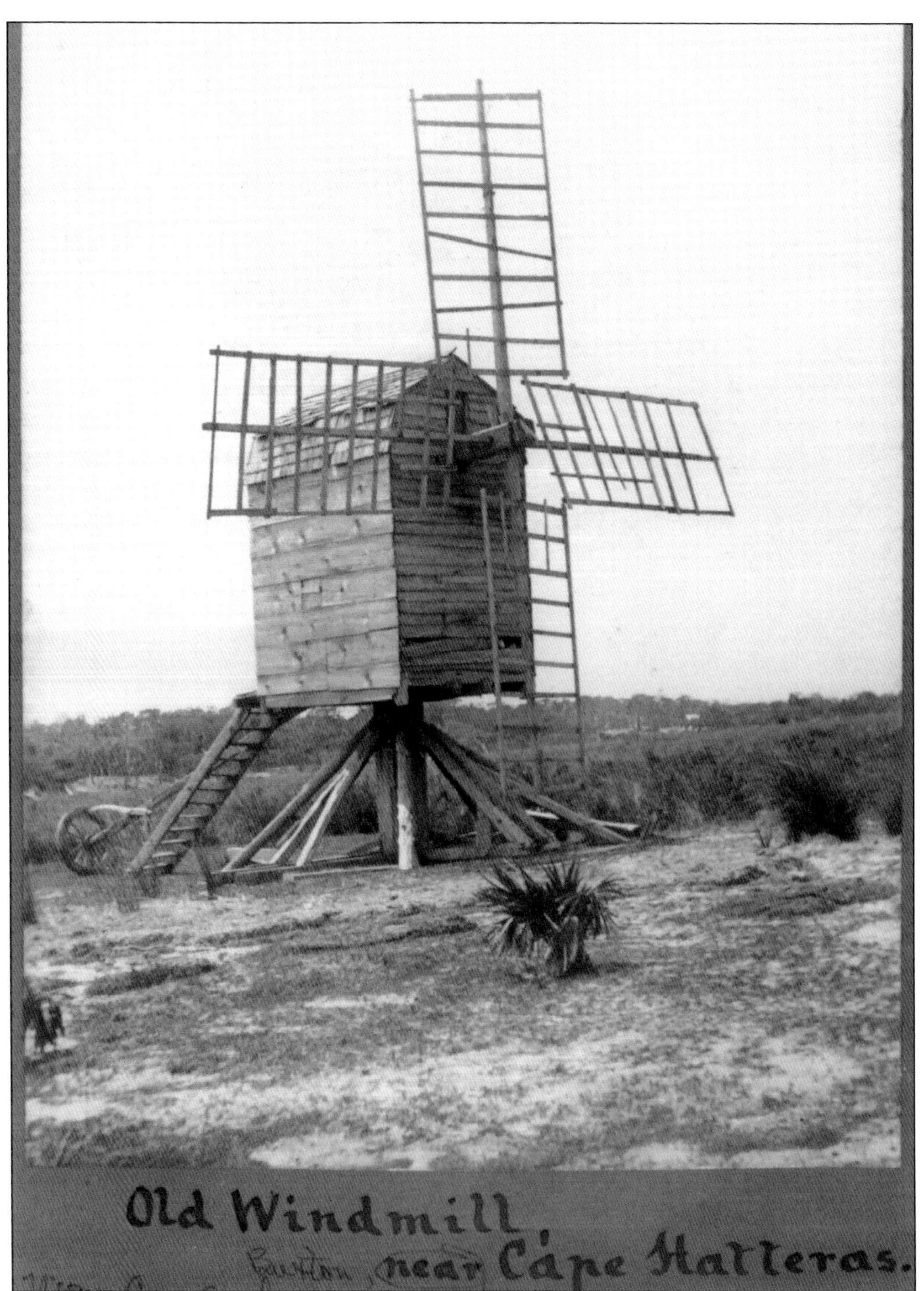

Historically, on the Outer Banks and Core Sound, windmills were a vital part of life. At least 25 windmills stood along Hatteras Island and a dozen were scattered throughout the villages of Avon, Buxton, Frisco, Hatteras, Ocracoke, and Down East. (Courtesy of the Cape Hatteras National Seashore.)

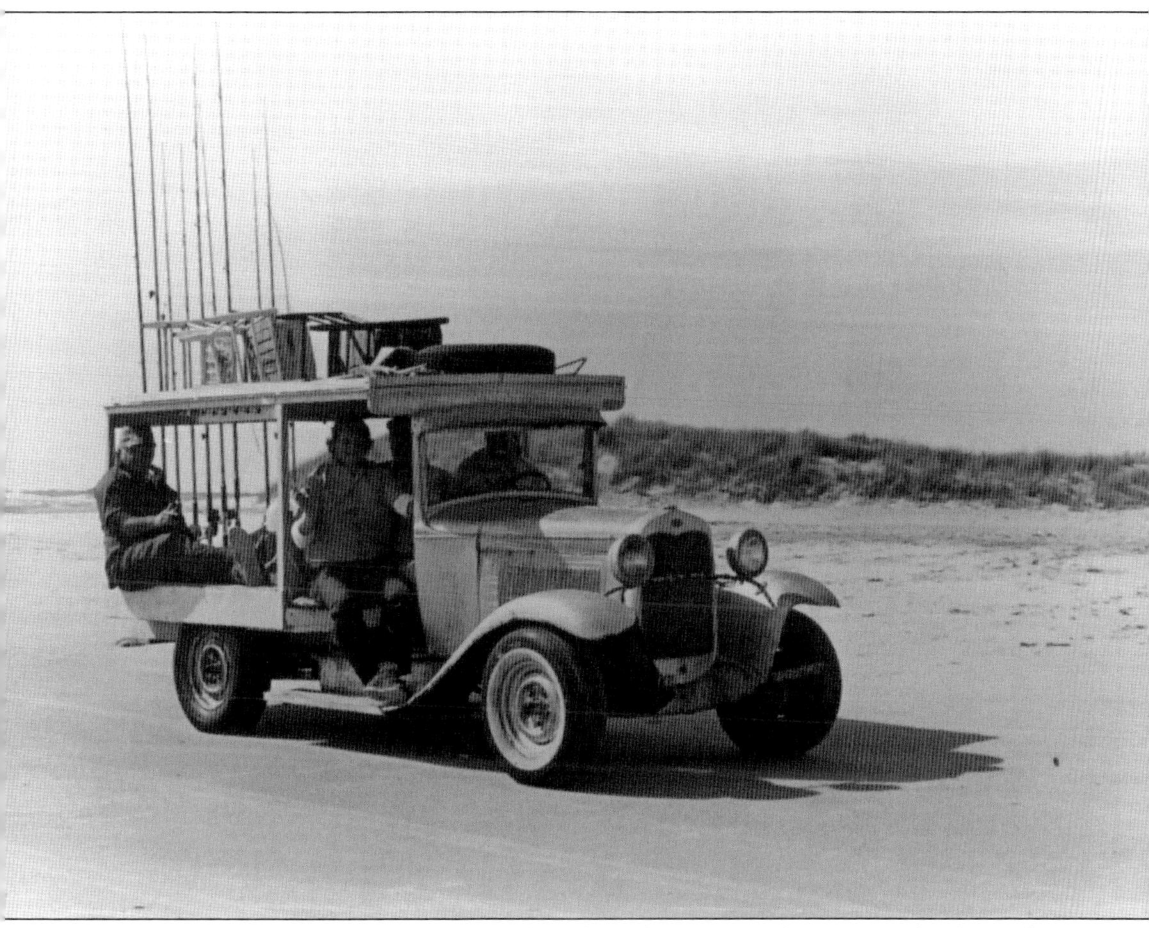

This 1975 photograph of a Ford Model A traveling along the Outer Banks is a reminder that early visitors were not afforded the luxury of a smooth paved road to visit this spectacular region of the country. Today, visitors can travel the byway for 142 miles in a much easier manner and still take advantage of an off-road experience to see the ocean beaches and sound-side waters while traversing 21 quaint coastal maritime communities. (Courtesy of the Cape Lookout National Seashore.)